Pedaling, Paddling and Pedes
Book 2

Pedaling, Paddling and Pedes

Biking twice around the World
Once below and once above the Equator

A Pronoic Adventure

by Means of 'Muscle Fuel'

Book 2 - Horizontal

Hans Frischeisen

All Rights Reserved
Copyright © 2023 Hans Frischeisen
ISBN 9798391108030

"Your task is not to seek for love, but merely to seek and find all the barriers within yourself that you have built against love."

Rumi

Dedication

I dedicate this book to the memory of my mother, with whom my fascination of traveling by means of 'muscle fuel' began. She taught me to live with gratitude, to appreciate nature and to care for our earth and all things on it. With mindfulness I wish to respect and honor the multitudes who love our planet, who live with the burning desire to preserve and protect our world from the destructive calamities brought on by thoughtlessness and carelessness; who act to educate, to encourage, give support, clean and groom our beautiful earth along their path of life and who make a dedicated effort to spread peace, love and friendship wherever they may be, for now and for all future generations.

Acknowledgment

There were times when my business partner and soul mate, **Lois Eckroat**, welcomed me at the airport upon my return from one of my exotic bike rides with laughter and hugs and while we were still in that initial embrace, she would ask: "When are you leaving again?" Fastidious or sarcastic? Not at all! Probably more humorous than anything. Whenever I expressed my wish to travel somewhere, never, not even once, had Lois voiced an objection or even a concern, not even when I left her in often challenging situations and fully in charge of the growing business we both fostered and furthered. Her support has been manifold and boundless. It was just amazing to have a wonderful partner and companion who fully understood and respected my aspiration and drives. She has gone out of her way to support and to encourage me. Here I am thinking, in particular, of occasions when I hiked the Pacific Crest Trail of her attempts to meet me, while driving her van to support my hike to locations where the highway, road or primitive jeep trail crossed my path. She also got into precarious and even life-threatening situations, yet she never complained, although, like most ladies, she preferred to stay in nice hotels when away from home. Still, she 'roughed' it with me, often sleeping in the wilderness on the ground, washing up in a small container or stream and cooking over an open fire with serenity and grace, all as though it was her usual and only way of life. Another very important aspect of her contribution to this book was her initial suggestion and encouragement for me to write it, offering to help me with editing and artwork. She often went beyond the scope of the adventures covered in this book, the writing of which was only possible through her sacrifices. Thank you, Lois, for your selfless support throughout these years of travel and adventure.

My deep thanks also to my good friend **Ragnar Kühnert**, who, as a former teacher, offered his talents to revise and help to edit my writings making suggestions that has made this book a better read. Thank you for all your hard work, my friend.

With all this support, this book could have been printed years ago. So, why was it not? I enjoy writing, but not anything between the written word and a final printed book. That meant it was at a standstill. Then something rather miraculous happened. My stepdaughter, **Christina Silone,** happened to read the beginning chapters of some of my writings. "This has to become a book," she declared and although she had no experience in the world of publishing, but loved literature very much, offered to take charge and to drive my 'book' forward and to find a way that it could be published. Thank you so very much my dear Tina, for your enthusiastic and energetic involvement to instill new life into the publishing process for my first book attempt. Now, as we advance into the second book in this series, all are written, just not yet published. I am still, ever so grateful for your advice, unique talents, input and labors. Thank you so much again my *Liebe Stieftochter* (my dear stepdaughter).

To my sons **Andreas and Mark Frischeisen,** whose admiration and pride related to my accomplishments had uplifting and encouraging effects. Thank you, my sons.

Then, I wish to extend my gratitude to all of those who, on my long and often exhausting journeys offered me hospitality, comfort, advice, information or just a friendly smile. Also, my heartfelt thanks to all who have attended my slide presentations, read my articles and chatted with me confirming that the earth, our home, is a wonderful, beautiful and exciting place to explore, protect, honor and love.

Lastly, above all, I wish to thank **God** for blessing me with the awesome privilege of experiencing these adventures and the ability to write about the many threads that make up this tapestry path of love, inspiration, peace, joy and good health.

Contents

Introduction 11
Preface 22

Part 1. Biking Horizontally around the World through countries of the Southern Hemisphere

I. Africa: Overcoming and moving ahead
1. Namibia 1: Starting in Cuba, a German presence, leopard encounter 31
2. Namibia 2 and Botswana: Large farms, cold nights, woken
up by a lion 41
3. South Africa 1: A wall, racial disparity, violence, luxury
in Pretoria 49
4. South Africa 2: Anglo-Boers War, giant orchards,
Crocodile River 55
5. Mozambique: Poverty, changing money, Maputo, 'Save the Children' .. 61

II. Australia: Across the driest of all continents
6. Australia: German pancakes, a cyclone, Ayers Rock,
Barrier Reef 81

III. South America: Into the land of gauchos
7. Chile: Bike trails, a German college, total exhaustion,
the Andes 105
8. Argentina 1: Rafts, sleeping in a gully, a French cyclist,
earthquake 109
9. Argentina 2: Mighty storms, a cow, bees, police, apples, the Atlantic .. 115

Part 2. Biking Horizontally around the World through countries of the Northern Hemisphere

IV. Europe: A view into European countries
10. Through France and Switzerland: Losing Lisa, Visiting Lourdes 135
11. Homeland Germany: Son Mark, my former wife, a basilica,
Bad Wörishofen 143
12. Germany 2, Austria, Italy, Greece and Turkey: There is
hope for mankind 149
13. Turkey 2: Lunch instead of prison, intestinal woes 154

V. Eurasia: Land of opportunities
14. The country of Georgia: Three thefts, a broken pedal and
George, my savior 181

15. Russia 1: Black Sea to Ural Mountains, a pact with the wind, 'Stalingrad', 'Pravda' 185
16. Russia 2: A side trip to former Insterburg, my place of birth 193
17. Russia 3: Ural Mountains to Omsk, Volga Germans, an illegal border crossing, ice cream 198
18. Russia 4: Siberia, from Omsk to Irkutsk, Mormons, a bike problem...204
19. Russia 5: Siberia, Irkutsk to Vladivostok, Lake Baikal, Buryats..213
20. China 1: Suifenhe to Harbin, high work ethics, police headquarters, turnpikes 225
21. China 2: From Harbin to Manzouli, a fancy dinner, getting lost, a haircut..231

VI. North America: Across the USA, land of the free

22. USA 1: Hawaiian Islands, The Macadamia farm on the big island 260
23. USA 2: Golden Gate Bridge to Wyoming, biking on I-80, separated, a deluge..270
24. USA 3: Wyoming, Nebraska and Iowa, antelopes, Buffalo Bill, visiting family..275
25. USA 4: From Iowa to the Atlantic, Civil War battlefield and people of peace 280
Conclusion 298
About the Author..300

Introduction

I have offered my books as not only a description of my adventures and happenings during each segment of my journeys, but a tutorial of how I have successfully completed nearly six trips around the world using only muscle fuel as described herein. I feel that you, the reader, may benefit by an explanation of how, exactly, I was able to do all this over my adult lifetime.

Pronoia

Before I share how it all got started, allow me to explain the word 'Pronoia' since it is probably a new word for most. You may not find it yet in your dictionary. I googled it and came upon this definition: "Pronoia is the opposite of Paranoia; how the world is conspiring to shower you with blessings, the declaration that evil is boring, the universe is friendly, and life is a sublime gift created for our amusement and illumination."

How did my love for biking and kayaking get started?

It must have been in the year 1943. I was two years old then. As an officer of the German air force, my father was stationed at a military airport in the town of Insterburg in the province of East Prussia *(Ostpreußen)*. Other than the soldiers at the war front, his assignment, for the time being, was rather safe and pleasant. He worked regular hours and had time off. At night he would come home to the comfort of our family and a warm bed. Food was getting in short supply. So, on some of his days off from work, he would grab his bicycle and place me on a specially mounted seat in front of him and ride to nearby villages and farms. The plan was to trade for food. What he offered in exchange for eggs, bacon, potatoes etc. besides money, I do not remember. I played a supportive role as well. With an outstretched arm and hand, I would approach a farmer or his wife and demand: "*Ei!* (Egg!)" Who can resist the innocence and charm of a toddler? Papa and I did well.

Years later, Papa told me with some admiration, that even when it was cold, I was eager to come along on these bike rides and that I would never cry nor complain. It must have been then that my love for biking was born.

Baptism by fire

Boom! Boom! Boom! The sound of artillery fire was drawing closer. There was panic everywhere. All able-bodied men, including my father were in the war effort with the German armed forces. My dad had been transferred away from us, my mother and me. Left behind, totally unprotected, utterly confused and terrified were women, children, the old, the sick and the many, many wounded. These were the last desperate months of World War II in Europe. I was just three years old when I first heard the thunder of war, saw people running and screaming. It must have been a traumatic scene for this three-year-old because I remember it clearly. I sensed that something dramatic was about to happen or was already happening.

Since their defeat at Stalingrad deep inside Russia in January of 1943, Axis forces were in desperate retreat as the Soviet war machine picked up momentum. In June of 1944, Red Army soldiers first invaded German soil in the state of East Prussia where I was born. A counter offensive by Nazi forces threw the Soviets temporarily back, revealing unspeakable brutality committed particularly upon German women and girls.

The Nazi propaganda broadcasted these atrocities widely, expecting to bolster the will of the civilian population to utmost resistance against the invaders. It did not work well, for terror had struck the hearts of the people.

There was another circumstance that led to the forthcoming human tragedy. Unless authorized by the German authorities, no one was allowed to flee and those who did try to escape could be shot if caught. Long before the Soviet artillery could be heard and felt, the 'heroes' in government offices who were in charge, along with their families, had escaped to greater safety further west. Back in East Prussia, in chaotic flight, an exodus of miserable humanity ensued. For most, escape was too late. All trains had been destroyed. Roads were blocked. A stream of horse drawn carts, tractors, wheelbarrows, hand pulled wagons, a few vehicles all loaded with pitiful belongings had brought the traffic flow to a snarl. Overrun by the Soviet war machine, tragically over tens of thousands of civilians perished.

What does all this have to do with biking and me? Everything! My mother and I were in the midst of all this. Our lives were in great peril. Besides me, among the most precious things my mother had, was her bicycle. Being young and athletic, with me on the bike rack, she escaped the death of East Prussia. Over one thousand years of German history and culture had violently ended. The townships destroyed, and what was considered the 'breadbasket' of Germany, lay in ruins. Later, the province was partitioned into three sections. The north became a part of Lithuania, the center, was annexed by Russia and the southern section was handed to Poland. In 1999, I visited the Russian enclave, the area where I was born. Sadly, almost all Germans had been killed or deported and all traces of German presence had been erased.

Growing up in a bicycle culture

In stages, my mother with me rode all the way into the state of Schleswig/Holstein, which was to become the 'British Zone'. We lived for a while in classrooms of a vacated school building. A few months later, my father rejoined us. When he was released from a British prisoner of war camp, he barely weighed 46 kg (101lbs.). Although the fighting was over now, these were still very difficult times.

I must have been 7 years old, when my father gave me my first bicycle. No, not a new one! New bikes were not available for a while after the war. My treasure was pieced together from parts taken from old bicycles. Nevertheless, with joy and pride, I felt I had come a step closer to the wonderful world of grownups as I perceived it, the freedom to go anywhere.

Then came Christmas 1951. By this time Germany's recovery had picked up momentum. Santa Claus' sack of presents had gotten larger. My gift did not even fit into it, for it was a new bicycle, a *real* new bicycle; my pride and joy from the German Göricke factory. Oh, was I ecstatic!

The bike now became my means of transportation to school, to the stores, beach, theater, to see my friends, to the football (soccer) field, everywhere! I was enthralled by this new independence within my little world. Either on my own or with Klaus, my close friend and also a refugee from East Prussia, I would explore our surroundings, venturing further and further. We 'discovered' new trails, roads, villages, woods and landscapes, learned where and when to pick raspberries and blackberries and how to harvest hazelnuts growing in the wild. Was this sensation of euphoria a biker's 'high'? Was this, when my desire to bike far beyond, to distant, exotic lands had begun? It must have been then, that my love for adventure began.

During my school years, we lived near the coast of the Baltic Sea, just about at the same latitude as Ketchikan in Alaska. Year around, I would bike nearly 5 km (3.1 mi.) to school. Winters would often be outright nasty with strong winds, rain, snow and ice. There was no school bussing. What a blessing! Nothing to spoil us pupils and rob us of our daily exercise!

When I later studied naturopathy at an extension of the University of Kiel, I resided 63 km (39 mi.) from home. As a student, living on a stringent budget, riding my bike home on weekends was good for the wallet and my stamina. Plus, I found it to be so much fun riding through the lake district known as the "Switzerland of Holstein".

For my first job, I moved into the foothills of the Alps. Bad Wörishofen was a plush health resort community, the kind I envision for the Reno, NV, area. Later on, you will read why these true health centers are such enormous health and financial successes. My job started at 7:00 in the morning. To get there, I had to ride 10 km (6.2 mi.) through beautiful forest and over two major hills. In winter, at times, I was the first to commute through freshly fallen snow. On one occasion, the snow was about 30 cm (9') deep. Biking became a struggle. I fell repeatedly.

Gravel had been thrown the previous day. Even though I wore gloves, sharp rocks punched through them and punctured my skin. I arrived at work with bleeding hands. This was the only time in 18 months that I arrived late; so reliable my relationship with my bike had become over the years.

Of all German cities, I know Munich best. Throughout the entire urban area, with almost 2 million inhabitants, there stretches a network of bike paths even far into the countryside often even connecting cities, towns and villages. In my exploration of other countries, I have found that it is very similar in many communities throughout the world.

Biking and kayaking in Canada

When I, in March of 1961, immigrated to Canada, of all my prized possessions my beloved bike was not with me. However, my loss was not to last. My first job landed me on the U.S. Air Force Base in Goose Bay, Labrador. One of the departing soldiers let me have his 'Hercules' bike for $10. What a deal! For the first time, I owned a bike with a three-speed shift. My commute from my new home to work, a mere 16 km (10 mi.), was primarily over sandy roads. This was an area where it could rain several days in a row. Puddles would form and the soil became soft and soggy. When I got stuck, I would hide my bike in the bushes and hitch a ride with a passing vehicle. Several days without precipitation would cause the opposite calamity. The sand would get dry and soft making biking impossible.

The following winter became the severest I had ever experienced. Labrador, on the far northeast coast of Canada lies across from Greenland. My biking activities 'froze'. Meanwhile, I had made friends with a German fellow, who owned a foldable two-seat kayak, a German made 'Klepper Aerius II'. I had marveled at these boats when I grew up at the Baltic Sea. I watched them elegantly and swiftly glide over the water and wondered what a wonderful sensation it must be to ride one. Later, I read a book written by Dr. Hans Lindemann, a German medical doctor, about his adventure of crossing the Atlantic in exactly the same model. During the summer in Labrador, I had borrowed canoes from Indians and with my friend Günter, explored the rivers and lakes of the region, most of all the mighty Hamilton River (later renamed to 'Churchill River'). Walter offered me his kayak for a very reasonable price. How could I refuse a dream coming true! The great adventure that almost cost me my life was not to unfold until next year. Meanwhile, in 1962, I had moved to Quebec City, a place I truly loved. I never owned a car and rarely ever took a bus. As usual, I met all my transportation needs by means of a used bicycle I had purchased.

What would it be like if I returned to Goose Bay and kayaked 2,000 km (1,300 mi.) along the entire coast to Quebec City? A risky undertaking indeed for this is said to be the second most turbulent coast on earth. Hence, by the end of August, I returned to Goose Bay. I needed some parts for the kayak, which had to be ordered from the manufacturer in Germany. Freight by air was not yet commonly done in those days. Anxiously, I waited for the shipment. The summer seasons so far north were short. I was running out of time.

It was almost October before the parts arrived. I refused to accept the danger of setting out so late in the season to dare the sea. With a large audience at the river, I finally took off. Three days later, fortunately less noticeable, I humbly returned. Still far from the Atlantic, where the Hamilton River widens to become Lake Melville, strong winds had whipped me around. Agitated waves splashed into the boat. Trouble! In short, I sat in ice cold water and ended up with a nasty case of sciatica. I turned around. With pain increasing, I paddled against the current all the way back to the place where I had started from. Good that I learned so early that it was far too late into the season. Had I gone out into the open sea, it most likely would have become my grave. I consoled myself, thinking I could try this kayak venture again in early summer. I left the boat behind with a friend, but as things turned out, I never saw him nor the kayak again.

Coming to the United States

Back in Quebec City, I resumed commuting by bicycle until, early in 1963, I moved to the city of New York and continued my colorful life. I did not need a push toward travel and adventure. Four months later, I embarked on ships to Iceland and Norway and around the North Cape. Overland, I traveled through Finland and into the Soviet Union, experiencing the sinister world of communism, during the height of the 'Cold War'. Next, I journeyed around the Mediterranean Sea. In 1964, and for the next 5 years, I moved to Alaska and began working as a sales representative for IBM. Taking advantage of their generous vacation plan as well as unpaid leaves of absences, I hitchhiked across the Sahara Desert, worked and studied in Israel, even got married in Germany and spent a one-year honeymoon traveling literally around the world.

Most significant was my hike of over 2,450 miles (3,920 km) on the Pacific Crest Trail, which extends between Mexico and Canada. Over a dozen times, I wandered to the bottom of the Grand Canyon, rim to rim through Zion

National Park. Repeatedly I hiked to the top of Mt. Charleston, Mt. Wheeler and Mt. Rose, in Nevada, Telescope Peak, overlooking Death Valley, Mt. Whitney, Mt. Lassen and Mt. Shasta in California, and Pico Bolivar, in Venezuela. In the Alps I climbed Grossglockner, the highest mountain in Austria, also the Krottenkopf and in Switzerland the Jungfrau. At least 7 times I ascended Germany's tallest mountain, the Zugspitze as well as the two next highest, the Watzmann and the Mädelegabel.

On one of those trips to Germany, I bought the same already familiar type of kayak directly from the Klepper factory. With Andy, my oldest son, we launched it on Alpsee, a lake in the Alps with a view of the famous castles of Neuschwanstein and Hohenschwangau. Following that, we paddled across a lake district and on the Baltic Sea in the section of my East Prussian home state that now belongs to Poland. Later we kayaked on Lake Mead, Lake Powell, the Colorado River, along the coast of California, along sections of the coast of Yucatan and Baja California, and around sections of Oahu. On my own, I paddled partly around Grand Cayman in the Caribbean, along the Intracoastal Waterway in Florida, to whale watching off Puerto Vallarta on the Mexican coast and followed the shoreline, around Lake Tahoe. Lastly, I paddled along the coast of Colombia and Panama.

The bicycle dilemma in the USA

Statistics show more bicycles in the USA than cars. There are, however, major differences in the use of bikes compared to the rest of the world. Here, bikes are mostly used for recreational purposes, athletic events as in races and, unfortunately, also in destructive ways in the form of mountain biking through fragile landscapes. In other countries, the bike is primarily a means of transportation to travel to work and for running errands. In Germany, for instance, even high-ranking government officials and business executives may commute using their bicycles.

This culture actually begins in elementary school. Traffic rules, safety concerns and bike maintenance are taught along with educational basics and fall under strict police enforcement. Every bike, for example, even in daytime, must have proper light fixtures, brakes etc. installed. If this is ignored, the rider will be fined when caught. Since all are taught to obey the laws regarding bicycle riding, it becomes easy to catch one who disobeys the law for he/she stands out.

One night that was about to happen to me. I do not remember why I rode in the darkness to the little suburb community where I grew up. Suddenly someone shouted, "Stop! Police!" I recognized the voice of the local gendarme who was overweight and slow on his bike. I was about 14 years old and in tiptop shape. No way could he catch up with me. Also, it was too dark for him to identify me, all factors seemed to be in favor of flight. The real reason for my escape, however, was not rationality but my fear of the lawman. I just panicked and dashed away.

There are more differences. Those relate to biking safety, which is a big problem in the USA and hence a deterrent to biking. Typically overseas, bikers are kept off streets and roads. It makes so much more sense to design and construct sidewalks to be shared by pedestrians and bike riders. What works so well elsewhere would function here as well. I have made corresponding presentations and petitions to city and county authorities here where I live, yet little is happening. It is just beyond my comprehension why the richest country in the world remains so stingy when it comes to the need of safe biking facilities.

My job with IBM, which had begun in1966 in Anchorage, Alaska, ended in1990 in Reno, Nevada. This early retirement opened up golden opportunities. Now, I was totally free to pursue what I wanted to do. But what would that be? I had lived what I had believed to be the 'American Dream': A wonderful family, a good job and income, a nice house, two cars, a kayak and, of course, a bike etc. So, was that it? Was that to be my destiny? What about my real dreams? What about the three things I am passionate about? Traveling by means of 'muscle fuel', health and peace? Of these three, peace to me is by far the most important, for without it, not only are my other two aspirations in danger, but everything on earth is in peril.

Sometimes in life, we come across an event that really gets our attention: maybe a deep experience we had, an eye-opening movie we watched, an inspirational book we read or a powerful statement we heard. In my case, it was a quote from Benjamin Franklin that struck a chord deep inside of me. At one time, he was asked whether he was afraid to die. After some thought, he answered that, 'he was not afraid to die, but that he would be afraid to die without having done something.' So, what could this 'doing something' be for me, I pondered? If I were to do something off the beaten path, something that not everybody would do, what would it be? How about something that I would also enjoy? I love biking, hiking and kayaking, and I love the earth and wish to protect it from further harm. And so, it occurred to me to travel around the earth as often as I could as a statement and an inspiration to others. Just imagine for a moment what the world would be like without vehicles and everybody riding a bike instead. On the positive side there would be no exhaust, resulting in a reduction of global warming, cleaner air, fewer and less severe accidents, preservation of fossil fuel, elimination of gasoline as a political plaything and cause for violence, improved health and physical stamina, a subculture for our young etc. Of course, this is Utopia at its best. It is too simple and therefore unrealistic. But is it really? Could a small-scale example not be an inspiration to start a global trend? I know that many of us will not just ignore the warnings of pending harm coming to all of us from the effects of global warming.

I use every opportunity I find to pass this message on to others wherever I go. It became part of my conversations with customers in our Everlasting Health & Professional Center, letters to newspaper editors, articles I write, slide presentations I give. It is very encouraging and heartwarming to me when I experience an echo. One of many of those responses I wish to share with you. I had approached a commissioner of the Regional Transportation Commission in Washoe County, Nevada, for help to speak in front of the commission about better biking facilities in the region. She said she would get me on the agenda but emphatically asked for me not to bother her by talking about bike riding. I honored her request and gave my presentation to what I perceived as closed ears and minds. Approximately two years later this lady came into our center for natural healing beaming, walked up to me and gave me a big hug. "I bet you don't know what this is for! I want to thank you for introducing me to the wonderful world of biking. My husband and I just returned from a bike ride along the Keys of Florida. We had the time of our lives and now we are hooked." And so, I challenge all of my readers and all who hear me at a speaking engagement: *'Try it. You may just like it'*. I want you to get 'hooked' on bicycling, optimum health and wellness, and I want you to be in love with our beautiful planet and the practice of peace.

Multitudes of benefits

Besides the inner satisfaction of serving the earth and humanity there is a multitude of benefits to traveling by means of 'muscle fuel'. Foremost to me is the adventure. I think of the thrill to observe and experience diverse lands and people. Imagine how much you can learn about how people live wherever you go, so far beyond what any typical tourist at fancy hotels and popular tourist sites will ever experience. How true this observation from Ernest Hemingway is: "It is riding a bicycle that you learn the contours of a country, since you have to sweat up the hills and coast down them. Thus, you remember them as they actually are, while in a motor car only a high hill impresses you, and you have no such accurate remembrance of country you have driven through as you gain by riding a bicycle."

As a 'westerner' humbly riding on a bike, people may reason that you are too poor to afford a plane, train or bus. They will readily accept you at their level and open their hearts and often their homes. You will make new friends and acquaintances. Their acceptance of you automatically will make you an ambassador of understanding and peace.

You will have a chance to practice and sharpen your language skills and expand your knowledge of geography and history. On long lonely stretches, in particular, you can think and meditate, maybe re-evaluate your purpose and destiny. At the start of a bike ride, I have all the same aches and pains anyone else would have. See me, however, at the end of my trip, when I have turned into a 'biking machine', developed strong muscles and reached a plateau of high energy. I often say, "If I were a doctor, I would prescribe bike rides."

Another advantage is the economy of this mode of traveling. Picture this: On my longest bike ride of 9 weeks through Russia and China, leaving from and returning to Reno, Nevada, my total cost was just $770. US. I would typically spend considerably more just staying at home over that same time period. Yet, I was never unreasonably hungry and never suffered a shortage of any kind. I even had purchased little gifts for friends and staff at Everlasting Health & Professional Center. I had one advantage; however, my flights were covered by my frequent flier account. "Oh", I hear people say, "I just don't have the time." Try to remember this if you remember nothing else from this book: *We have all the time there is!*

A golden opportunity presented itself when I received an early retirement package from IBM in March of 1990. Freedom! Now I could pursue the things I had dreamed of, namely to travel non-motorized "by muscle fuel", a phrase I coined, across the Americas: from South America's most southern tip to where the land ends in northern Canada. That very year, I embarked on my first major segment by kayaking from central Canada to the Arctic Ocean. As I progressed along the route, first the thought and then the desire for more began to grow. Besides adventure, as I stated earlier, I am also passionate about the pursuit of health and peace. Actually, the two, in my opinion, are related, for violence is not conducive to good health.

In later years, I had the privilege of inviting Patch Adams M.D. to come to Reno. You may have seen the movie 'Patch Adams' in which Robin Williams portrays the young medical student, Hunter Adams. The real Dr. Patch Adams began his lecture in the crowded auditorium of UNR's Medical School with a surprising statement: "I came here to seduce you!" Then he paused. I could sense that the young women and men in the audience were surprised if not shocked by his opening. Frankly, so was I, for as the moderator I was wondering what I had gotten myself into. Then he continued: "I came here to seduce you to become political activists. As doctors we are obligated to oppose and counteract bloodshed and violence for it hurts, wounds, maims and kills on all levels of our being." Right on!

In 1991 I had undergone a very painful divorce. Reading the book "Your Erroneous Zones" by Wayne Dyer Ph.D. helped me to pull myself out of the depth of appearing insurmountable trauma. What, in particular, guided me out of the state of despair was the realization that happiness is not the result of achievement. We just have to decide to be that, namely happy. How often have we heard someone proclaim: "I would be so happy if I had that red Porsche or that gorgeous house, that nice job or that wonderful woman or man! Yes, there is some happiness associated with acquiring those things, but how deep is it and how long does it last? Just to be that, namely happy, became a powerful discovery for me and has since, significantly affected my life. However, being happy was not as easy as hitting a switch to lighten up. Slowly, with constant practice my happy disposition took on permanence. Some people who know me have even stated that I live a pronoic life.

I was still a novice at it, when one day I had lunch with an attractive lady. She shared a little about her life with me. A good education, a good job, a nice house, a great car, good looks and health, an impressive wardrobe, many friends... a life like the top of the "American Dream". Yet, she was the saddest person I knew. Maybe, I can help her, I thought, by suggesting to her to practice something I do. When I get up in the morning, it makes me laugh when I see this sleepy, silly face of mine in the mirror. As I related this to her, I noticed the lady's eyes getting bigger. She seemed horrified. "What's the matter?" I asked. "When I look into the mirror, I see my growing wrinkles," she cried out. I laughed out loud. "So, are you telling me that your vanity is more important than your happiness?" We do have a choice. This was hers. Which one is yours?

Attached to the mirror glass, I keep 'smiley face' stickers to remind me of my morning ritual to sing to a certain tune: "I am happy and healthy, and I love myself and Wombina (nickname for my soulmate) too and that is true." Thus, I practically sing myself into a good start of the day. Besides the cheerful disposition, I feel, this is a major factor in support of my ongoing good health. Both, in my opinion, play an important role as it relates to long distant biking, namely a positive attitude toward everyone and everything and to maintain my immune system at optimal levels.

As it relates to the immune system, I believe, if we restore it to maximum levels, we should never be sick. It is not so very long ago, so I learned, that man did not know disease. Thus, when the white man came first to these shores, the Native Americans were still free of sickness. I believe it is not difficult to return to that blissful state of good health even as we age.

To maintain happiness and health, to me, is the most important component of any ride.

Often at the beginning of my slide presentations, I asked my audience, "Let's see by a show of hands, who has heard that the French do not like Americans?" Normally almost everyone's hand comes up. To that I respond, "If you elect to believe that, it just might become your reality when you are there. But if you come with loving kindness, understanding and cheerfulness, because you brought those things with you as your gift to France (or wherever you go), that attitude is now there with you. I have never experienced a lack of a corresponding echo. In fact, in all my travels I have never been refused hospitality. This is the practice of *pronoia,* the perception that the world is a friendly place. The opposite would be paranoia, the fear that 'they are out there to get me'. There is nothing wrong with applying a little wise prudence. I prefer to bike on back country roads, where the tourists normally do not go. Not only is this to be more interesting and safer but there, you would find the very soul of the country you are visiting.

Preface

I happily offer my writings outlining what I have learned over the span of my adventures, to be used by any fellow adventurers or by any readers who love to read about adventure.

Getting Ready

Now let us look at the physical side of preparing for a bike trip. Naturally, it is very advantageous to get into shape. Yet, I do not believe it to be critical. I do not venture out much beyond riding my bike from home to work and running errands. I also have a stationary bike and a trampoline at home, ideal for times of inclement weather. At the beginning of a ride, when I reach my comfort level limit, I stop, confident that I will be able to add a few more miles tomorrow and a few more the days after until I reach a realistic and appropriate schedule that will allow me to finish this sector of my trip within the time frame I may have elected. Throughout most of my global rides, I have managed to average close to 165 km (100 miles) a day.

The Route

Once I determine where I want to go, I acquire road maps which are detailed enough for my purposes. Next, I do a little research in order to get a good understanding about what lies ahead. In what condition are the roads? Do I prefer level terrain and if so, how can I avoid mountains? If not, how high are the passes? What kind of landscape should I expect? Desert, forest, coastline, lakes, pastures, agricultural fields, townships? I normally like to avoid big cities. What scenery and points of interest can I anticipate? Am I willing to go out of my way for them? Do I want to stop somewhere and for how long? The climate can be very critical. So, I want to know what temperatures to expect. Do I have to be prepared for rain? What is the direction of the prevailing winds? That could determine the direction I choose to travel. What cultures, traditions and religions are prevalent? Are there particular holidays and festivities to know about? What is the expected dress code? Do I need an entry visa?

Food & Lodging

As part of the adventure, I almost never make advance arrangements as where to sleep or eat. Typically, I play it by ear as to whether to look for a hotel/motel. When I have found a place that looks suitable, I halfway seriously ask for a 'cyclist special'. Surprise, surprise! I often have been able to negotiate a substantial discount. Past successes have made me less shy to ask.

Believing that a good nutrition bar can replace a meal, I like to begin my ride with nine of them as a three-day emergency supply. Once on route, I like to shop in local stores for basics such as bread, cheese or salami, fruit and vegetables and then carry a little supply along. I shun cooking on my travels because of the inconvenience and extra weight of utensils. I rather eat in restaurants here and there, eager to sample the local dishes. I carry little water with me, yet I have never been seriously thirsty. As you read on you will see how I stay hydrated.

Money

You do well to know the currency and the present exchange rate for the country you intend to visit. Principally, you are better off to change in that country rather than back home. Airports commonly do not offer the best exchange rate. Banks charge a commission. Therefore, I often asked locals for the best place to change. I carry three forms of payment with me. Cash I distribute in $100 bills over four locations in my clothes. Some in little zip lock bags, I place under both shoe inserts, more in a little pouch sown into my underwear. That is also where I keep miniature copies of my identification documents. The remainder along with my passport, I carry in a money pouch under my underwear. In a pocket of my slacks, I keep a few small banknotes along with traveler's checks, so as not to arouse suspicion should someone attempt to pickpocket or to hold me up. My bank, at home, issues American Express traveler's checks free of charge. At times, when exchanging them, I have received a better rate than for cash. Lastly, I carry two credit cards. Since one is tied to my frequent flier account, I use it as often as possible. The other, I keep for a possible ATM emergency cash advance which I, incidentally, have hardly ever needed.

The Bicycle

I have found that a 'hybrid' between a mountain and road bike universally most suitable. With two exceptions, I have purchased all my bikes used. That has the most advantages such as high cost avoidance to begin with, being less likely to attract theft and less 'pain' of loss if at the end of a ride I want to give my bike to some poor soul. As you read on, you will see the method I often use to make my bike even less attractive. In fact, it turned out to be so unsightly that the owner of a local bike shop proclaimed it to be the ugliest bike he had ever seen. Right on! That was my intent.

At times, I have found it convenient to travel in darkness. It can be somewhat cooler then, and traffic is often lighter than in the daytime. For night biking, I use a red flashing light attached to the rear and a lightweight but strong headlight in front. Both of these lights are powered by double 'A' batteries. In order to take my bike on a plane, I pack it into an empty bike box, which I pick up at most any local bike shop. I remove the wheels, pedals, seat post and the handlebar and wrap a plastic bag around the chain. In the past, I have never been asked to pay for transporting my bike on international flights. New regulations require a hefty fee. I have never received an answer to my following request to stop victimizing cyclists:

American Airlines 30.6.2011
Customer Relations
P.O. Box 619612 MD# 2400
DFW Airport, TX
75261-9612

Ref. Bicycle transportation costs
Aadvantage Platinum account holder

Dear Sir/Madam,

On occasion, your 'Americanway' magazine carries articles which imply that the airline has an interest in ecological concerns and solutions. With great interest, for example, I welcomed the article "Cycle in the City" page 18 of the June 15, 2011, issue. I am a cyclist and am about to complete my 5th bike ride around the world. (Two horizontal, two vertical and one diagonal circumnavigation) To discourage theft, I prefer a used bike normally priced around $200. I am writing articles for various publications to further the interest in this ecological and wholesome mode of traveling and experiencing the world. Over the years, I have flown with your airline and/or your partners to and from segments of my journey. To avoid oversized handling, when I take a bike along, as my only check-in baggage, I have reduced the size of the bike box to the dimensions of 48x36x10 and the weight to 35 lbs. There had never been any charge to take a bike along.

Hence, I was shocked when your agents told me that there is now a fee of $150, and if I were to interrupt my flight for more than 24 hours another $150 would be charged. If I faced the same scenario on my return flights, I could end up with a total of $600 on just one single trip for a bicycle barely worth $200. This is not reasonable.

Other institutions actively promote the benefits of biking by constructing and maintaining meaningful biking facilities. The attached German article, for instance, relates to the building of a 'freeway' for bike riders. While many communities seek ways to 'go green', airlines counteract this progressive momentum making it prohibitively costly to take a bike along. Rather than asking you to explain the contradiction between your articles of environmental consciousness and punishing bike riders, I petition you to take the lead in dropping transportation charges for any reasonably packaged bicycle.

Respectfully,

Hans Frischeisen
Hans Frischeisen
Reno, NV

My Luggage

It is my contention, no matter how good my bike, the weight and wind resistance factor have a major bearing on performance. I find three pieces of luggage ideal for my purposes. A small lightweight knapsack tied with two strings to my bike-rack offers the convenience of instant removal. When strapped to my back, my hands are free to carry the bike to my hotel room or into the bushes for the night. The second piece of luggage is a pouch attached to the handlebar, basically for bicycle tools and parts. Lastly, I carry my fanny pack which I wear around my waist where it stays with me at all times. Over the years, I have developed the art and science of bringing my total luggage weight down to about 5 kg (11 lbs.). When, on occasion, I encounter other long-distance bikers, they often do not take me for 'real' because according to them, I do not carry enough 'stuff' with me. At times, I have met cyclists with 50 kg (110 lbs.) of luggage weight. Speaking of 'science and art', I have meticulously listed and weighed every item I take along. See for yourself whether I am missing anything outside of, perhaps, a little more comfort. You may appraise what I customarily carry with me as I have listed below each item of necessity:

The List

1. Knapsack:
a) Camping Articles:

Tent poles and spikes	305g
Light sleeping bag	695g

Tent	284g
Rain fly	278g
Therm-a-Rest	384g
Total	**1,946g**

b) Extra Clothing:

Rain jacket	128g
T-shirt	194g
Underwear	96g
Socks	54g
Total	**472g**

c) Miscellaneous:

Small towel	124g
Mosquito hat	40g
Extra plastic bags	24g
Knapsack	712g
Bike pump	132g
Maps/writing material	78g
Total	**1,110g**

2. Bike Pouch:

Tube	108g
Head lamp	78g
Lock chain	94g
Patch kit	30g
Two Allen wrenches	
Pliers, other wrenches	
Spoke adjust, tire lift	142g
Nine nutrition bars	252g
Total	**704g**

3. Fanny Pack:

Miniature Calculator	14g
Two writing pens	8g
Nail file	8g
Wound patch/Band Aids	4g
Spoon	6g
Laundry soap	4g
Matches	2g

Flashlight	70g
Camera	220g
Toiletry bag, creams	50g
Supplements (30-day supply)	140g
Total	**526g**

Grand total luggage weight   **4,758g (10.5 lbs.)**

4. **Wardrobe:** (*What I Wear*)

T-shirt	194g
Socks	54g
Sandals	864g
Underwear	96g
Light sweater	130g
Slacks	342g
Gloves	34g
Wristband	28g
Biking shorts	194g
Money, passport, pouch	44g
Baseball cap	
Total	**2,069g (4.6 lbs.)**

Above is a complete list of what I carry along while biking in tropical regions. For subtropical areas I add the following items:

Rain suit, slacks	84g
Sweater	194g
Down vest	506g
Heavier shoes	140g
Warmer sleeping bag	668g
Added Total Weight	**1,592g (3.5 lbs.)**

The Kayak

I know a couple of fellow globetrotters who travel to exotic places for the purpose of kayaking. They seek to rent boats upon arrival at their destinations. It had worked well for them in Siberia, Canada and Sweden among other places. I prefer to travel with one of the two foldable kayaks I own. Both, my Klepper Arius I and II each fit into two bags of which one is more of a knapsack and the other resembles an oversized duffel bag. Here are some of the advantages I see in this approach: Great flexibility and transportability. I have traveled with either of my kayaks by plane, bus, train and automobile. I have even hitchhiked with them and was thus able to take them to places where no rentals were available. Then there is also the matter of storage capacity and familiarity. These boats are manufactured of collapsible wooden frames and skin made of a tough fabric with a waterproof coating. This hull design allows ample storage space normally not found with hard top kayaks.

Besides the emotional benefit of feeling 'at home' in your own boat there is the acquired knowledge to optimally pack and distribute luggage. Basically, I stow camping gear a little deeper into the stern and leave the area right behind my seat to keep clothes for easy access. Food and related items, I move into the bow but leave my next meals handy for easy reach. Between my legs, I place a well sized fanny pack with containers for two water bottles. Inside, I keep my camera, cellphone, toiletry items, charts, writing material and a few nutrition bars.

Knowing your boat can also relate to greater safety. Having flipped over a few times, I have a pretty good idea when the size of waves mean trouble and will take appropriate action.

If cost is a consideration, in the long run it may be more economical to purchase than to rent a kayak. Incidentally, only once when I traveled with a kayak on a plane was I charged for overweight. That was within Russia when I traveled with a large supply of food items. I had to pay $50 US.

Though weight on a boat is not as critical as when biking or hiking, my luggage differs only slightly from the list above. Typically, I would take a larger tent, have fishing tackle and a larger supply of food on board.

Now that we have thoroughly prepared ourselves, we are ready to go! On the following pages, let us travel twice horizontally around the world, once below and once above the equator. Take your love along for your brothers and sisters all over the world, your love for our beautiful planet and travel with pronoia by means of 'muscle fuel'. Are you ready? Then, let's get started!

Hans, on a break in Reno, NV

Part 1:

Biking Horizontally around the World through Countries of the Southern Hemisphere

Chapter 1

Namibia 1
Starting in Cuba, a German presence, leopard encounter

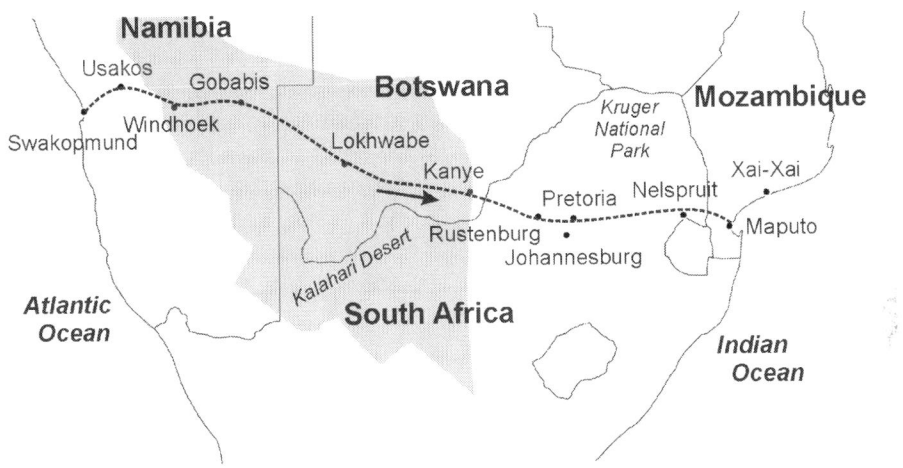

The year was 1976 – the bicentennial year of our great nation. Time to celebrate our freedom in style, except, for the moment, I was in Communist Cuba. For 5 days I stayed in an aging hotel right on the Malecon, the famous sea promenade in Old Havana. I was never informed of any restrictions. Hence, I wandered about exploring the island. That, however, is a different story. Besides, what does this have to do with Namibia? In a moment you will see.

When I ate at the hotel, I normally had my own table in their in-house restaurant. On one occasion, though the large hall was empty, a blond, Caucasian woman was directed to sit with me. Why? I wondered. Simply because we were the only ones who did not seem to ethnically belong here or was this part of some communist recruitment attempts? I never found out.

Probably in her mid-thirties, the woman wore thick glasses that made her eyes appear huge. They never seemed to directly look at me. She was a small, frail person and spoke Spanish with a strong American accent. "So, what got you here?" I began our conversation. First, she was a bit hesitant, but then as she got going, became louder and increasingly more agitated. Here is her story as I remember it. During anti-Vietnam War demonstrations at Kent State University, several students were shot. One of them, her husband, was killed, so she said. Chased by US authorities, several students with apparent communist leanings, narrowly escaped into Canada and found a safe haven there until some of them, like this woman, moved on to Cuba.

By this time, her sharing her experience had become dramatic. I felt the pain of her memory. I could not discern whether it was her dedication to the cause of communism or her disdain for our government or both that was driving her so strongly. Did she know who I was and why I was here? I was an immigrant happy to live in America, temporarily held up here in transit from Germany to catch planes to Mexico and home. That, however, I did not share with her. Did she assume, I was here in training for a communist mission like herself? "So, what is your function then or what will it eventually be?" I asked. "When I am ready, I will be assigned to Namibia to set up an underground print shop to produce and distribute fliers and pamphlets. The purpose will be to form resistance cells against white, fascist tyranny in Africa." Hmm!

As Angela was talking, I sensed flashes of anger increase in her eyes. "So, what would you do if you get discovered and cornered by the authorities?" "Oh yes, I know how to use a pistol or a hand grenade and I would kill as many of them as I could." Wow! I shuddered feeling enormous hatred from this little woman. I decided this was not the right place nor time to point out the ineffectiveness and senselessness of violence. Though I feel strongly that violence is an expression of incompetence, I kept quiet. Ironically, without much bloodshed, on March 21st, 1990, Namibia gained its independence.

Beginning in 1890, Germany claimed most of the region as one of its colonies, known then as 'Deutsch Südwest Afrika' (German Southwest Africa). Shortly after the outbreak of World War I, in 1915, the white-controlled government of South Africa, 'iron-fistedly' took over the colony. Most German settlers stayed on and over the years new immigrants arrived, all maintaining a strong connection with the motherland.

So, what could Fidel Castro, Robert Mugabe and Otto von Bismarck (a remarkable German statesman in the 19th century) have in common? Whatever conclusion you may come to, most likely it is not that major streets in Windhoek, Namibia's capital, are named after them. Incidentally, the German word 'Straße' for street, road, avenue and drive is still being used on street signs after their names, rather than the English or Afrikaans equivalents.

"You picked a bad time for your bike ride across our country", said the driver of a pickup who took me to a bike shop in Windhoek. "We are now heading into summer and it will get increasingly hotter." How come then I almost froze to death during my first night in the country? This was September 2nd, 2008. It was supposed to be the early part of spring. I had arrived at the airport at 13:00 h. When I set out to unpack and assemble Wilhelm, the name I have given my bike, and my luggage, I realized that I had forgotten small sized Allen wrenches which I needed to fasten the rack to my bicycle. For now, I used a string to keep it in place to hold my knapsack of 4.5 kg (10 lbs.). I was ready to roll into the Namibian desert, not unlike ours in Nevada. In the distance, barren mountains simmered in the heat. Ironically, just a few days earlier, my good friend and business partner Lois and I had stopped at a town in Germany that was advertising rose quartz, yet we hardly found any. Their rarity made them precious and pricey. Here rose quartz was all over and was so common that it was even used for the construction of roads.

Was I wasting time trying to make it to the bike shop before it closed at 16:30 h? It was already after 15:00 h when I got started. I still had 45 km (28 mi.) to go and did not even know where in town I would find such a store. In addition, I faced rather strong headwinds. As so often on my trips, it just worked out fine. A few kilometers along a pickup had stopped. I talked with the driver, an 'Afrikaner', meaning a Caucasian settler. Lucky me, not only did he give me a ride into town but also dropped me, just in time, directly in front of a bike shop. That was when I was told that the timing of my bike ride was not favorable temperature wise.

The driver had been on his way to a clinic for an antibiotic shot for his flu. I told him I would fire any doctor that would administer antibiotics unless it was the last resort in a matter of life-or-death situation. Antibiotics do not resolve problems but may only address symptoms, thus, drive them deeper, as I have come to understand.

English is the official language of the country. For the pickup driver, Afrikaans, a Dutch related language, was his mother tongue. Here at the bike shop, I was addressed in German. The owner was a recent immigrant from northern Germany and others like his manager, though born here, had attended one of the German schools in town.

I bought a set of wrenches. All adjustments to Wilhelm were made free of charge. With a fully functional bike, I felt more confident to take on African city traffic, alas, riding on the left side. Though I saved exploring Windhoek for my return, I noticed how orderly, clean and modern it was. In particular, residential areas looked much like in my native Germany.

My objective as part of my fourth ride around the world, in this case below the equator, was to bike across the width of Africa, namely from the Atlantic to the Indian Ocean. Though the folks in the bike shop told me it would be dark in an hour, I was anxious to get started and left town riding westward. Soon, I was back in the bushland which I had already experienced when I left the airport. It was still warm but totally dark when I made camp about 30 km (19 mi.) along. Was I in for a surprise! In the middle of night, I woke up shivering in my thin sleeping bag. Though I put on all the clothing I had, I just could not get warm. Hence sleep was my best solution. My joy to see the sun in the morning did not last long. Before noon it was already so hot, I was outright miserable. I estimated the temperature to be above 40 deg. C (104 deg. F). I drank plenty of water adding spirulina for energy. It did not help. Was my strength drained for lack of nutrients, like carbohydrates or proteins, maybe? I ate the tuna sandwiches I had brought along, yet I was getting worse. I found a little shade under a tree, where I stretched out on the dirt. Quickly I was reaching a point where I did not care anymore. Fortunately, I fell asleep for a while. That helped a little. There were road construction workers out in the blazing sun, laboring hard with pick and shovel. Some of the native Africans did not even wear a headcover. Amazing! Was I just out of shape, simply a wimp or was I, at 67 years of age, getting too old for this?

By midafternoon, it began to cool off. My spirit returned. Now, I could more fully appreciate my surroundings. Herds of baboons, in wild flight, would occasionally cross the road. To them, I must have been a strange sort of animal. The sound, sight and stink of vehicles they were accustomed to. Now, what kind of threat is this big and quiet thing coming toward them, they must have wondered? They were not tall enough to see me when they were running through the high, yellow grass growing on both sides of the highway. It was so amusing to see them jump high and turn their heads toward me while in the air and then immediately looking back into the direction they were racing. Mothers would carry their little ones on their backs. All this, though fairly close, happened so fast that I never had a chance to take a picture. It was similar with warthogs. I thought pigs were supposed to be smart. Well, one did not appear to be. While the herd of a dozen dashed away into the bushes to my right, a single one ran parallel to the road. Why that, I wondered? "You can't get away from me that way, little pig!" I mused. More amazing yet, the porker now ran back toward the road and crossed it just a little ahead of my bike. Maybe it decided it was safer on the left side of me.

This was *"safari"* country. Actually, the word from the Swahili language simply translates into "trip" or "travel". Its meaning in our world relates to the adventure and experience of wild game watching. For that purpose, tourists typically frequent game parks like 'Etosha' here in Namibia, still about 500 km (310 mi.) to the north. I had my own "safari" right here. I could watch giraffes, kudus, elands and gazelles right from the road. That however was not to last. The further west I headed the sparser the vegetation became. Eventually, I rode through full-scale desert. Though I could see far now into the distant hills, I no longer observed any wildlife. Also, the vehicular traffic had become very light.

So, what business would leopards have here? Two fellows who I believed to be local ranchers stopped their pickup next to me. "There are two leopards just ahead of you!" The driver stepped from his vehicle to point them out to me. There they were about 500 m (1,650') ahead. Before I could ask them: "Are they dangerous? What would you suggest for me to do?" they had left. I had hoped the ranchers would take my bicycle and me beyond this potentially challenging area. Why did I think there could be a problem? Because the majestic cats were within the fence which flanked both sides of the highway. Here I was, the complete novice, alone with these so formidable animals of prey. What was I to do now? I remembered the advice when one faces a mountain lion in our neck of the woods to appear 'big'. Would that work here too? I sat as tall on my bike as I could and slowly advanced. I knew that these wild cats could develop enormous speed but only for a short distance. Cheetahs are said to be even faster. One has to be fairly close to tell them apart from leopards. Ultimately it did not really matter whether the ranchers were right. It would not have altered my course of action.

I was about 400 m (1,320') away when they noticed me. Was that safe enough should they decide to attack me? Of course, I would not wait for them, but turn and ride away as fast as I could. I must have appeared tall enough. The cats ran away from me. Why would they not simply jump across the fence and be gone? Its height was at most only 1.25 m (4'). Even I could jump that high, well at least in my younger years. I would, however, have to take a run to clear it. Maybe the leopards were too close to the fence to consider that route of escape? Now they were just walking and then turned around to face me. I just kept advancing slowly on them. Good, they took off again running, but only a little stretch. Were they exhausted? Where would they get their water here anyway? As far as I could tell there wasn't any far and wide. Only later I learned that they can go 3 days without a drink. Also, they get moisture from eating the game they kill. But, I thought, not even a springbok could live in this arid terrain. Would that increase the odds for them to consider me for a meal?

How long would this go on? "Come on guys, jump the fence and get this over with for you and me!" No such thing! They had meanwhile stopped to look at me again as I, as tall as possible, approached. Were they considering me for dinner? They ran away again for a little while, but again covering less ground this time. Then they slowed down, faced me and ran a little more. Eventually they only trot. When they ran out of strength would they then feel cornered and make a stand? This went on over distance of 2 km (1.2 mi.).

Ahead, I could see an overpass over railroad tracks coming up. Oh no, the fence on both sides made a 90 degree turn to continue under the overpass. Unless they jumped across, this created a dead end for them. Did we have a situation here not unlike wild mustangs being driven into a corral?

As I approached the bridge, I could not see the beasts. They must have been in the tunnel section. "Just stay there until I cross over the bridge!" They did! Good animals! As I descended on the second half of the overpass, I knew I was safe. Later a tour guide of game reserves told me how lucky I had been. No, not because no harm had come to me, but for having had a close encounter with these wild cats, often so difficult to track down. I will always treasure this great experience, the kind that is sort of reserved for cyclists. I thought of an African proverb: "Until lions have their own historians, tales of the hunt always glorify the hunter".

The highway, all along, had been sealed and was excellently maintained. Not once did I come upon a pothole. I had no problems biking after dark. Obviously, it was pleasantly cool then. So, I did a lot of it. Eventually, I came upon a dried-up river bed. By again lifting my things across the fence, I could now walk a little 'upstream' and made camp on a surface of fine sand.

It was on my third day when I left the community of Usakos by late morning. The heat was back in full force and getting to me. No, it could not have been for lack of nutrients depleting my energy. I had enjoyed a great breakfast at a restaurant in town. Now, I had to bike slightly uphill for the next 16 km (10 mi.). No shade anywhere! The thoughts returned to me: Maybe this is not a good time to be riding here. Why don't you go home and come back at a cooler time of the year, I kept telling myself. I knew this would not be an easy decision. Good, I did not have to make it now. So, on with the struggle! I started to get shaky. I needed to rest. When I crossed the Atacama Desert in Chile under similar conditions, I had occasionally found shade next to parked trucks. Ahead stood what looked from the distance like a huge vehicle. Ah, the trailer for a tar tanker! When I came closer, I noticed the spills below. I did not care anymore. I just dropped on the ground where there was some shade. I must have dozed for about an hour. It helped. I felt better now and continued the ride.

That night, while biking until late, there were two things different from the nights before. Besides the beams from occasional vehicles there had been no lights, no signs of man anywhere. Now there was a bright glow coming from behind the hills to my right. Mines! I remembered reading that diamonds, gold, lead and copper were being mined in the country. Why was there so much activity at night? I came upon a crossing with heavy truck traffic. Next day, I discovered these were said to be the third largest uranium mines in the world. I shuddered. Had I known that, maybe I would not have slept so well in the area.

The other thing different was the temperature. I was not cold anymore. When I woke up in the morning, everything was wet. With this heavy layer of dew, I thought flora and fauna could thrive. Instead, the closer I came to the sea, the more arid the terrain became. Finally, right along the coast stretched an enormous expanse of sand dunes.

When I had this bout with heat over the last days, I comforted myself with the vision to soon dive into the Atlantic Ocean to cool off and to rest on balmy beaches. It all happened a little differently. I had not seen a single cloud thus far. Naturally, when I had an early start, namely by 5:00 h, it was still dark. With increasing daylight, I became aware of the extent of fog over the land. A stiff breeze from the sea increased the chill factor. I had similar sensations coming from brutal heat in Vacaville, CA and within an hour reaching numbing cold in the Bay Area.

All bundled up, I arrived at the ocean by 8:00 h. No, this was not for swimming! Or just not yet? I asked local folks when, typically, the mist would lift. "Anytime or not at all" were sort of the answers. I bought a few food items and settled for breakfast on a bench facing the sea. I watched the mighty surf with never ending fascination. A class of black school children passed me. Was it so unusual for a white man to picnic like this? First, they just stared at me, and then they laughed and poked some fun, most likely in Oshivambo, the major African language spoken in the country.

Similar to Windhoek, though much smaller, Swakopmund was a very orderly, clean city with even stronger characteristics of its German past. I set out to explore the community. By the time I settled in a park facing a historic lighthouse and the old imperial court, the sun had come through. The cool air from the Atlantic did not allow an 'explosion' of heat. This was a good time to ponder a decision I had to make. After a bus would take me back to Windhoek, would I bike on into even greater heat deep in the Kalahari Desert or would I head home to return at a cooler time? Since I do not consider myself a quitter, this was extremely difficult for me to decide. Of course, there was also the consideration of the additional cost of coming back. How about if I would make that dependent on the outcome of attempting to change flight arrangements! My return from Johannesburg was scheduled for 3 weeks from now. Since, I was traveling based on my 'frequent flyer' account, there were considerable limitations, in particular, on short notice such as this.

Before Wilhelm and I got on a bus, we visited the enormous, endless appearing sand dunes just south of town. 35 km (22 mi.) further on lay the town of Walvis Bay. The road to that community led right along the coast between the sea of water and this 'sea of sand'. Breathtaking! From the pier back in town, I had seen a little freighter near the shore. Isn't that too close, I had wondered, and concluded that there must be some loading facilities. Wrong! Now that I was near it, I saw that it had beached. According to the advanced state of decay it must have happened a long time ago. I wondered how many of the early seafarers and explorers may have shipwrecked here since Bartolomeu Dias sailed along the shore in 1488 on his way around the Cape of Good Hope, where the African continent ends.

Shortly after 17:00 h, I was back in Windhoek. A campground had been recommended to me and that was where I headed. Even if there would have been another tent, it probably would have dwarfed mine. Alas, I did not see any. All other campers in this huge facility had arrived mostly in slick RVs. There was one kind that intrigued me – the kind I had never seen nor heard of before. A tent was mounted high on the level roof of a van. A ladder on the side served to get up and down. How clever I thought! This certainly would optimize the safety aspect when camping out in the wild. Another attraction was the space conservation. The tent was not transported inside the vehicle but folded down into a box-shaped package right on top of the van and stayed there while the vehicle was driven.

I did my laundry in the washing facility where I met a joyful family originally from Switzerland. The parents retired a few years ago and moved to South Africa. The son still lived in Europe. He was visiting for now, but also planned to move to South Africa. So, what is the great attraction, I wanted to know. I had thought since black Africans came to power, many white folks felt threatened and left the country. Is the trend reversing? These folks, ever so happy with their move, shared with me that their life was very costly in Switzerland and that they could stretch their pension so much further here. They had sold their home in Switzerland and from the proceeds bought a larger, nicer house with swimming pool. And now they had all the sunshine to enjoy the latter, something so rare north of the Alps. Also, taxation was more favorable in South Africa, so I was told. Needless to say, they were happy. As it seemed, they were not the only ones with their discovery.

I was up early next morning, a Saturday, primarily to locate the bike shop which had been so helpful and also to explore travel possibilities. Unfortunately for me, most businesses closed here over the weekend. Though I pride myself with a good sense of direction, I could not find the shop. Ah, a police station! Maybe I can get help there. I did and much more than I could have expected. The black officer in charge patiently listened to my questions and concerns. Then, after repeatedly warning me about high levels of theft, he radioed Abraham to come in. Abraham was a trainee and 20 years of age. The officer instructed him to take Wilhelm and me in his police pickup to the places I wanted to go. What a surprise and why all this courtesy? Did the officer think he needed to protect me against thieves or did Abraham need this sort of training exposure? In any case, we had a great time. My bike was loaded onto the pickup and Abraham chauffeured me all over town for the next three hours at no charge, alas, with marginal results. We never found the bike shop. Good enough, we came upon another one that had a bike box for transporting my dear Wilhelm. Though British Airways was closed until Monday, I was glad that after a long search, we had at least discovered their location.

When I parted from Abraham, I thought I would try one more time on my own to locate that bike shop. Again, I was unsuccessful, but I discovered something even greater, much greater, namely the Chameleon Backpackers Lodge. Jackie, who with her husband owns the lodge, gave me a tour. First, I was shown an advanced, large self-help kitchen, also with restaurant services. In between the bungalows, built in typical African style with reed thatched roofs, was a swimming pool. Lush tropical vegetation with a wealth of colorful blossoms adorned the surroundings. There was a lawn, a bar and a computer center. The rooms were clean and equipped with all bathroom conveniences. And even though the lodge was conveniently located just a few blocks from downtown, it was peacefully quiet. Would 90 dollars per night with breakfast in this little paradise be reasonable? How really reasonable it was you can appreciate when you realize, these were Namibian dollars. They related to a mere $12 US.

Sunday morning, I left with Wilhelm to explore some of the sights I had noticed in passing with Abraham just yesterday. In a dominant position, on a grassy hill overlooking the downtown area stood the *"Christus Kirche"* (Christ's Church). Most German settlers were of the Lutheran persuasion. Sadly, in its history, religion has frequently been involved with violence and often even was the cause of it. A little further on stood the *"Reiterdenkmal"* (Horseman's Memorial). It was dedicated to the fallen soldiers of the German occupational forces fighting and subduing the Herero and Nama tribes (1904 to 1908). Next to it stood the *"Alte Feste"*, a sort of fortress. A film crew was busy setting up their equipment. The fellow running about in the attire of the early German settlers, I assumed to be one of the actors. Most likely this would be for a movie to reenact historical events. Still a little higher up on this hill, I marveled at the country's government complex, surrounded by well-maintained parks.

On the way back to Independence Avenue, the main thoroughfare through the impressive business district, I passed a Methodist church. Beautiful sounds reaching me made me stop. It was the choir of African youths I heard. I stopped at the open entrance door to enjoy masterful, harmonious tunes. If angels like music, they must have been very pleased.

Speaking of angels, was it my guardian angel that helped to arrange for my flight back to Reno the following morning? That became the response to the alternatives I was wrestling with. I gladly accepted the answer thus given me: Wilhelm and I flew home the following day.

Chapter 2

Namibia 2 and Botswana (2011)
Large farms, cold nights, woken up by a lion

Was I to have another encounter with leopards or even lions? I could not see them for it was pitch dark on a moonless night. To protect myself against subfreezing temperatures, I wore everything I had brought along and crawled extra deep into my sleeping bag. Seldom had I seen the stars so bright as here in the middle of the Kalahari Desert. Beyond marveling at the beauty and wonders of the universe, I had been dead tired from an exhausting day of biking through Botswana and was soon asleep.

Blood curdling hisses and growls in the middle of night got me quickly wide awake. Khauauh…! I instantly knew this could mean trouble. As I hastily rushed out of my sleeping bag there came another one of these terrifying sounds. Now, I watch animal movies as often as I have a chance, which gives me some idea of the sounds made by the major beasts. Who else of aggressive nature could be out there but a lion? Or maybe more than one? Now, what could I use as a weapon? I turned on the lamp I wore attached to my forehead. A nearby bush was all I could see. Was the beast just behind it ready to pounce on me? And what then? The end? I hoped it would go fast and not with a lot of pain. Why were there no rocks around, just sand? Even before I stood up, I threw a handful into that bush and let out the most powerful yell I was capable of. Then another one of these scary hiss/growls. I imagined it was a little further away or was that just wishful thinking? I had to get out of here! Somehow the beam of the light gave me a little sense of safety, for I knew, the animal could not see me.

While I quickly grabbed my things and stuffed them into my knapsack, I kept the light moving to where I had heard the beast. Were there more than one? Now my bike and I started moving toward the highway. Animals of prey attack from the rear, right? My little lamp had to perform double duty by me moving it quickly to shine in front of me and then behind me. Ah, the big cat followed me. Now, I could see the light reflecting in his/her eyes in very bright green barely above ground. Was the lion in crouch position ready to pounce? It would be nice if a vehicle would drive by right now. But there was nothing but silence at half past midnight. Now on the road, I got on my bike and pedaled away, securing my escape by rotating the light beam from front to back.

Africa: Overcoming and moving ahead

I rode for about 25 km (16 mi.) and came to the edge of the village of Kalkfontein. At a petrol station a sign read that it was open for 24 hours. It was closed. I bedded down behind the building and continued my sleep undisturbed by any critter. Later, when I thought back about the event, I concluded, if the lion did not mean business, it was rather rude to wake and terrify me in the middle of night. Now, wasn't it silly on my part, the first thing I did when I was so inconsiderately woken from sleep that I looked at my watch? It was 32 minutes after midnight.

Three days prior, I had returned to the airport of Windhoek in Namibia to finish this section of my horizontal, subequatorial bike ride around the earth. I had assembled my bike at the same bench at the airport as I did four years earlier. Like then, I had an audience of black folks, helpful but incredulous. In fact, I was asked why I wanted to bike to Johannesburg when there were planes right here at the airport and why when I had just come from there? My answers only increased their disbelief and the shaking of heads. Oh yes, the general perception is that all white folks are rich and like in my case are also very strange.

This is going to be easy I thought when I got out on the highway heading east. It was 15:30 h. A nice breeze helped me move along swiftly. The pavement was good, the terrain level and the traffic was very light. With the sky deep blue and the air pleasantly warm, I dressed down to biking shorts and T-shirt. For the moment, I enjoyed that feeling again that this was life at its best. I sang it out loud. Since the theft of my bicycle with all my camping gear, clothes, maps, bike parts and tool bag only two weeks earlier in Norway, I had replaced it all while still in Europe. Now, I was eager to try out my spanking new and shiny stuff. With plenty of food and water along, life could not be any better as here in the African bush.

The airport terminal would be the last building I would see for the next 200 km (124 mi.). On both sides of the road, approx. 50 m (165') from the pavement a barbed wire fence about 1.5 m (5') high was maintained. The areas between fence and road were grass covered with only occasional bushes and trees. Far apart giant gates indicated the enormous sizes of cattle ranches, here referred to as 'farms'. Dirt roads lead to their buildings normally out of sight deep in the 'bush' most likely all of them owned by white, Afrikaans-speaking folks.

Here and there, I came upon herds of cattle, reminding me of Texas Longhorns. However more than cattle watching, I wanted to experience something of the kind of 'Safari' Africa is so well known for. It began with a huge brightly colored owl sitting on a fence post, watching me intently with its big eyes. Yes, riding silently through nature had some advantages. A little later, I surprised a herd of elands. They reminded me in size and shape of our elk in North America. Ironically, the noise of cars seemed to trouble them less than my quiet approach, which caused them to take off in wild flight. A springbok is a gazelle belonging to the family of antelopes. *'Spring'* is the Afrikaans' word (like in German) for 'jumping'. In fact, they are capable of long jumps as far as 15 m (50'). This one gave me an elegant performance of his/her talent, albeit away into the bush.

The evening was approaching and with that an unpleasant surprise: It turned disturbingly cold. Now wait a minute, I was even as close to the equator as Cuba or Mazatlan in the Northern Hemisphere, where it never gets cold. I had abandoned my first ride through Namibia because of the tremendous heat and now I faced subfreezing temperatures. I was not prepared for this. There was another drawback: By 18:00 h it was totally dark and would only light up by 6:00 h in the morning. What would I do with 12 hours in my small tent? I could hardly sit up in it. For now, I kept biking into a moonless night trusting that the lamp shining from a strap around my head would reveal occasional potholes or any obstacles, hopefully just in time.

There was no shoulder on either side. The traffic, however, was so light that I considered the road 'all mine'. Left hand driving is the rule and would be all the way to the Indian Ocean. When I was ready to call it a day or more accurately a night, I lifted Wilhelm over one of those gates, climbed over it and followed a dirt road a little way to put the new tent up and crawled into my lightweight sleeping bag, placed on top of my new, thin Therm-a-Rest. In the morning I discovered why I was so miserably cold all night. Frost crystals covered my surroundings. Somewhere, years ago, I read that the action of shivering, similar as intense exercise, can warm the body. Several times during the night, I had given the shivering 'full throttle' until I fell asleep again.

Long before the sun rose, oh was I glad when she finally did, I was back biking, wearing everything I had brought along. It just was not enough. The sun had been shining for at least a couple of hours before it got warm again. Now, two more unpleasant phenomena developed: A nasty headwind and a disturbing cracking noise in my left pedal.

By noon, I reached the town of Gobabis, the only town I would come through in Namibia. "Excuse me, please, where might I find a bike shop?" There wasn't any. I had to go on, hoping the pedal would last. What if it broke seriously down? I did however locate a store where I could buy a blanket to insert inside my sleeping bag. I still froze the following night for it was even colder. The moisture of my breath combined with dew caused ice crystals to form on the sides of the tent and the sleeping bag. Since I could not relate to any warming effect inside the tent, I no longer put it up. I just spread it out on the reddish sand and slept on top of it.

Years ago, a fellow in Venezuela had shown me how to locate the star constellation of the 'Southern Cross' in the nightly sky. Lying in my sleeping bag, peeking through the tiny opening of its hood, I gazed at the stars ever so bright, filling me with awe and wonder. A deep sense of gratitude overcame me for being so privileged and blessed to so ably pursue what I love…and now back to shivering which I don't love.

The country of Botswana (2011)
The Kalahari Desert, a night in a bungalow, jackals

Again, I biked deep into the night for that was when the wind died. Next morning, approximately one hour after sunrise, the nasty headwind was back. Dealing with this weather pattern became my daily routine for a while.

So, where does the Kalahari, one of the largest deserts on earth, begin? Many years ago, I had seen the movie "Sands of the Kalahari". Something like that, namely sand, was what I had expected. When I entered the country of Botswana, I could not detect any difference in the landscape. It was 'bush' all over. Alas, there was a difference. The endless fences along the road in Namibia, at least for the time being, were missing. There was, however, the same sort of high brown grass strip on both sides of the road. Rather than a lion stepping out of it, one would more likely encounter cattle, horses, sheep or goats.

In various forms, Namibia showed evidence of having once been a German colony. One of them were the names of communities. Steinhausen, Hochfeld, Blumfelde, Uhlenhorst, Hochwald are actually names more German sounding than one would find in Germany. That changed abruptly with entering Botswana. Though there were some white land and business owners (3%), this was said to be 'black' Africa.

Besides the absence of fences in the beginning, the construction of the road also differed. The highway was wider and sported a shoulder on each side of at least 1.5 m (5') width. There was, however, a drawback. The surface was not sealed. The gravel differed in size from one section to another. Besides exposing me to constant vibration, it slowed me down.

Those animals grazing in a meadow-like clearing were strange looking cows. Was it really cattle? I looked again, happy to have come across a herd of fifty or so wildebeests. I stopped to take pictures and left my bike lying on the ground. Though they were over 200 m (660') away, I seemed to make them uneasy. They moved further away.

The temperature gaps between day and night were just amazing. By midday it would easily exceed 30°C (86°F). As soon as the sun was about to dip below the horizon, the temperature rapidly dropped down to the freezing point. Brrrr!

Biking again into the night, I heard bells ringing. It sounded like I was back in the Alps. These familiar rings, however, came from the necks of goats. I could well imagine lions killing a fully grown cow. Now it was probably the goats they were after, and I got in their path here as described in the beginning.

Slowly I was running out of food. I had brought Mountain House dehydrated meals from Everlasting Health along, actually a delicious, practical and nutritionally well-designed solution with meals like 'Chicken Teriyaki, Beef Stroganov, Pasta Primavera, Spaghetti with Meat Sauce' and similar. Ideally, they would be reconstituted in hot water. Since I did not carry cooking utensils, I mixed it with water in a plastic container. When it was all consumed, I bought bread and cans of corned beef, ironically labeled 'Texas', in stores in some of the rare communities. I mixed the two in said plastic container with water until it formed a stew. That became breakfast, lunch and dinner for a while. Life is easy if we keep it simple.

Though I kept a little water in reserve, I resorted to a proven method to re-supply myself when there wasn't any around, which was just about always the case. While biking, I would hold an empty water bottle upside down with an outstretched arm into the traffic when one of the rare vehicles approached. Already the first car stopped. Besides two bottles of water, the driver also gave me a nutrition bar. And one more thing: I had overlooked to exchange Namibian currency. Though it is at par with money used in Botswana and South Africa, it was not readily accepted here. This fellow exchanged what I had left for South African rands. That helped.

My road map must have been of an older date. It showed the next section of 220 km (136') in the heart of the Kalahari as 'unpaved'. Any moment now I expected to bike over rocks and sand. To my pleasant surprise all of it had been meanwhile paved. The wind, for a change, was in my favor and, the going was good. Could I reach the community of Kang after a long stretch void of human habitations? While I gave it all I had, just then I had to have a flat. Unfortunately, having a different valve, my pump was useless for my spare tube. The puncture was so tiny, that I could not detect it. I needed a container with water if I wanted to fix it. Of course, there was no such thing anywhere. When I pumped the punctured tire up and rode with it, it would last for about 1 km (.62 mi.) before I had to repeat the process. That is how I proceeded for I was determined to make it to Kang. I had seen road signs advertising lodges there. After four nights out in the cold, I felt ready for a nice, cozy hotel room. For that to become real, I had to find a way to fix that flat. Sadly, like back in the United States, some people here have the habit of throwing garbage items onto the edge of the road. I picked up a large, empty plastic bottle. From the first vehicle which stopped, I collected about .3 l water and a little more from the next. When I eventually had enough, I sliced the bottle lengthwise in half and filled it with the water I had thus gathered. There you are! Now inflating the tube, fine air bubbles revealed the location of the puncture, which I could easily patch now. I was actually proud about the solution I had come up with in the wilderness. Time for a happy song!

Fairly exhausted, but still in daylight, I reached Kang. The first lodge I approached with requesting a 'biker's special' actually came down from 550 to 300 rands ($45 US). Not bad! Could I improve that? Using the same approach at the next even nicer lodge, I faired indeed much better. The owner let me have one of his cabins free of charge. I was delighted and touched by this human gesture. Still, the cabin was not quite what I had envisioned. It could not be heated. It turned very cold that night. Using all the blankets on hand, I was still chilled. There was, however, hot water in a separate bathhouse. While I took a luxurious shower, I also washed my clothes. I then strung the customary string across one section of 'my' cabin, hung my things to dry and directed the airflow of a fan towards them.

As the following day went on, the usual warmth returned. Thus far the sky had been totally cloudless. Now, I noticed some haze on the horizon, which grew into sporadic clouds. The nights became milder, the days more temperate.

In sections, the old road, which ran parallel to the new gravel-surfaced highway, was partly sealed. Not only was it easier to ride on it, but also trees and bushes protected me more effectively from strong winds coming from the left. Riding a while on it presented a surprise, I would have otherwise missed: a condor; at least that is what I thought this huge bird to be with a wingspan I estimated at 2 m (6.6'). Before I saw the vulture, I heard some flopping in the bushes only 10 m (33') away. I had surprised the giant bird which hurriedly tried to get away.

I had meanwhile reached the eastern half of Botswana. It was basically still 'bush' used for livestock grazing. A white rancher, to whom I had waived while he was closing the gate to his property, stopped next to me with his son in their pickup. "Would you like a lift?" "No, thank you, to me that would be cheating." I accepted some drinking water out of a huge container on the back of their vehicle. "In this area the water in the ground is salty. It is good enough for our livestock but not for irrigation." That statement I had confirmed a little later by an elderly Bushman. I had meanwhile entered some agriculturally more versatile land. He seemed to be the owner of a field of 'maize'. That is what he called this kind of corn. To me the stalks and leaves looked awfully shriveled up. "No, we cannot irrigate on account of the salt content in our groundwater. We depend on rainfall and often experience drought. Maize is the staple food in this region."

For a while I watched a group of locals in the process of harvesting. Though they used a tractor and some harvesting machine, the process was still very labor intensive. "We pay our people well," said the Bushman, "these women earn 20 rands a day." Wow! That relates to a little over $3 US. These were all young women and men hard at work. Their little children were playing at the edge of the field, staring at me with wide eyes when I stopped to talk to them. "I am not happy being called a 'Bushman'", said the Bushman. "The people of Namibia are called 'Namibians' and those of South Africa 'South Africans'. Since all of this is Kalahari (statistically 70%), I would prefer to be called 'Kalaharian'". Well, when I said goodbye, with a smile, I called him 'Kalaharian' the name he preferred, and he smiled back.

I had seen simple huts off the road. Some were traditional, circular adobe structures with reed covered roofs. Others were primitive imitations of western styled, rectangular shaped buildings with sheetmetal roofs. This was, I assumed, where the field hands lived in tiny spaces with large families. It was just beyond my comprehension why people already so impoverished bring so many more children into an environment of suffering and misery. To me that is the height of irresponsibility and carelessness.

Actually, Botswana is moving rapidly ahead developing its enormous potential. The further east I rode, the more often I saw mining operations. Best known are the diamond, gold and uranium deposits. More recently oil had been discovered. Meat exports and tourism are other important components of the country's growing financial wealth.

Jackals for a saying-goodbye party? These canines sort of remind me of coyotes. They were just a little smaller in size and similar in appearance. That they also howl in like fashion, I was to find out during the night, my last one in Botswana. I had, as usual, set up camp a little beyond a gate in the fence and bedded down in some grassy area. Oh yes, I delighted that it was not as bitterly cold as earlier and felt comfy in my sleeping bag. Then, in the middle of the night, I heard a lonely howl. Seconds later came the response from multiple throats nearby. Then total silence. I looked at my watch. Interestingly, it was 0:32 h, on the minute the same time of my lion experience. I hoped jackals also behaved like coyotes and not bother humans. Not until a few hours later did this chorus of jackal voices reoccur to again be followed by total silence.

There, where I saw hills in the distance must be South Africa. It was. It still took me most of the day to reach the border leaving the country behind, I had come to enjoy so much.

Chapter 3

South Africa 1 (2011)
A wall, racial disparity, violence, luxury in Pretoria

A tall fence, probably 5 m (16') high, topped with barbed wire, marked the border between Botswana and South Africa. Is that what the border between Mexico and the USA in parts looks like? This drastic measure is not as much to keep folks from Botswana out, but more so desperate refugees from Robert Mugabe's Zimbabwe. Later I was told that there is hardly a plantation in South Africa which does not employ illegal immigrants from Zimbabwe.

It was a pleasant change of scenery to enter hills though they required greater biking efforts. It had turned dark by the time I entered a village that did not want to end. Its existence was not yet shown on my map. I was ready to call it a day, but the row of houses just continued. I had inquired for accommodations, but there did not seem to be any. A car was parked in a bus turn out. For some reason, I decided to pass it to the left. Big mistake! What I, in the darkness, had thought to be a highway/shoulder separation line was the concrete curb of a sidewalk. Bang! I landed on the gravel. Ouch, that hurt! My mishap seemed to be someone's entertainment and enjoyment. Some youths must have noticed my fall and laughed hysterically. Momentarily, I did not feel like joining them. I touched my body parts. Nothing missing, nothing out of place and the bike was okay too. Only next day, I noticed the hole in my slacks.

Facing the wind, I smelled the fire long before I saw its glow. The row of houses had finally ended. Now this: Either freshly burnt, still burning or yet to be burnt grass areas to allow new grass growth. It prevented me from finding a suitable campsite. And I was so tired!

Then I passed a junction. No burning beyond it. I made out a utility building of some sort. Behind it, protected from the wind and somewhat from the noise of vehicles, I finally found a place to sleep.

It was still early when I rode into the town of Zeerust in the morning. Good news for me! There was a bike shop, where I could replace the pedal which had been squealing rather threateningly. Now, I did not have to fear breaking down somewhere in the wilderness.

For a change, I enjoyed breakfast in a restaurant. While I was talking to the waitress, through the window, I could see a gust of wind whipping up a cloud of sand and blowing it across the street. This nasty headwind I had to face all day long. Hence, I barely made the 60 km (37 mi.) into the town of

Swartruggens. Rain had been forecast. All day long, I had watched the build-up of clouds, increasingly getting darker and more threatening. A tempest was eminent. At the second lodge, named Villa Luca, I was able to negotiate the rate for my room from 300 to 200 rands ($26 US), just by asking.

My timing was perfect. I was just taking a shower when I heard the first crashing sound of thunder. Minutes later a ferocious deluge hit the land. Wind driven rain whipped the window. I crawled into 'my' bed and just felt good, so very good that I was not lying out there flooded in the bush. The misery would have been beyond imagination. It rained all night and still a little when I took off in the morning.

Unfortunately, with the eventual clearing of the sky, the headwind returned. Gradually the landscape changed from bush to farmland. Less attractive were the frequent mining mounds. One huge one, surrounded by high fences, processed silica. It seemed, wherever there were buildings, they were heavily protected either by high walls with broken glass pieces cemented on to the top, barbed wired fences or wires with an electrical charge. This was particularly noticeable around white neighborhoods. I got the picture: Crime rates must be high. I already had been told that and soon was to get a little taste of it.

Meanwhile, beyond the town of Rustenburg, the road turned into something like a speedway. So far, I had held the shoulder next to the roads to be 'mine'. It troubled me that vehicles used it as another lane, even though there was an obvious solid yellow no-passing line. There was really no room for a biker. Why did drivers honk at me, when they were not supposed to be riding on the shoulder strip? Trucks scared me most when they barely cleared my handlebar. It became rather clear to me: I had to get out of here. When I chose an off-ramp, I noticed signage indicating that biking was no longer allowed anyhow.

Incidentally, the ring of the community's name 'Rustenburg' reminded me of a town in the former German province of East Prussia (where I was born) called 'Rastenburg'. It became famous as the location of Adolf Hitler's stronghold hideout known as *'Wolfschanze'* (Wolf's Lair in English). The historic event of the unsuccessful assassination attempt on July 20, 1944, on Adolf Hitler by Colonel Claus von Stauffenberg in this bunker is acted out in the movie 'Valkyrie'. Tom Cruise plays the role of the colonel whose action could have changed the course of history. What if he had been successful?

The lodge I chose for the night was called 'Grace Point'. The white owner pursued some ministry work with his black neighbors. Again, I was warned of crime. "They have killed people in this neighborhood for their cell phones. There is no respect for human life," the paster lamented. Maybe it was good then that I did not care to have a cell phone.

"Did you hear that loud bang last night around 23:00 h?" he asked me in the morning. I had not. "I thought there was an accident on the highway," he told me, "I ran down to offer help. This was not an accident but a robbery. Bandits had bombed the ATM booth next to the BP petrol station. While some were loading the money into a vehicle, others stood by toting automatic weapons. God must have blinded them," said the minister, "for had they seen me, they would have shot me." And this happened so close to me, just across the street. I went to the crime scene and took a picture of the mess.

The clergyman had drawn me a map showing how to reach Pretoria, the country's capital, by avoiding the freeway. It had rained during the night and was still sprinkling when I took off. It felt so cold as if it would snow any moment. The road was narrow and without shoulder. That meant, I had to be extra vigilant, particularly when two vehicles passed each other. Then the dirt next to the road was my only option. I passed huge orange orchards heavily secured with high fences. The oranges appeared ready for harvesting. They shone like baubles on a Christmas tree. Occasionally, I could see impressive villas at the opposite ends of the orchards, where they bordered forested hills. Growing oranges must be lucrative business, I assumed.

From an area of wealth, I abruptly entered the extremely impoverished, rundown and dirty neighborhood of black Africans. I had seen this contrast between black and white before, but never to such extreme. Many of the black folks would work in these orchards for a pittance, making the white owners even richer, while the latter lived on a 'high horse'. Not all that long ago there were no white people here. When they came, the natives, like our American Indians, had no concept of land acquisition and land ownership. Colorful glass beads, other trinkets, alcohol, broken treaties and brutal force came to mind.

From rich to poor to beautiful! First, I saw the colorful, steep rock formation. Next followed a lovely lake surrounded by attractive homes, resorts, restaurants, shops and all sorts of tourist facilities. To get there, I had to cross a one-lane dam. The released water tumbled powerfully foaming through a narrow rock-bed, barely missing little islets and heading into jungle-like bushland. Time to stop, marvel and to draw a little from that energy!

It was still raining and bitterly cold when I reached the outskirts of Pretoria. This was not a city built with any consideration for cyclists. Remembering what a hard time I had on a previous ride through the city, I looked for side streets to make my entry. Alas, I ended up again on a high-speed 'motorway'. This was scary. There was no space next to speeding

Africa: Overcoming and moving ahead

vehicles. I was forced to share a lane with fast moving vehicles. I had to get out of here and fast! I could see the high-rises of downtown coming up. Hence, I took the next exit. Oh no! Not a good move! An array of messy little shops, street vendors and a swarm of people, all black. Propelled into bitterness by injustice, I could see it in their faces: A white man had no business here. 'White man, are you nuts, daring to show up here? Get lost!' It rang inside of me. And yes, I tried my best to do just that namely disappear. I had truly picked the wrong welcome party.

Then happened what was about to happen. I first felt heavy resistance while pedaling. No stopping now! I pushed on even stronger. Someone held on to the rear of the bike somewhere. I glanced back for a split second. A man had grabbed my knapsack, which was firmly tied to the bicycle rack. Did he try to rip it off, stop me altogether, go after the bike as well and/or me? All I thought I could do was keep pedaling as hard as I could. Was that my guardian angel in action? I saw the man stumble. He released his hold on the knapsack. Hurrah! He fell landing on the pavement. For a moment I wished the car driving behind us would run right over him. Now, that would not show gratitude toward my guardian angel, would it? So, I sent him love instead, believing that he needed a lot of it.

I hurried on. Three, four more blocks and I was out of the worst. I caught my breath at a police station. No, not to report the incident! That would have been not only utterly useless, but also outright silly. "Can you help me to find out whether American Airlines has an office in town? I have just arrived, and I am a complete stranger." This was not the welcome committee either. The female officer was rather curt. "They are on Park Street." "Where might I find that? Is there a city map somewhere?" But the lady was already bent over some papers and kept ignoring me. Not only was she rude but also wrong. American Airlines did not sport representation here, as I was soon to find out.

In search of a travel agency, I biked through this metropolis of high-rises. I followed Shoeman St., one of the main drags. Just before it crossed Nelson Mandela Ave., I noticed a hotel of interesting design. At least 8 stories high, it was round and correspondingly called 'Coliseum'. Maybe I can get some information there I thought and entered. It was truly a plush place and probably prohibitively expensive, I assumed, being in the heart of a capital. As usual, I asked for a 'biker's special'. Their going rate was 650 rands. The reception clerk offered me 550 rands, but then called on the manager. She lowered the rate for me to 450 rands ($58 US), which included a generous breakfast plus her offer to take a package of food along upon my departure.

Well, I was not quite ready to move in. First, I biked to a nearby travel agency. "No, American Airlines does not have an office here ... and yes, you will have to pay twice transportation costs for your bicycle of $150 each since on your return trip you will be spending a night in Miami." Fortunately, I escaped from such ridiculous charges, as I will share later. "Yes, we believe that you can get a visa for Mozambique at the border. To make sure, we suggest you contact their embassy directly. They are located not far from here." When I inquired about reasonable accommodation, Paula, after making several phone calls for me, recommended a Backpackers Hostel. Their rate was around $30 US.

So, what should it be? Economy or luxury? After the attempted robbery, I felt deserving of a special treatment and that is what I got. My room at the Coliseum was actually a luxurious suite with spacious, individually separated living/dining room, a fully equipped kitchen, a bedroom and a bath. It was still afternoon, giving me plenty of time to give myself the pleasure of this luxury. I became my own 'welcoming party'. Sometime in the middle of night, I awakened and looked out of the window. The wind seemed to attack a battery of flags and it looked forbiddingly cold. Happily, I snuggled back into 'my' warm bed.

Sunshine in the morning warmed up the world which appeared so much nicer now. First the breakfast buffet, a festive celebration to me. Moslems owned the hotel. Hence no pork, no alcohol! The staff provided boxes and bags for my take-along foods for lunch and dinner.

Assuming the Embassy of the Republic of Mozambique would open at 9:00 h, I arrived shortly thereafter. Paula from yesterday was right. The visa could be obtained at the border at less cost, without picture requirement and a half-day wait time as was required here at the consular section.

With that information, I was ready to head for the last country on my ride, except no one could tell me how to get out of downtown Pretoria. "No, as a cyclist I am not allowed to ride on the freeway", I responded when everybody, including police officers, directed me there. Interestingly, someone from the German embassy over the phone told me how to proceed, and it was not even difficult.

With glorious sunshine, I was soon out in the country. The road was shoulder-less, but the traffic was light. Maize fields alternated with cattle ranges. Though the landowners did not appear as well off as I previously had observed, they seemed to be still exclusively white. The ethnic composition alternated. In the town of Whitbank, for instance, I did not see a single white person. Just before I entered the community, I had passed some huge mining and processing operation for coal, steel and vanadium. I stopped at the entrance gate to inquire about taking a tour. In particular, vanadium interested me. Combined with a sulfur compound, we keep it available at Everlasting Health to counteract diabetes. Alas, it was a weekend. The administration was closed. I saw only black workers and surmised this was another way to enrich the white man.

Around noon the following day, I arrived in Middelburg, a white dominated community. A lady was selling some homemade candy in front of a hardware store, reminding me of our 'girl scout' cookie sales. When I asked her for directions, she whipped out her cell phone and called her husband. "Yes, beginning from here biking east you can use the freeway," she shared with me. "How can your husband be so certain?" I asked. "He is a traffic officer," she responded with a reassuring smile. That was good enough for me, and I headed for the freeway. More recently constructed than the country roads it was more direct, hence shorter, avoided mountains and was free of potholes. But where was the shoulder? 30 cm (12") was a bit skimpy. I was a little uneasy as the vehicles whizzed by me ever so close. Eventually it widened to twice that size and more or less remained that way as far as Maputo at the Indian Ocean.

Chapter 4

South Africa 2 (2011)
Anglo-Boers War, giant orchards, Crocodile River

There seemed to be an agreement between the countries of southern Africa to standardize highway construction, their maintenance, signage conformity and, of course, the six-layered barbed wire fence, 1.5 m (5 ft.) high. Except for a section in western Botswana and when passing the rare and isolated communities, there was an ongoing fence from the Atlantic to the Indian Ocean on both sides of the highway. Though it helped to keep livestock and wildlife in, it also kept me out.

The wind, for a change, was with me. I moved speedily along. The sun was approaching the western horizon when I came upon the first structure along the freeway: A giant rest stop with all sorts of facilities, except there were no accommodations! Fascinated, I approached the miniature game reserve consisting of a herd of African buffalo, zebras, ostriches and kudus. "And what are you doing here?" I asked the large birds known as emus. "You are imports from Australia!" Talking of imports, I suppose the vast forests of eucalyptus trees originated from the driest of all continents and the evergreens from Europe and/or North America. I could see that before the white man came here all this land was the kind of bush I had experienced all along, where man and wild beast interacted.

It was getting dark. I became anxious to find a place to camp. I stopped at overpasses looking for a way to get off the freeway but could not find any possibility to get over that fence which would have been a risky business. Then there was a bunch of bushes and trees. I saw a potential for a camp. No cars for the moment coming from either direction, I dashed behind them. In the process I scared two huge birds into the air. They later returned. I smelled something unpleasant and related it to the birds roosting above me. Only in the morning I realized that I had spread the tent out over some fresh human feces. Certainly, the experiences on adventures like these are varied. So far only the bottom of the tent was affected. There was no way to begin the cleaning process here. So, in the morning, as carefully as I could, I rolled the tent up and placed it into a plastic bag in my knapsack and took off probably with a stench trailing me.

The front of a petrol station became the center of my cleaning operation. Between two picnic tables, how convenient, was a faucet for my laundry action. A partial roof over the picnic tables served as my clothesline.

I wondered what the black employees of the station might have been thinking of this white man's strange behavior. Even in our world it might have caused a few to wonder. I could not very well tell them what I was dealing with, could I?

A huge monument near the town of Belfast caught my attention. It was dedicated to a major battle in the year 1900 between British forces of 20,000 soldiers and 40 canons against 5,000 Boers with 4 canons. Why so dissimilar? What lead up to the ensuing, senseless carnage? For a better understanding, I delved a little into history. Two African tribes are known as the earliest inhabitants of the region: The 'Khoikhoi' also called 'Hottentots' and the 'Sam's', better known as 'Bushmen'. These were hunters and gatherers. Somewhere between 2,000 and 3,000 years ago, Bantu tribes moved in from the north bringing along cattle. They also knew the use of iron to make plows and developed agriculture, primarily growing maize. With their expansion the Khoikhoi and Sam tribes were driven west into the Kalahari. That is where I had come upon them.

Beginning in the middle of the 17th century the Bantus faced a similar invasion. Immigrants from Europe, mainly from Holland and Germany, began to arrive in the Cape Town area. Originally calling themselves *'Burghers'* (citizens), they became later known as *'Trekboers'* or just *Boers* (farmers). These pioneers cultivated the land by developing vineyards, orchards, grain and vegetable fields. To claim more land, they expanded northward, culminating in the 'Great Trek' of 1834 to the early 1840's at the loss to the native population. It was a time when a Dutch based language evolved known as Afrikaans, which today is widely spoken by white folks in countries of southern Africa. Calling themselves Afrikaners, most were members of the Dutch Reformed Church, which is based on Calvinistic theology. The perception that God favors the white race eventually led to the legalization of apartheid (separation) in 1948.

British presence began to expand in 1806. Were they envious of the Boers' accomplishments? Was it their imperialistic ambition to conquer the world or both that brought them with military might to South Africa, like securing the chain of Cape-to Cairo Colonies? The later discovery of diamonds and gold caused another wave of foreigners to flock into the area under British control. Conflict erupted and led to armed confrontations. The First Anglo-Boer War (1880-1881) lasted only 4 months and ended with the thorough routing of the British forces. Even after a tremendous build-up of their military might, the British suffered tremendous losses in the beginning of the Second Anglo-Boers War (1899-1902). Eventually the British with new re-enforcements and superior weaponry began to triumph and conquered most of South Africa. The area of Bergenthal, the place where I now stood, was the site of the last open battle. Poorly placed, the 4 canons of the Boers were ineffective. The outcome was predictable.

The Boers withdrew. They had learned that confronting superior British forces would turn out disastrously. But the war was not over for another two years as the Boers resorted to highly effective guerilla tactics. Their surprise ambushes caused considerable harm to the British. The war might have lasted even longer and could have ended with a different outcome was it not for the ruthless implementation of the 'scorched earth policy'. Unable to defeat the Boers militarily, the British, under the command of General Horatio Kitchner devastated the land of the Boers. They burned their fields and crops as well as their homes and poisoned their wells. Women, children and the elderly were herded into concentration camps. No, not the Nazis but the British invented these heinous forms of incarcerations. Under most deplorable conditions 26,000 inmates were said to have died. It was these cruelties that brought the Boers to surrender and to accept the British peace terms.

Thousands of soldiers and civilians had died. Many more were wounded, physically and/or emotionally, fields and houses destroyed, the land devastated. As I biked on, I pondered the senselessness of it all, here, or with any violent confrontations. I see the frenzy of nationalism stoked and enflamed through mind-conditioning propaganda. Patriotism, we are led to believe is not only a virtue but also our duty. Deeply implanted in us, we don't question it. Hence, we cannot see it as immoral, selfish and irrational. It distorts our judgment, divides the world, contributes to militarization, causes wars and contradicts the practice of love, which is the core of all major religions and philosophies. Albert Einstein so wisely observed: "Nationalism is the measles of mankind." I felt, the greatest learning experience of traveling around the world is that I accept all people as my brothers and sisters, including those that are still misguided. Only when we come together and act on the basis that we all belong to the family of mankind can there be lasting peace.

A fellow was casting for fish at a lake where I had stopped for a lunch picnic. He had not been successful on this day but had previously caught bass and carp. "Do you eat carp?" I asked him which he confirmed. Like in Europe they are considered a delicacy. In some regions of Germany, for instance, carp is the favorite dish for Christmas. In contrast in America: "No, we do not eat them. They are scavengers, living garbage," I was told at Clear Lake in California. An annual event takes place there, a competition as to who can hunt the most carps using bows and arrows. I witnessed two truckloads of

Africa: Overcoming and moving ahead

carps being taken to the dump. I grabbed one, had it cooked, but no one else including in my family would eat it, though we were all Germans. Was that part of the 'Americanization' of us? Here America's influence was rather evident with McDonalds, KFCs and several other fast-food establishments. Competing with Pepsi, Coca Cola was clearly the winner from Namibia through South Africa. I even came upon a popular beer brand that I knew from the USA: Black Label.

By midafternoon, I came upon a junction. Both highways, according to the signage, lead to Nelspruit, the next larger and my last city in South Africa. I was in wide-open country. There was no one to ask which of these two options would be best for a cyclist. In the distance, I saw a couple of houses. I had to choose a side road to get there hoping to get some advice. An older white couple invited me into their home and offered me a drink. They described the road veering to the left as more worthwhile, meaning more mountainous and thus rather scenic as well as shorter. It actually led through dense pine forest for the next 20 km (12 mi.). Oh, did I like the smell and sight of those conifers! It was like a touch from our neighborhood at home, raising homey sentiments.

I had to ascend to higher regions, but then coasted down through a narrow canyon. Darkness was approaching just too early on this beautiful day. Riding into a valley flanked by wooded hills, I followed a sign leading me to a lodge. My negotiating skills failed me here, but only partly. The lady owner would not come down from 350 rands ($50 US). When I was about to move on, she offered me to camp free of charge on their beautiful lawn surrounded by tropical flowers and bushes. I camped next to their swimming pool.

As the valley widened, I came upon a large orange orchard next morning; in fact, the biggest I had ever experienced. It seemed I passed at least 10 km (6.2 miles) of deep rows of orchid trees. I stopped to buy some oranges. They were sold in large, long bags. "Can I just buy three oranges?" I asked the lady managing a kiosk. With a big smile she handed me four large ones as a gift.

Orchards of pecans followed. Their leaves had turned color and were dropping to the ground, reminding me that it was autumn. Macadamia, banana and papaya orchards and huge fields of sugarcane were next. This was truly a land of plenty, a contribution that originated with the white settlers.

Around midday, I passed Nelspruit, just a little south of the famous Krüger Park. Memories returned of my visit there in 1971. I had flown from Rio de Janeiro in Brazil to Johannesburg, from where I set out to hitchhike through the region. First, I traveled to Cape Town and then along the Indian Ocean to Port Elizabeth, East London and Durban. Oh yes, I got to see the ugly face of apartheid. I wonder what would have happened if I would have gone swimming in the designated section on the beach for blacks. In Nelspruit, I had met some very hospitable and trusting folks. They owned an automotive repair shop and lent me a car for a few days. Imagine that! It was free of charge. Were those 'the good old days?'

The vehicle had just undergone a major overhaul when I took it into the Krüger Park. So that was what Africa was like before white settlers changed it into something like an extension of Europe. I stopped and turned off the engine when a herd of elephants, slowly grazing, approached the road about 200 m (660') ahead of me. They were leisurely moving towards me. When I thought they were close enough, I wanted to back away. To my horror nothing happened when I turned the ignition key. The car was absolutely dead, and the elephants were coming closer. If there had been one, now would have been the time to hit the panic button. What would these huge beasts do to the car and me? Push us around, walk over us, and flip the vehicle? And closer they came. Could they smash the window and go after me?

Nothing of this sort happened. Totally ignoring me, they trot around the car and eventually disappeared in the bush. What had happened? The generator was not charging the battery. A vehicle which had stopped a good distance behind me, approached. Folks inside, probably wondering whether I was nuts, inquired why I had not moved out of the way of the herd. Though it was not allowed to get out of the car, we did and they jump-started mine. The smart thing to do now would have been to return the car. How could I though when I had so much fun? It was just too beautiful and obviously too exciting to be sensible. To continue, I either let the engine idle or stopped the car on an incline so I could kick-start the engine. Lastly, I relied on people to jump-start me again with cables. This game reserve was a paradise for wildlife, but also for the folks who came to experience it. I felt so blessed to enjoy this animal kingdom on the turf of the beasts and was eager for more: the zebras, the giraffes, the buffalo, ostriches, antelope, monkeys.... a long list.

I spent the night sleeping in the car in the parking lot of the lodge. I could not just leave the park, could I? So involved was I watching, learning, enjoying that I left the nature reserve almost too late. With my semi-dead battery, I could not use the headlights. I had to hurry now. With the last bit of daylight, I returned the car to my generous hosts.

That was then. I would have loved to visit the park again, but I had a different objective this time. Through a project called 'Save the Children', Lois and I supported the education, meals and clothing of three impoverished children. One of them lived in Mozambique. My plan was to visit Jerson,

Africa: Overcoming and moving ahead

learn about his life and the program designed to lead the poorest of the poor on a path to self-help. I would take pictures to document my findings and share the story in our part of the world. Years ago, I had done this sort of thing visiting a girl I sponsored in Guatemala. I was very pleased with what I observed and glad to be a part of it. Daily 40,000 children are said to starve to death. Is there any excuse for that? What are $20 a month to you and me when it can propel a child into a life of opportunity! I feel this concerns all of us.

One more time the country surprised me with breathtaking scenic beauty. The road led into a gorge reminding me of the Grand Canyon. Wild and untamed, the Crocodile River ran through its base. When the valley widened again the wealth of plantations continued.

My last night in South Africa was upon me. Expecting bugs in the sugarcane fields, I erected my now odorless tent, actually only for the second time on this trip. However, I never encountered mosquitoes and hardly any flies. The highway had lost some of its rigid structure. When it led through a small town, I stopped at a supermarket. Across the street, I noticed some sort of travel service. Maybe I can obtain some information there, I thought, and entered. Tracy R. became sort of my guardian angel. She allowed me to use my prepaid phone card and to call home. Then she provided me with the location of Maria, the owner and manager of a sightseeing company in Maputo. I left with 2 bottles of water and the promise that I would later share some of my articles with her.

Several times the road had crossed the Crocodile River. By the time I was just a couple of kilometers from the border, it had grown into a formidable stream. Two white youths were casting from the bridge. Proudly they showed me their catch of three catfish. Two black boys were silently watching. I could see it in their eyes that they too would like to have such advanced fishing rods, which they certainly could not afford. "Are there crocodiles here?" I asked. "Oh yes," said one and pointed to a section of rocks and bushes in the river. "Yesterday one tried to get our bait. Hippos are a little further upstream." I lingered a while, hoping to make out a 'croc'. Since they typically stay motionless for a long time, I could not discern them from rocks sticking out of the water.

Chapter 5

Mozambique (2011)
Poverty, changing money, Maputo, 'Save the Children'

Crossing the border into this former Portuguese colony was easy. I paid for my visa, had a picture taken and was clear to go. Besides their Bantu language, almost everybody knows to speak Portuguese and many are fluent with English. Road signs were written in both these two European languages. People were friendly and appeared happier and more relaxed than folks in South Africa.

I was surprised that there was no money exchange on the Mozambique side of the border. "Not to worry, you can do that at the banks in Maputo." Even that was not so as I was to discover during the next day. "Okay," I said, "but that is still 100 km (62 mi.) away. What if I need local money to buy some food?" I was then directed to a lady who exchanged 100 rands ($13 US) for me, probably at a horrible rate. Such is the nature of the 'black market'.

The difference between South Africa and Mozambique was shocking to me. The land was totally arid and barren. Are locals denuding the bush for firewood? The country appeared empty. Occasional, little huts were far apart. Had I re-entered the real Africa?

The moon was almost full when I camped out. I kept being amazed at my ability to sleep up to 11 hours when the most I could manage at home would be 7. Since it was dark by 18:00 h and remained so until about 6:00 h in the morning, there was little else to do but sleep. Still, after all that, I surprised myself, when I turned over at daybreak and said: "Oh, just a little more sleep."

On the last 10 km (6.2 mi.) into the capital, industrial complexes and modern housing projects alternated, while obvious poor folks were teeming on and next to the street. I wondered who can afford to live in any of these fancy homes! When I later inquired, I was told primarily white South Africans, executives of industries investing here, embassy staff members and corrupt locals would occupy those. Hmm! It sounded all too believable.

My first stop in town was the Barclay Bank, which I knew to be worldwide. I stood a long time waiting in line to be told that they would exchange currency only for account holders. Since that seemed to be the rule for all banks in town, I thought about on calling on Maria. I had mentioned earlier that friends of hers in South Africa had given me her name in case I needed help. The park, where I stopped to munch on my bring-along lunch, was the filthiest I have ever seen. I could imagine dumps elsewhere to be more attractive. Later, I made my way past shoes for sale spread out on the sidewalk. Everywhere someone tried to sell something or just asked for food and/or money. I have often wondered in various places on earth, when there is so much space elsewhere, why do so many flock into the streets densely overcrowding them?

I managed to make it to the ornate railroad station, a building dating back to the early part of the last century. This is where Maria's office was located. She was temporarily out. Hence, I did a little exploring. "So, when can I catch a train to Johannesburg back in South Africa?" I asked one of Maria's assistants. "You cannot. All passenger trains were shot up during our civil war." Of the folly to resolve issues by means of violence I hold 'civil wars' to be the most uncivil and heinous. So, what happened here in recent history? I am quoting from Maria's brochure: "In the early part of the 20th century, vast tracts of land were rented to and administered by private companies. Agriculture became the main activity, creating huge numbers of poor, rural black workers, while a policy of white supremacy was pursued. Repression and exploitation provoked a backlash, which led to the growth of the independence movement and the founding of freedom organizations like Frelimo in 1962. Armed struggle led to independence (from Portugal) on June 25, 1975. A 17-year-long civil war, which then broke out was only resolved in 1992..."

While we were talking, a long freight train moved out of the station, towards South Africa, I presumed. It will probably return with massive amounts of imports for Mozambique produces very little on its own. That explains the inflated prices which have also affected accommodations. So why is a country with so much potential so impoverished? Again, I heard government corruption blamed, meaning instead of circulating funds into developing agriculture and other industries, the powers that be fill their own pockets.

Maria, a white Portuguese lady, was a person of action, in a country where that is rare. Within a few minutes she had made a list of where I could change money, the address of a jewelry store and the location of a backpackers hostel. Next, she got me in contact with 'Save the Children'. The latter was a disappointment. "Your 'son', Jerson, lives in Xai Xai, a town 220 km (136 mi.) north from here. Only minibuses travel there and they were not equipped to transport a bicycle. We can come and pick you up. That will cost you $250 US." I had her repeat the amount, for it sounded offensively high to me. I had to do some thinking. Of course, I could ride my bicycle to Xai Xai. By this time, I had biked approx. 2,400 km (1,488 mi.). I was tired of it and was not in the mood for anymore. I will now rest and recoup. When a representative from Save the Children in the USA later inquired about my meeting with Jerson, I responded with the following letter:

"Dear Cassandra,

Thank you for your follow up note. No, I did not connect with Jerson. I had the impression that your organization really did not want me to meet him. First, there were unnecessary delays in the documentation process of which you and Cindy were a part. Then I was left with the impression that the boy would be in Maputo. Xai Xai, his location, is still another 220 km from Maputo. Your representative there, Monica, told me that for $250 US, arrangements could be made to take me to Xai Xai. That to me is an obscene amount. I felt offended that the Save the Children program appears designed for the rich while my wife and I struggle every month to come up with the funds to support 'our' three children (2 in Bolivia). If you practiced empathy and understanding, you may sense my disappointment after I rode my bicycle across all of Africa to be turned off like this. But actually, this is your loss as well, for I would have donated my bicycle, tent and various other items to your organization in Mozambique. Since I am a writer, I had planned to inform my readers about Save the Children and would have urged them to become sponsors themselves..."

Though I expressed my frustration over recent communication shortcomings hoping to encourage greater diligence, I still think it is a great project.

I felt even better about my decision to stay in Maputo after a counselor for orphans I met at the Back-packers Lodge, told me that my bike and tent etc. would have been too large as a gift for a boy in a group of children who owned practically nothing. "It will create feelings of envy in the group and would harm Jerson emotionally or even physically."

Backpackers' lodges are very simple. Though for $30 US I had my own room in 'The Base', it was Spartan. I had to share bathroom, kitchen and dining area. Actually, a little company was quite desirable after having been alone for so long. Though age-wise, I could have been grandfather to all of them, I did not feel like one. To the contrary, I turned young again in their midst. I was also the only person traveling on a bicycle. Often, I was drawn into sharing some of my adventures. Two very pretty girls from Holland invited me to share their spaghetti dinner so they could listen to my story. I gladly obliged my beautiful audience. Almost all the visitors were white and

Africa: Overcoming and moving ahead

mostly from Europe. Several were engaged in some volunteer service for the needy. How commendable!

On my first full day, I set out to explore on my bike. When I came to the harbor area, I noticed a ferry in the final state of departure. I rushed to get on, having no idea where it was headed and when it would return. We crossed a bay and docked at the pier of a sandy beach. I followed a sign pointing to a lodge and made a great discovery. 'Katembe' was not only clean, but also beautiful and reasonable. A free of debris, white sand beach in front of the indoor and outdoor restaurant was a rarity and hence precious. When I arrived, I had paradise all to myself. Sitting at thick wooden tables under pinion trees offered a spectacular view over the entire city of Maputo only 1 km (.62 mi.) across the waterway. The rate for their neat cabins at $50 US was truly a bargain. Later, a South African couple told me that they spent ten times as much in the tourist area for a hotel half as nice.

A little later, three pretty young ladies from Portugal arrived and the 'Garden of Eden' became even nicer. I spent almost all day between the beach and the lodge reading, writing, looking, beach combing for shells, eating, drinking and just enjoying myself.

The following day I explored the Costa du Sol, the beach to the east and north. I pedaled what seemed to be a stretch of 10 km (6.2 mi.). The section closest to the town center was where the rich had their formidable villas. Among them I made out a few embassies. Then followed a few upbeat hotels and restaurants for tourists able and willing to spend a lot of money, lots of it. There was even a casino helping along to rake in tourist funds. Lastly, just before the road turned inland, I came upon the homes, kiosks and markets of the general public. The beach was disappointingly dirty, being covered with bottles, plastics and all sorts of other debris. It was a relief when the low tide revealed large sections of clean sandbanks, in some places extending more than 1 km (.62 mi.) into the sea. Here and there, mainly women, bent over, would scrape and dig in the sand. What were they looking for? I walked up to one to find out. It was exactly what I had thought: Clams. This lady had about a dozen in a little bucket and had probably spent several hours to find them.

At the backpacker's lodge, I had boiled some eggs and had prepared some rolls with sliced lunch meat. Along with some fruit I had brought along, I was having lunch. While I ate, I looked over the Indian Ocean. Occasionally, larger ships would pass further out at sea. This is where and how my horizontal ride below the equator (my third ride) around the world ended. Two days later Wilhelm and I caught an overnight bus to Johannesburg where my flight home was to begin.

We arrived at the bus terminal in downtown Johannesburg shortly after 4:00 in the morning. I was the only white person sitting among hundreds of black folks in the waiting hall. Though police officers were constantly patrolling, I locked my bike to the bench I was sitting on. To combat the bitter cold, in addition to wearing everything I had with me, I covered myself with a blanket. The next four hours I spent in a state of semi-sleep.

It was nice and sunny when I entered the streets and biked towards the airport still over 30 km (19 mi.) away. There was an easy, direct freeway connection, but that was not an option for me as a cyclist. Had I known that since I was here last, a city train connection had been built, I might have chosen it. By the time the stores opened, I had come upon a huge shopping center, actually the largest I had ever seen. There things fell into place for me as it relates to preparing my bicycle to travel home with me. In a bike shop I obtained a box used to ship new bicycles. The axle of the rear wheel was not removable for me. So, I had their mechanic exchange it for an easily removable axle. I slid the box partly so I could fold it and tie it firmly to my bike rack. At a hardware store, I bought see-through packing tape and a black felt pen marker, which I added to the string I had already picked off the road somewhere.

At the giant supermarket it was a pleasant change to have a wide range of food options at reasonable prices. After a generous picnic, sitting in the warm sun, I continued my ride to the airport. There I sought out a corner where I could get to work undisturbed. First, I took the bike apart as much as I could with ordinary tools. Then I sliced about ¼ off the bike box and re-taped it. Now I was ready to insert the bike components into the shortened box. Before I did the final sealing with tape, I wrote in large letters on the sides and top of the box: "Wheelchair". Finally securing the package with my string, I placed it on a luggage cart. I was now ready for check-in.

My Aadvantage Platinum membership allowed me to check in at the business class counter. There was no waiting in line. Now heavily limping, I approached the ticket agent, who took it upon himself to request a wheelchair for me. Such fine service! Meanwhile my bike was checked in, unquestioned as a 'Wheelchair', meaning there was no charge. During my layover in Miami, I repeated this drama with the same results, even without the use of a wheelchair.

When Lois welcomed me back at the Reno airport, we were still hugging and kissing, when she asked me: "Where are you off to next?" Well, we shall see, for I still have a lot of dreams and at age 70, I am much too young to stop.

Africa: Overcoming and moving ahead

Arriving at the airport of Windhoek - Namibia's capital

Opposite: Wilhelm in the African bush

66

Achtung
Attention

Africa: Overcoming and moving ahead

Approaching the Kalahari Desert

Local transportation in Botswana

Pedaling, Paddling and Pedes 2

A bushman's mother with child

Precious Botswana children

Africa: Overcoming and moving ahead

Home sweet home

Opposite: Beans – a staple food

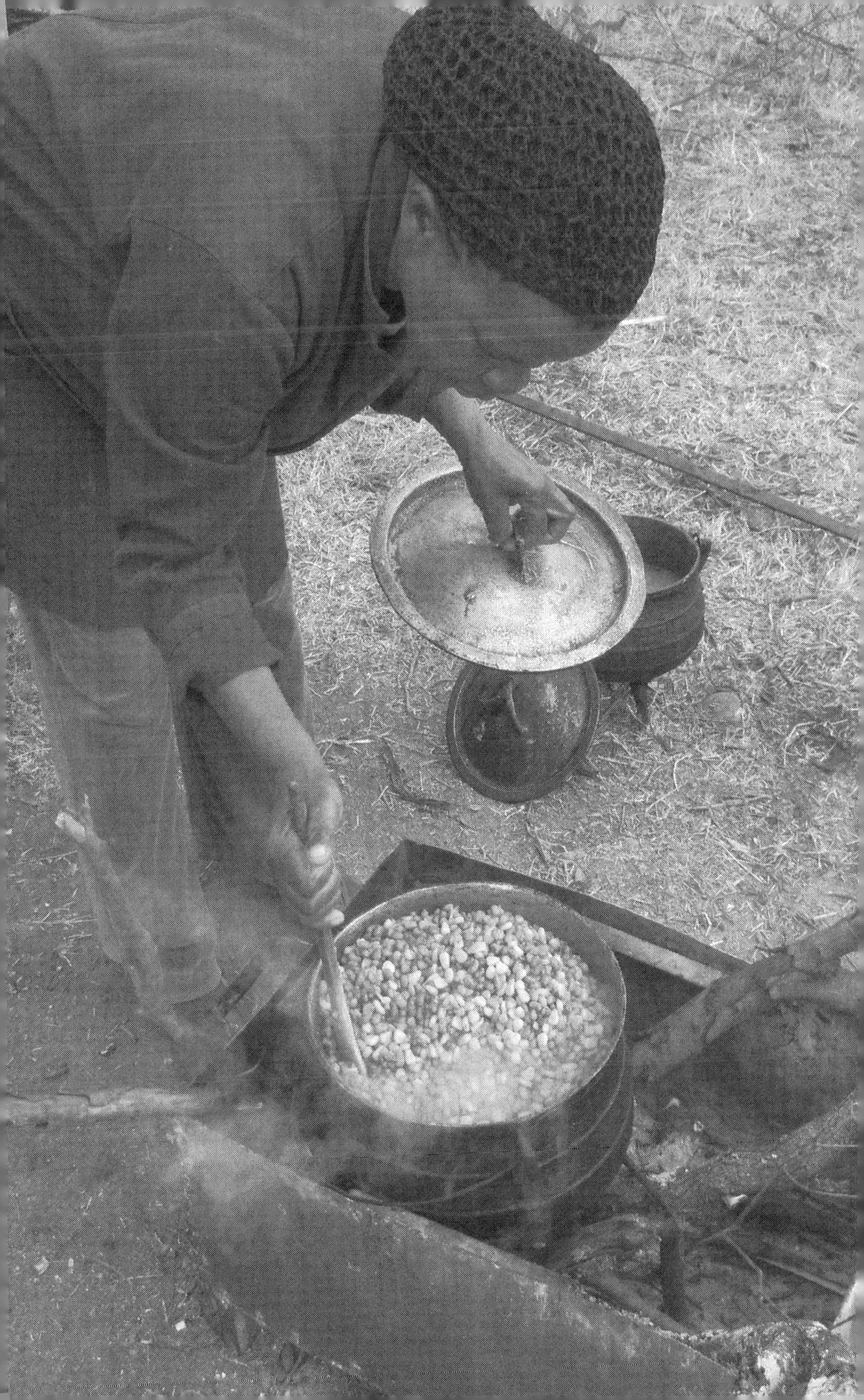

Indulging in needed proteins

Comped to stay in this cabin

Pedaling, Paddling and Pedes 2

My campsite visited by a lion

Fixing a flat

Africa: Overcoming and moving ahead

Africans struggling to survive

Opposite: ATM blown up by bandits

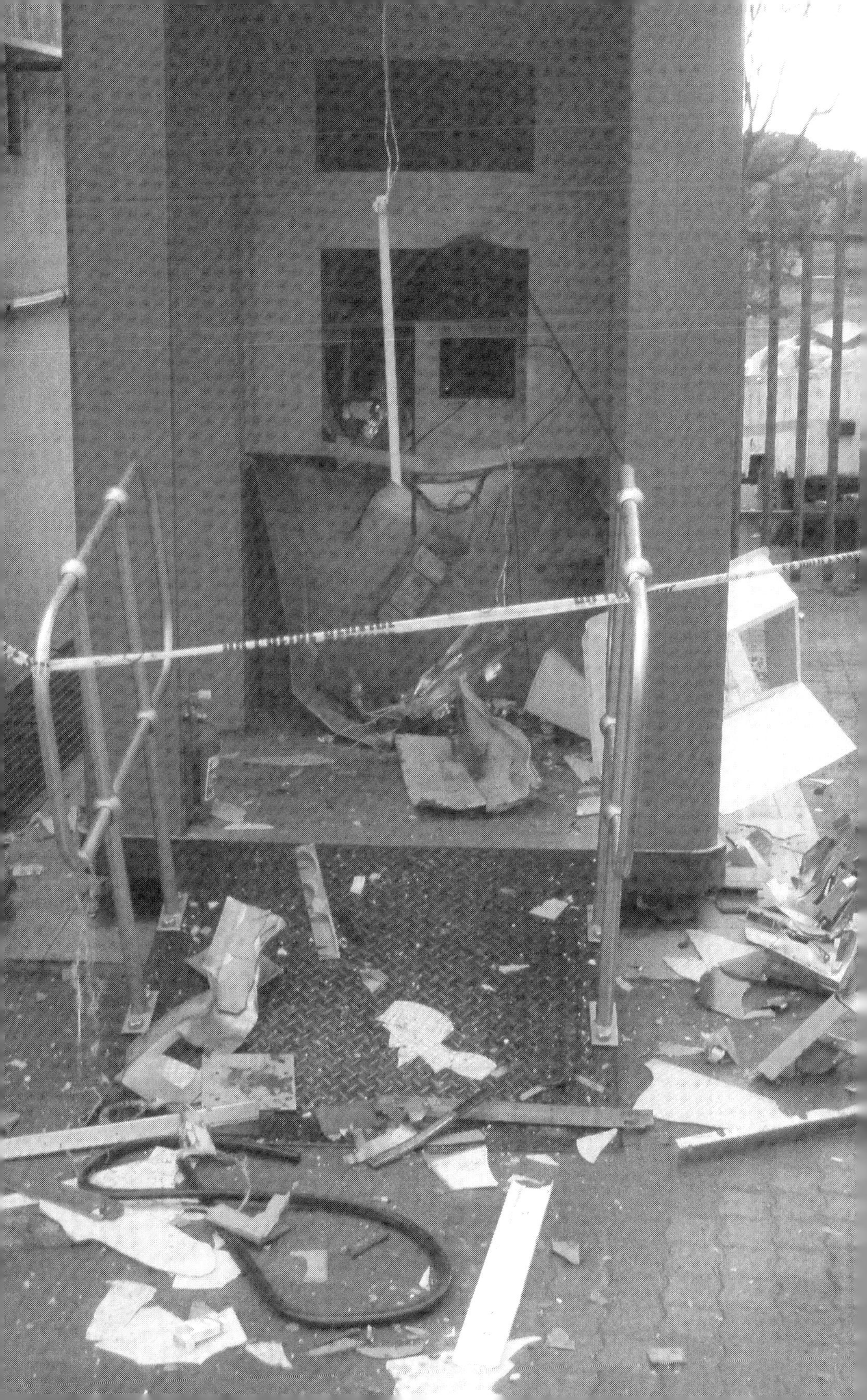

Africa: Overcoming and moving ahead

A generous breakfast buffet offered in 'my' hotel

Oranges galore

Papayas

Drying laundry in my hotel room

Market in Maputo, Mozambique's capital

Maputo's fishing harbor at low tide

Arriving at the Indian Ocean ending the ride across Africa

II. Australia
Across the driest of all continents

Chapter 6

Australia (1997)
German pancakes, a cyclone, Ayers Rock, Barrier Reef

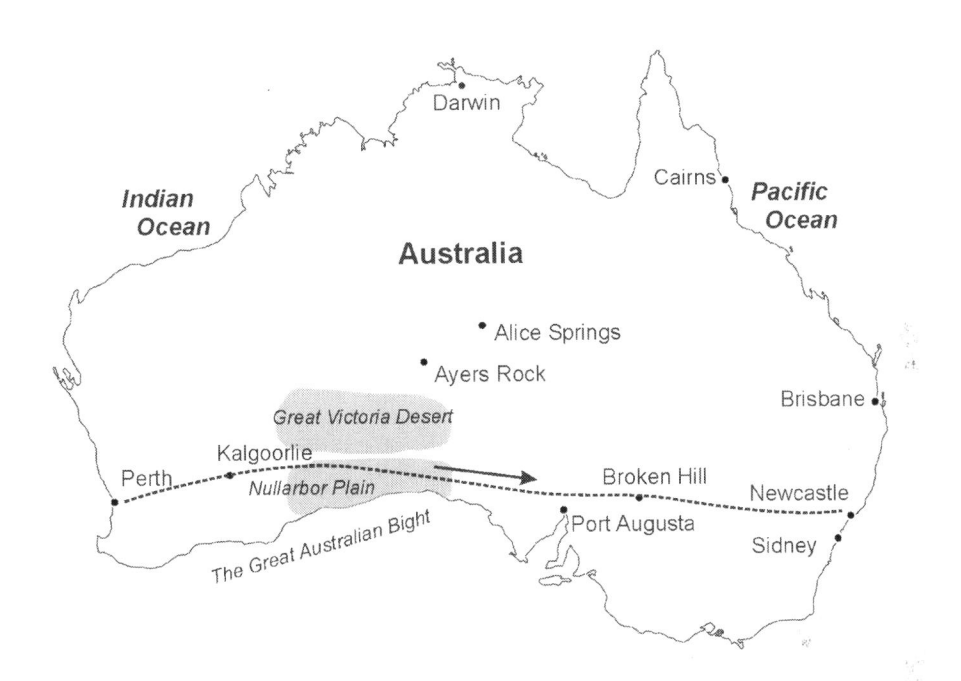

"Good day, mate", I was greeted, and the "mate" sounded like "mite" and I actually felt like a little critter in this vast, empty land. The continent of Australia is almost exactly the size of the continental United States but has only one ninth of our population. There was a road sign which related to 144 km (89 mi.) of absolutely straight highway, meaning there was not a single bend. That was within the 'Nullarbor Desert' (Latin for 'zero trees'), an expanse over 1,600 km (1,000 mi.) without communities and water. Even the lonely service stations along the road posted signs reading: "No water, don't even ask!" Well, I did not ever ask. I did not have to for I was not traveling alone. My friend Lois, who later became my dear business partner and companion, was riding along with me, alas, not on a bike but in a support vehicle, the very car we were now both riding in. Naturally, we could and did carry plenty of water in the car for us to use.

We had rented the vehicle upon our arrival at the airport of Sidney. I fitted a car rack I had brought in my suitcase onto the roof of the vehicle. That

Australia: Across the driest of all continents

was where we tied Wilhelm, my bicycle, down. "Let's just get out of town and then make camp" I suggested. Were we ever ready for some sleep! It was late at night. We had traveled over 19 hours since Reno, NV. Though we were awfully tired, we still had a big laugh when I got into the left side of the car where I was accustomed to sit and drive. What was this? There was no steering wheel. Of course, this was a left-hand traffic country. Correspondingly, the driver would sit on the right side of the car. That addressed, we took off into this large city, in darkness and totally unknown to us.

Driving on the left side was a strange and a bit scary sensation. My friend, who was traveling with me, was sitting on the left side of the vehicle which was so close to the left edge that she kept saying: "Watch the telephone poles! Don't hit the curbs!" I think she was serious. Later she told me that of course she was serious.

As planned, we managed to drive beyond the city limits. Unfortunately, the place we had selected for our camp was close to railroad tracks. Several times throughout the night, trains would rumble past us, waking us each time. Our plan was to drive across the country to the city of Perth on the Indian Ocean. Near there, from the town of Fremantle, I would begin my bike ride across the continent to Newcastle, a city a little north of Sidney. My friend Lois would drive a little ahead or behind me in this rental car.

Only two months prior, I had sort of casually invited her to come along. She was my immediate neighbor then. I did not seriously expect her to join me on this adventure. Lois does not have any difficulty making decisions. It was only three weeks later that she told me, "I am coming along!" Now, I became a little uneasy. Could I dare to take an American woman used to all the conveniences of her home, into the wilderness and most primitive back country of Australia? She would have to go several days without shower and laundry facilities. Alas, this determined lady could not be discouraged from coming along now. I assumed that she was ready to show me, and maybe herself, how tough an American woman can be. And indeed, she was that, at all times, beyond my wildest imagination.

It was a good choice to begin this adventure in early May (1997) for 'Down Under' the summer had just ended. Temperatures can easily reach 40° C (104° F). Now, in Perth it was cool and rainy. Having been settled first by the British, 'Fish & Chips' was still a popular dish and that became our first meal in a restaurant on this trek. It had taken us three enjoyable days to cross the land. Now, for 4,500 km (2,790 mi.), we would follow the route we had just gotten to know. We had spent the night in Perth in one of the most comfortable Youth Hostel's I had ever encountered. It even sported a swimming pool. We had taken my bicycle along to the beach of the Indian Ocean and dipped its wheels into the water. Exactly 28 days later I would perform the same ritual across this continent at the Pacific coast.

For now, we traveled through fertile farmland that looked not much different than Missouri and Iowa, Lois's original home. The wind was with me. We made good speed. I would first ride ahead. Lois would relax a while, break camp a little later, then catch up and pass me to wait a few kilometers ahead. Every 20 km (12 mi.) or thereabouts, we would rendezvous and chat a little, listen to some fine classical tunes we had brought along while I enjoyed a drink and a snack.

The rain had stopped, but it was still overcast when we prepared our first lunch. From the wire of a coat hanger, I had made some 'feet' for a little grill grate. This we placed over a small wood fire and Lois would bake German style pancakes in a frying pan. They differ in that they were prepared without any leavening thus they did not rise. That became our staple along with purchased jam for breakfast and canned meat or sausage and cheeses for lunch and dinner. The latter we kept light for obvious health benefits. We always carried plenty of fruit and vegetables with us.

In the township of York, we had seen an old colonial style mansion which intrigued us. It had been converted into a bed and breakfast establishment. That was where we spent the first night. We were given a tour and marveled at how the original pioneers kept their household.

Slowly we left the cultivated land behind. It had turned more arid. The soil now consisted of reddish sand in which eucalyptus trees seemed to thrive. It was easy to find a suitable campsite. Riding ahead, I would normally scout for a place to pitch our tent a little away from the highway. Then, surrounded by trees, we were less likely to be noticed by anyone passing by. Satisfied for having typically biked 150 km (93 mi.) per day, we would relax at a campfire and enjoy the ambiance of our surroundings. This was outdoor life in the Australian bush at its best.

In the town of Kalgoorlie, we replenished our food and water supplies. Do people eat kangaroo meat we wondered? When we saw some salami-like sausages made from kangaroo, we just had to try it. Not bad! In the parking lot of the supermarket, we noticed vehicles with an arrangement of iron bars in front of the hood. That was protective 'armor' against hitting animals when driving the enormous distances. Australians would typically travel at high speed even in darkness. We, however, were never in a hurry. Hence, we drove more cautiously with more respect for the sanctity of life. Kangaroos and emus are very social beings. When the first animal in a single file would cross the road, all those belonging to the clan, would certainly follow, even in the face of death by a rapidly approaching vehicle. Regretfully, we saw thousands of their carcasses spread along the highway.

The huge birds known as 'emus' were not as common. At this time, we did not know the astounding health benefits of their oil, so beneficial to treat psoriasis, acne, eczema, arthritis, sore muscles, dry skin, cold sore, rosacea, sport injuries, wrinkles and puffiness.

As we traveled deeper into the desert, we wondered where the wild animals found water. Well, they just did. Would the morning dew be sufficient? Beyond that, we also imagined they would chew moisture-containing plants. Because of the scarcity of water, we made sure we always kept an ample supply in the car. After a few days, Lois was ready to do some laundry, washing by hand, of course. To dry, she spread the clothes over some nearby bushes. Passing truck drivers seemed to show a keen interest in her underwear, which they manifested by powerful honking. She learned quickly to 'hang' her more private washables on the backside of the bushes away from the highway.

We were intrigued and amused by the sounds made by the local ravens, so different from what we hear back home. It ended in a mocking-like singsong, which we took pleasure to record. With all the road kills, there was no shortage of food for them. Other animals, like the dingoes of the canine family, joined to share the bounties though we imagined not always peacefully. Similarly, gray cats survived in the wild. On occasion we saw foxes. Riding a bicycle had a great advantage. I could quietly approach animals, often only noticed by them sort of at last minute. Among the imported critters were also eagles and hawks. Certainly, there must have been rodents or snakes for them to live on, yet we never saw any. So, the road kills had to do. They had turned vulture.

At Mundrabilla Roadhouse, which was not much more than a petrol station, a miniature zoo had been established. Most animals present were native to Australia. The dromedaries from Africa, erroneously referred to as camels, had found a new home here.

One evening, we saw a wombat, a cuddly little bearlike beast. Sadly, a vehicle had killed it. We returned in the morning to take another look. It was gone. In the sand we noticed obvious signs that it had been dragged. We followed the tracks for 50 m (165') and there it was. We surmised only a dingo could have been strong enough to do that. Most likely the canine was watching us from behind some bushes. We kept a watch out for koala bears. Alas, we never came upon one, except later in the zoo of Sidney.

Was it not ironic that on the driest spot of the driest continent, we were inundated by a cyclone, one of those mighty rainstorms? The normally friendly skies had turned dark and sinister one morning. Lois had driven ahead to prepare, as usual, a pancake breakfast over a campfire. Just a little before I caught up with her, the torrent came down. I had expected her to find refuge in the car. But no, I could not believe it; this determined little woman steadfastly continued flipping pancakes. "Please come into the car. We can eat something else." I called out to her. She refused saying, "I am already totally soaked through. It does not make any difference now." And thus, I got pancakes for breakfast, just a little more moist but still delicious. We sat and ate in the car in our wet clothing.

What next? Would we have to experience some flooding? Could our vehicle get stuck in wet sand which was turning into mud now? I drove the car back onto the pavement. Good so far! We knew there was a motel with restaurant and convenience store at Eucla about 20 km (12 mi.) further on. Considering this tempest, should we just drive there? No, I was not about to cheat! Lois, whom I now called 'Wombat' due to finding one of these interesting small creatures we both thought was cute and cuddly looking, had just given me a demonstration of toughness. So, back on the bike I jumped and pedaled until the elements simply forced me off my bike. Even pushing it became a struggle. Oh misery! Would this not strike you as a time to sing? Ballads maybe? And still stronger the tempest blew. Despite my raincoat, I was totally wet and my strength was fading. At last, out of this enormous dampness, I walked into the reception of the motel. The owner, a Lithuanian and thus a 'neighbor' to my native East Prussia, welcomed us with warm hospitality. The long hot showers followed by a long sleep-in midday in cozy, warmth while it continued to pour and blow, belonged to the highlights of this trip. Meanwhile, on strings I had tied across our room, we tried to dry our wet clothes.

By midafternoon the rain had stopped. We went for a long walk across giant sand dunes nearby which met the Indian Ocean. Visible to the east was the 'Bight', a spectacular rock coastline. The South Australian plateau came to a sudden end and dropped over 150 m (500') for a length of over 1,152 km (720 mi.) of coastline. Beyond Eucla, the highway ran so close to the 'edge' that we could see the agitated sea from lofty heights, pounding the mighty granite walls below. The desert landscape had been so thoroughly watered by yesterday's typhoon that a layer of mist lay over the land, filling the air with a wondrous refreshing scent. First, we only heard the surf. After a while the sun broke through. All day long, we could take in this grand experience with all our senses. I kept 'pulling over' to watch, listen and smell in deep awe. We walked along the edge and finally camped right there for the night to wake up to a glorious sunrise. We cautioned each other to be careful of that perilous edge should either of us leave the tent in the night.

While we were picnicking at a rest stop, a rather overweight lady came over from her car and sort of interrogated me, the cyclist, in particular. Why would anyone (in his or her right mind) want to bike across a whole continent, when it was obviously so much faster and easier in a car? Good grief, what a question! Later I kept dwelling on my answer and all those I could have given her as I biked on. Yes, why did I do this? Was it to build a healthier, stronger body or to see and to learn more of land and people? Was it for the love of adventure and fun or forthcoming attention and recognition? Was it to demonstrate a wholesome, ecological, economical alternative to motorized transportation and to promote biking? Was it, as a health practitioner, to lead by example, to inspire others to raise their own consciousness by connecting with the great outdoors? It was all of that and so much more: A deep emotional and spiritual experience, vibrant love for the earth and a zest for life.

By now I was 'broken in' to biking in Australia. It also helped that I had lost a little weight. The road was level and the wind kept supporting me. We made excellent time. Just before we reached the end of the Bight section two days later, we passed through a reservation called 'Yalata Aboriginal Land'. It was strictly forbidden to enter with any alcohol. We were very safe in this respect. This was my third year without a drop of liquor. Ironically, it was right here that I found a full, still sealed, can of beer next to the road. Ignore it? Would that not be sacrilege here in this giant, waterless desert, where every drop of liquid was precious? I could not possibly leave it to waste, or even worse, risk having it fall into the 'wrong' hands. Thus, we took it along to a most delightful place named Fowlers Bay: A community of about twelve homes overlooking a picturesque bay with small rock islands. We wondered how locals could afford such nice houses and assumed that retired folks from far away came here to be gone from hectic life, for this was the ideal place for that. By walking out on the pier, we sent swarms of waterfowl into the air that had been resting there. We spread out on a picnic table on the beach and had lunch. It was here that I enjoyed the beer I had found.

Slowly we came into agriculturally developed areas. The next day was a Sunday. Surprisingly, it was overcast, and it even rained a little. I had seen street and road names in German leading us to believe that immigrants from central Europe settled this area. So, was this it? When the British, who came here first, grabbed all the fertile areas, they left the rest to later waves of immigrants. Here, next to the desert was certainly not the best soil, yet it had been turned into productive farmland. I stopped to take a picture of a huge tractor pulling an even larger plow. Later we passed a small Lutheran church. A few cars parked nearby meant some sort of service was going on. Lois was waiting for me there and on the spur of the moment, we decided to attend. I strive to be more a spiritual rather than a religious person. As I have observed it, ideally religion and spirituality would overlap. Unfortunately, so often they are opposites.

There were about 30 parishioners seated inside. The pastor must not have been accustomed to seeing strangers come in. When he noticed us entering, he stared at us, paused and repeatedly lost his train of thought. Of course, that drew the attention of the whole congregation on us. We sat down in the last pew. Heads kept turning around towards us. Then the pastor apologized! We thought this was hilarious but neither of us wished to disrespect the church or the ministry by even a smile. When the service was over, we became the center of attention in earnest. One older lady and her son Tim invited us to join them for lunch on their farm. Great! Lois grew up in the farm country of Missouri and Iowa. This was in some sort of way, her turf. She was amazed that this farm consisted of 6,475 ha (16,000 acres). After a great Sunday noon time meal, we retired to a large living room where we were offered tea. We were entertained by the many mice who ran about the room with no fear of those who lived there.

We were told, it took over two weeks away from home just to check the fences. On our way out, we were invited to pick all of the oranges in their backyard we wanted to take along on our trip. We did accept a small bag of the delicious tree ripened fruit quite different from what we buy in supermarkets in the US. We were both intrigued by the natural sweetness and vibrantly strong and delicious orange flavor.

About 100 km (62 mi.) before reaching Port Augusta, something unpleasant happened. The derailleur of my bike broke. It had loosened itself, got into the spokes and parts broke off. I could no longer ride. We found a bike shop in Port Augusta. "It takes three to four days for me to get a new derailleur sent from Sidney to fit your bike," I was told. Hmm! Stuck? Here we were right by the sea and that was nice. What if we used the rental car to drive up to famous Ayers Rock, considered to be the largest monolith on earth. We studied the map. 1,270 km (787 mi.) one way! That should keep us busy to be back in three days.

It rained lightly when we entered the 'Ururu Kata Tjuta National Park'. For now, we ignored the village dedicated to tourism. There were hotels, a museum, restaurants, a supermarket and gift shops, postal service, housing for employees etc. As we approached, we had a glimpse of 'Ururu' the aboriginal name for Ayers Rock. It was midday. We had the good fortune

Australia: Across the driest of all continents

to come upon a picnic area. From here, at a distance of 2 km (1.2 mi.), we had a great view of this natural wonder while we ate lunch. What made it so unusual was that it just was there in the middle of red sand desert, dotted with bushes and occasional small trees.

For about 20 km (12 mi.), we followed the road around the monolith. Here and there we stopped to marvel and to take pictures. People from all over the world were doing the same. Once we came to the east side, we walked a path through a stand of trees and past ponds leading to a narrow canyon. Similar red rock formation, I had experienced in Zion National Park in southern Utah. Here 'Silence' was posted to respect this aboriginal sanctity. Would we be able to climb the approximate 400 m (1,320') to the top of the monument? I was eager to do so. When we came to the spot where this is traditionally done, a sign forbade us the ascent. The authorities had decided it was 'too slippery' for the time being.

We spent the night at a local Youth Hostel and returned to Port Augusta the following morning. On our way, halfway back, we came through Coober Pedy, the opal center of the world. This town looked so much like a community of the Wild West of the USA. It seemed to have had a similar history. Walking through the many gem stores, we got a little education of what to look for. Only after we had become a little 'educated', did we begin our final negotiations and purchases.

Our timing was excellent. "I just received your derailleur an hour ago and installed it. Your bike is ready to go," I was told. As we headed further east, it seemed to get colder. Was that because we were getting deeper into winter or was it related to the geography? Probably both! On our way to Broken Hill, we came past giant earth excavations caused by the strip mining of iron ore. While I kept biking, Wombat went to explore. When we rejoined, she had purchased all sorts of jewelry made from polished iron ore which had a similarity to black pearls.

I remembered having read that there were skiing areas in the eastern section of Australia. Would we have to get over some high mountain pass where there might even be snow? Well, if there was, we missed it and that was good. In Broken Hill we stayed at the Youth Hostel. For the next nights, we were fortunate to find simple hotel rooms. In Nyngan, we made an interesting discovery. We had lunch on a picnic table in a city park surrounding a lake. While local trees and bushes stayed green year-round, here stood some trees of foreign origin. They had turned color and began losing their leaves. Of course, this was June. Autumn had advanced south of the equator. Back home it would be late spring now.

Then came our last night on the bike ride. It was already dark when I rode past meadows and fields of a very fertile region. Where could we spend this cold night? There was a sign pointing to a youth camp of a church group. We followed it and came upon a clearing in a patch of forest. First, we heard a bunch of youthful voices, then we saw a village of tents. We mingled with the throng. No one paid any attention to us. That was good, for I was worn out and ready to be left alone. All we wanted was to pitch our tent somewhere, and so we did at the edge of their encampment. Later Wombat told me that two grown-ups had come to investigate. When they heard me snore, one of them said: "They are sleeping already" and the other added, "let them sleep, we will see them in the morning."

They never saw us, for we were anxious to reach the Pacific this day. We had a long stretch of 150 km (93 mi.) to go. So, we got up early. There was frost on our tent. I used a pair of socks as mittens. Every once in a while, we stopped, and I warmed up in the car. The closer we came to the sea the warmer it got. First, we passed a huge coal mining operation with a lot of heavy trucks on the road. Once we got beyond that, we had to cope with denser urban traffic. Not only would that slow us down, it also increased the chance of losing each other. It had already occurred a few days earlier in the town of Cobar, where we were to meet in front of a supermarket. Lois had been ahead of me to do some grocery shopping. When I had stopped at some road construction, the crew was just having a grill party. I was promptly invited and fed steaks, sausage and rice along with beer. I could not have missed out on that, could I? So, it delayed me a little. When I came into town, I could not see the now so familiar car Lois was driving. Had she gone on? If not, I figured since she drove a car, she could easily catch up with me. So, I continued biking on the only possible road. Fortunately, a couple of hours later, we happily reunited and promised each other to be more diligent with our rendezvous.

It was slowly turning dark. By now we were in rush-hour traffic. Only 10 km (6.2 mi.) to go! I was giving it my best and the wind was with me. This was the 28th day since leaving Perth on the Indian Ocean. Oh, what a strange sensation to have the Pacific on the east coast! Where was that beach now? I could sense it, smell it and then I saw it, heard it and felt it. In darkness, I took Wilhelm down to the beach and as I had done at the start in Perth, lead him into the water. Finished! The bike ride from ocean to ocean thus ended. It was time to celebrate.

We were in the city of Newcastle. So far, when we had stayed in a hotel or motel, the rooms had been very modest, even primitive because that was all there was. Now we were back in civilization. Unforgettable, after so long, was our stay in the first-class hotel named 'Noah's By the Beach'. When I approached the reception, I asked for a "biker's special. Certainly, you must have a better rate for someone who just biked across your whole, beautiful country." Well, they did not have a discount program for such event until now but came up with one just for us. The hefty price break given us made our rooms even more enjoyable. We slept long, but not so long as to miss out on the outstanding breakfast buffet. It was so good it could almost compete with Wombat's daily pancakes. We had a table right by the window, looking out over the ocean and sat there in awe, wishing time would stand still. Long hot showers, fantastic food and now the unobstructed view of the ocean I had pedaled so hard to reach, a beautiful finish to this adventure and even more rewarding with a wonderful travel companion with whom to enjoy the finale.

Though the bike ride was finished, it was not quite yet the end of our Australian adventure. To reward ourselves, we flew to the town of Cairns, the jumping off point to the spectacular Barrier Reef. Would you believe, as we walked over the pier to catch 'our' tour boat for the 30 km (19 mi.) out to the Reef, that there was actually a sign reading: "KEEP TAHOE BLUE!"? Right on! We felt at home already and continued on to enjoy the last part of our adventure exploring the Great Barrier Reef.

In the land of kangaroos

Biking on the wrong side of the highway?

Australia: Across the driest of all continents

Emus – their oil is used for skin disorders

Vastly empty savannah

Wallaby, a kangaroo cousin

Great Australian Bight 1,160 km long

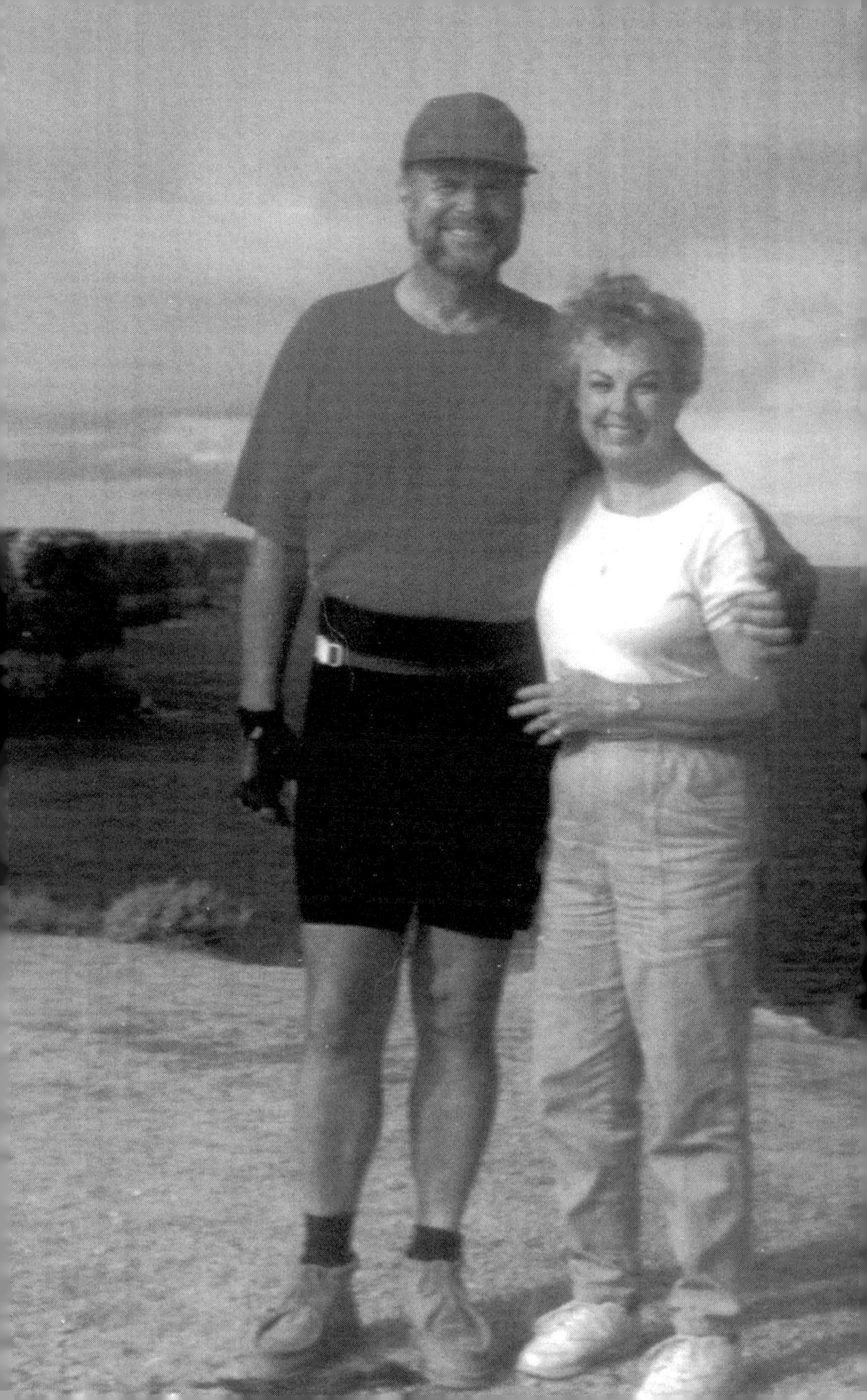

With Lois, halfway across Australia

Opposite: Hans and Lois, a happy couple at the Great Australian Bight

Australia: Across the driest of all continents

Please, read and remember the local road signs (distances in km)

Opposite: Aboriginals

96

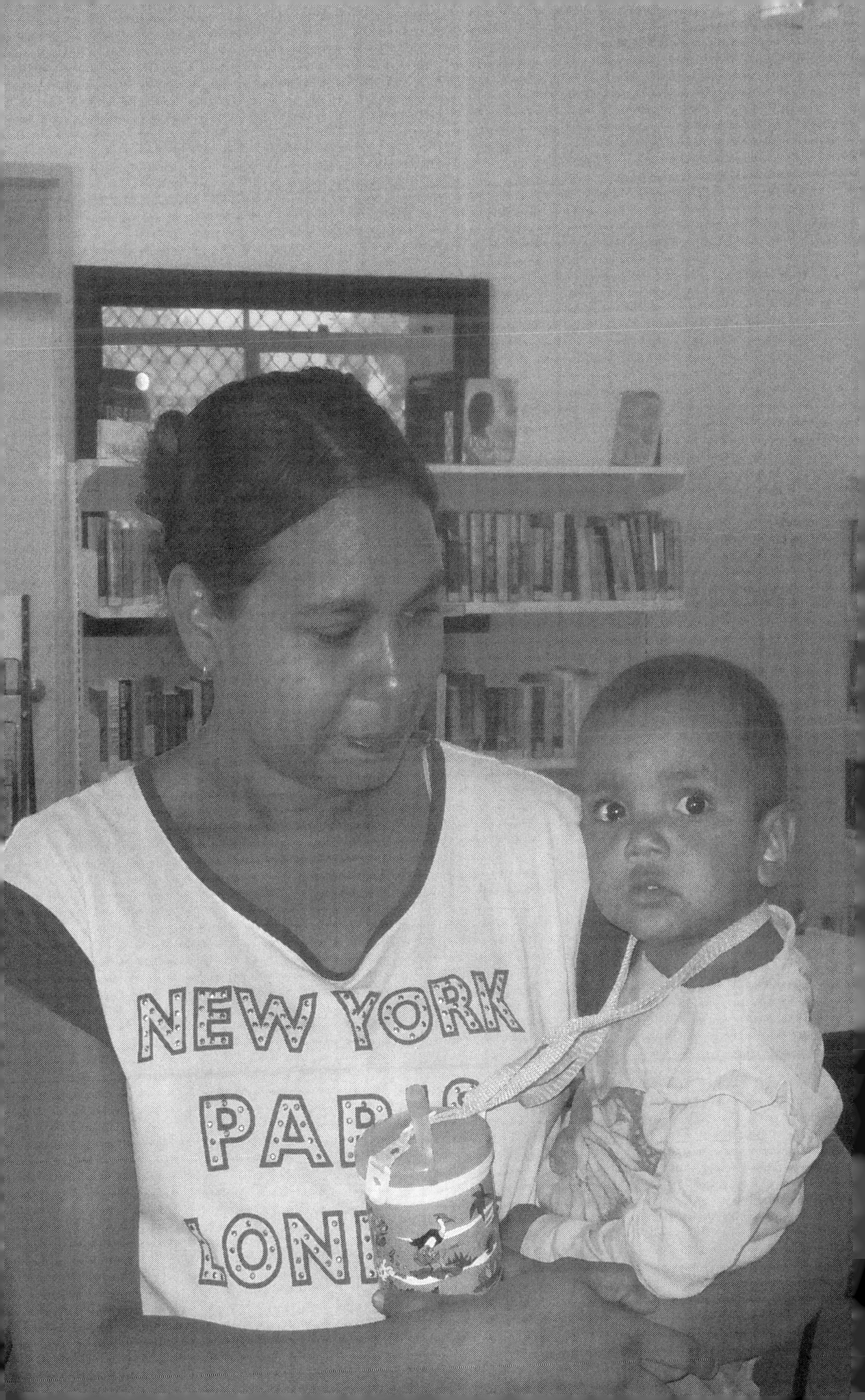
NEW YORK

Australia: Across the driest of all continents

Truck train up to 53.5 m (160 ft.) long

The highly poisonous brown snake

Sadly, most kangaroos we saw were road kills

In the land of eucalyptus trees

Australia: Across the driest of all continents

Baobab tree and Hans' bike

Termite column

Pedaling, Paddling and Pedes 2

Magpies which attacked me

Farmland in eastern and south Australia

Bike facilities on a turnpike offer safe biking

In downtown Newcastle

Noah's by the Beach where our tour ended

III. South America
Into the land of gauchos

Chapter 7

Chile (2010)
Bike trails, a German college, total exhaustion, the Andes

It helped that I worked out quite heavily on a stationary bike of the Holland American cruise ship 'Veendam'. What did not help were the ice creams, fine pastry and other questionable and tempting foods on board, one is so continuously exposed to. I had brought my road bike along and was anxious to go for a ride on the Falkland Islands a couple of days out from Buenos Aires and Montevideo. Argentineans typically call these islands Malvinas and claim them as theirs. Unfortunately, the sea, so the captain said, was too rough to allow us to go ashore. Cape Horn, the next point of interest, was known for foul weather and rough seas. Here, however, we were fortunate to have glorious sunshine and a friendly ocean. As we marveled at the rock islands where South America literally ends, the captain made us aware of a pair of condors soaring high in the sky.

The good weather held on the next morning when we reached Ushuaia, in Argentina. This time on my bike, I must have crossed the path of my 1971 hike several times which became the first segment of my trek across all of the Americas. It was winter then, cold and rainy. Obviously, a lot had changed in these almost 40 years since. I had heard that Ushuaia was the fastest growing community in Argentina. Touring the community, I could well believe that. Known as the southernmost town on our planet, flanked by gorgeous mountains, breathtaking glaciers and being the starting point of cruises to Antarctica, it attracts tourists from all over the world.

It was a festive moment for me to bike into the forested mountains beyond the town, on the road now nicely paved and well-traveled. Four decades ago, it was not much more than a jeep trail. At most I would see 3 or 4 cars in a day. On my return to the ship, a hitchhiker showed up carrying a huge knapsack. He looked sort of Anglo-Saxon. I later regretted that I did not talk to him. Thus, I could only wonder whether the island of Tierra del Fuego, like for me, became the beginning for him for the long trek to Canada or Alaska, and I could have suggested: "Young man, how about trying a bicycle!"

It was raining lightly when the "Veendam" anchored in the harbor of Punta Arenas in Chile. Riding my bike into town, I came upon the junction to the airport. That is where, a few years ago, I set out to bike to Antofagasta in northern Chile. When I was here in 1971, I met with some Germans connected with the local German Consulate of the Federal Republic of Germany. The 'Democratic Republic of Germany', also known as East or Communist Germany, sported a consulate in town as well. Interestingly, though both were Germans in a small, remote town, they would not talk to each other. Politics can be really absurd!

Early on February 23rd of 2010. Our ship had reached Valparaiso, just 5 days prior to a devastating earthquake. We were sitting in the stateroom waiting for our turn to disembark. Wombat called me to the window and said: "Look at that green house up on that steep hill. It looks like it is to fall down any moment." During the earthquake which measured 8.8 on the Richter scale it most certainly did.

After we had cleared Customs and Immigration, Wombat got onto a bus to take her to the airport of Santiago for her flights back to Reno. Hence, she would not get to see the beautiful beach resort of Viña del Mar. That is where I headed now on my bicycle, glad that for most of it I could ride on a trail dedicated to bike riders. Separating cyclists and motorists, this way assures maximum safety and convenience for both. The rule "Build it and they will come" certainly applied here. This was a weekday, and the biking traffic was heavy. Sadly, my attempts to prompt local authorities to consider the safety for the growing number of cyclists in the Truckee Meadows of Nevada have thus far shown only marginal results.

The area I biked through reminded me of Miami Beach and Waikiki:

Long rows of condominiums, elegant hotels, restaurants and fancy homes, all in a setting of gorgeous, tropical landscaping facing the beach and the sea. I must have biked along a stretched-out bay for when I reached the end of Viña del Mar, far in the distance, I could still see the "Veendam".

I followed along the coast for another 16 km (10 mi.) and then turned inland towards Aconcagua. At 6,480 m (21,384 ft.) it is the highest mountain in all of the Americas.

Who is to drink all that wine? Vineyards everywhere! When my former wife and I lived in La Paz, Bolivia, we traveled down to the coast to renew our tourist visas in Arica, Chile's most northern city. Starved for fresh fruit on the high plains of the Andes, we indulged in the wealth of huge grapes, juicy apples and pears, plums, peaches and others that must have come from the area I was now biking through.

The road was constantly climbing. Late afternoon I entered a canyon through which the Aconcagua River was running. Approaching the community of San Felipe, I came upon the well-maintained compound of a German college. In the town of Puerto Montt at a tourist office, Wombat and I had been told that there are still 18 German schools in Chile. So, this was one of them. I was hopeful to learn more about this institution, its history and direction, but also to request permission to place my tent on their lawn for the night. Alas, it was vacation time; of course, February is summer here. Neither the principal nor any teacher could be reached. No problem! I camped between some bushes just a little outside of their entrance gate.

Los Andes was the name of the next and last town in Chile, built in typical Spanish colonial style. Horse drawn carts mixed with trucks and cars in the streets. This was farming country. I had spread out on a park bench in the center of town, watched the busy life around me and ate sandwiches for breakfast.

While the ascent had been gradual thus far, that changed now. The rock walls on both sides rose higher and steeper. The highway snaked along the north shore of the river. On the other side, I made out railroad tracks. I thought it must be quite a chore to maintain them, seeing traces of so many rockslides. I had seen freight trains but then assumed that there must have been a junction where they traveled into a side valley. From that point onward the tracks had been abandoned. It appeared as if the mountains had their fun destroying this creation by human hands.

It was getting hot. Around noon, I stopped at a restaurant. I envied the two long distance bikers who leisurely coasted downhill while I ate. My major uphill efforts were still ahead of me. I left the establishment with a fresh supply of water, ready for the uphill battle.

South America: Into the land of gauchos

In higher regions, what I would call 'semi-tunnels' had been built over the highway to protect it from avalanches and rockslides. They were partly open on the side facing downhill. Inside of them it was cool. They became my 'magic markers' as I headed from one to the next. I was pushing the bike more than I was riding it, glad that the weight of my luggage did not exceed 5kg (11 lbs.) Each time I reached one of these tunnels, I was wet with perspiration and so exhausted that I thought this is as far as I can go. But then after 15 or 20 minutes of rest, some of my strength and spirit had returned, and I labored on.

The last 10 km (6.2 mi.) were most brutal. They were, in fact, the most demanding, I thought, I'd ever encountered. It seemed to me that the incline was possibly more than 12%. Even the engines of vehicles going up or down were whining and tires crying when negotiating the needlepoint switchbacks. My lungs, as recent as a day and a half ago, spoiled with oxygen rich sea air, now had to deal with an altitude of 3,000 m (9,900'). Every one of my cells must have been in shock. Three or four steps then pause. And again, a few more steps and pause to catch air.... Lungs, muscles, my whole system cried for a halt. Was I at my end? I thought of the incredible survival story of Captain Earnest Shackleton in Antarctica which I had read about while on the cruise. The airplane crash, not all that far from here, of a Uruguayan football team came to mind. The survivors struggled for months to reach civilization. The thought of these events related to extraordinary efforts propelled me on.

The sun had disappeared behind the snow-covered peaks. It turned rapidly cold. How and where could I spend the night? I finally reached the border post of Portillo. I completed formalities and exchanged my remaining Chilean currency into Argentinean pesos. I also learned that just a little over a kilometer away there was the tunnel of 3 km (1.9 mi.) in length connecting with Argentina. Since, we cyclists were not allowed inside the tunnel, a service was provided to chauffeur us in a van to the other side. And that was how I crossed the pass at 3,185 m (10,511') altitude into Argentina.

Chapter 8

Argentina 1 (2010)
Rafts, sleeping in a gully, a French cyclist, earthquake

I received a cold reception when I entered Argentina on February 24th. Coming out of the tunnel which connects with Chile high in the Andes an icy wind hit me. I fled into a lone public bathroom where I put on all my clothes I had brought along. Very helpful was a bright yellow rain suit, which was lightweight, waterproof and yet breathable. Besides blocking the wind, its radiant color made me rather visible now that it was turning dark. I engaged my red blinking rear light on Wilhelm as well as a strong headlight in front.

"Get off the road! The highway is ours!" kind of was the message aggressive truck drivers seemed to convey to me as they approached with gusto often honking wildly. In such cases, I had to get off the road even though there was no shoulder to escape to. One truck driver in particular was either sleepy or was overly eager to show me who the boss was. His maneuver could have gotten him in trouble. He approached me from behind, came awfully close to me and then at last moment spun his rig to the left away from me. When he was a little ahead of me, he overcorrected to the right, his right wheels leaving the pavement. How easy it would be to avoid these moments of dangerous confrontations for both cyclists and motorists with a proper shoulder. A 1-meter (3.3') pavement extension would dramatically enhance safety for both.

My next concern was to find a place to spend the night. I tried a hotel in 'Puente del Inca', a cluster of buildings where the canyon had widened a little. No rooms were available. I biked on into the night, careful to stay out of the way of trucks, in particular, when two passed each other. The cold and the fierce wind were not the only challenges. Another one was to find a level place in the darkness for my tent in this rocky mess. I must have biked about 30 km (19 mi.) when I crossed a bridge over the Mendoza River. At the opposite end I came upon a widening of the road. After a little further investigation, I discovered a hollow in the rocks just big enough an area to pitch my little tent. Lucky me again, for here I was wind protected. For a while I sat on the edge of the embankment leading down to the river. Moonlight reflected on the water's surface and the mountains up on high.

The sun was just trying to 'creep' over the mountain range to my right when I got going on the following morning. Biking downhill on a sunny day with massive mountains on both sides, it should have been a wonderful day.

South America: Into the land of gauchos

And it was for the first part. Cheerfully singing, I rode on, the sound of the wild river to my right as the background. Occasionally, I looked back, hoping to see mighty Aconcagua again. I never did. The canyon walls blocked the view. So different from the Alps, the mountains and valleys were dry and arid. When it got warm, I said goodbye to my old shoes in favor of the sandals I had brought along. Maybe some poor soul would come upon them and find them still useful.

Eventually, the valley widened, at least for a while. The landscape became even more desert-like, a bright beige in color. What a surprise then when I came around a bend upon a sudden 'wall' of green! There was no transition. Abruptly at the edge of desert grew rows of trees rich with juicy green color. This was the 'oasis' of Uspallata, a farming community and center for tourism. A stream ran through town providing water to irrigate the fields. After buying a fresh supply of food, I ventured into a park and leisurely indulged. Next to me was a booth where tickets for rafting tours were sold. Not for rides on the wild Mendoza River, I surmised. Wrong, as I was to find out later.

Biking on a few more kilometers, and the green ended just as abruptly as it had begun. I was back in the desert. The valley narrowed. I entered a canyon with the river now to my left. It was hot. To rest up for a moment, I found shade under a lone tree in the wilderness and promptly fell asleep. The touch of a cold breeze woke me. Heavy clouds had moved in. The strong headwinds returned. On and off it rained. Then, out of the corner of my eyes I saw something yellow bobbing up and down in the torrent of the river. I moved into a better position to look, and behold it was one of those rubber-rafts. It appeared that two men were frantically paddling. At times they disappeared in the rapids. Were they in trouble? If so, how could I possibly help? Now they steered into an eddy where they would be safe. Moments later they headed right back into the fiercest current. Ah, no trouble, these guys were just having fun.

I raced about 500 m (1650') ahead of them to be able to take pictures of this adventure. When they were close, I waved. Both enthusiastically waived back as if to have me participate in their exciting journey. And I would have loved to do just that.

Late afternoon it began to rain in earnest. While wind and cold presented a challenge last night, it was now rain making it difficult to camp out. In situations like this, I would have preferred to stay in a hotel, but any community was far away. My little tent was 'waterproof'. The problem was putting it up during a downpour like this. By the time it would be erected, most everything would have been soaked through. Maybe if I was creative, I could avoid getting wet and miserable. A white plaque with red stripes next to the shoulder marks the spot where gullies allow water in times of flooding to run under the highway. I examined one of them. It was totally dry inside and had sand on the bottom. It was just large enough to accommodate my erected tent. Cozily huddled in my sleeping bag, I contently watched the rain pound the world 'outside'.

Dense fog in the morning! The rain had stopped. The last hills of the Andes stayed behind. The sun broke through when I entered the huge plains of Argentina. When the blanket of clouds also lifted over the mountains now behind me, there on high, to my amazement, everything was white. New snow! This was a moment to rejoice, for would I have been just a day late, I would have been caught in what would have most likely been a powerful blizzard.

Here on the plains, it was pleasantly warm. The wind had slowed down. In short, I came past a string of vineyards known as *'bodegas'*. Signs invited passersby to stop for some taste-testing. To my delight they often included the words 'natural' or 'organic'.

Shortly before reaching the city of Mendoza, I turned south on Highway 40. In the community of Zapata, I passed a parked Nissan RV with French license plates. That certainly was a little unusual so far away from France. No one in sight, I rode on. I had been seen, however, by the occupants inside: Paul, a Frenchman, his German wife Marike and their little children Mako and Yoshka. Fifteen minutes later, Paul was riding his bike next to mine. His odyssey, if I remember correctly, had begun two years earlier in Halifax, Nova Scotia. They had their RV shipped to that Canadian port city. While he zigzagged biking across the Americas, Marike with the children drove their support vehicle. Both parents felt this was the highest level of education and bonding they could offer their children. Of course, besides seeing so much of the world, they were exposed to home-schooling.

We switched from Spanish to French and rode most of the day together. For me it was quite a challenge to keep pace with Paul. I thought him to be half my age, he was in top notch shape and free of luggage. Every 20 to 30 km (12 to 19 mi.), we reconnected with his wife and children for a little rest, chat and refreshment and on we went. After nearly 100 km (62 mi.) we separated in the town of Pareditas. Paul stayed within the 'Green Belt' just west of the Andes while I headed southeast into the desert-like pampa. There would be no habitation nor any water source until San Rafael 100 km (62 mi.) further on. There were, of course, *haziendas* (ranches), but they and their cattle were rarely visible. An ongoing 1.5 m (5') high fence kept livestock from roaming onto the highway.

I lasted another 20 km (12 mi.) before I lifted bike and knapsack cautiously across this fence. Just then, on a dirt road leading to a gate I saw the approaching headlights of a vehicle. Since I was about to enter private property, I was not keen to be seen. I lifted my stuff back up and stayed behind some bushes until the truck had cleared me and had taken off on the highway. Now I crossed the fence successfully.

When I walked Wilhelm into the desert, I noticed several entrances to what I thought to be fox dens. I did not pay any attention to them, yet they played a role in what was soon to happen. In the process of pitching the tent, I broke the joint of one segment of the bow that holds up the mosquito netting. Things like that can more likely happen when one is overly tired. Trying to keep the tent properly erect, I tied the broken pieces together with a string, alas not efficiently enough. That too had some bearing on what happened later during this unforgettable night. I fell asleep before I finished arranging my bedding. Never mind the flash of lightening and rolling thunder in the distance!

Three shots, really close in the middle of the night, got me out of my best sleep. How rude! No respect! What was going on out there? How had I been discovered? Cattle rustlers? Hunters? The rancher? There had been something strange about these shots. They were sort of 'soft', more like from a BB or pellet gun. I stayed in 'bed' figuring anyone having some business with me would make himself known. Nothing, however happened. Promptly I fell asleep again.

More rudeness! It was around 3:30 h. The tent and the earth below me started to move. What was going on now? I remembered the foxholes. Were the animals now expanding their den below me? The thought that I might break through the ground into a narrow trench dug by them woke me fully. I got up and moved the tent and bike 20 m (66') further on. No more shots, no more foxes – just the usual silence and peace.

When I broke camp in the morning, I could see why one section of the tent was hanging down. The string I had tied in the evening around the joint had come loose. The tension on the bow had caused the joints to catapult against the rainfly, once, twice, three times. In my sleep, I had held the noise thus created for 'soft' gunshots. That explained the first of the nightly mysteries. For the other one, I had to wait a few more hours. Passing them, I could not detect any sign of activity around the fox dens.

Early afternoon I rode into San Rafael. Pffff! I heard the air escape through a puncture in the rear tire. I walked across the street to a petrol station. Talking with the attendants, I now learned why the earth below my tent shook during the night. It was caused by the devastating earthquake near Valparaiso about 250 km (155 mi.) as 'the crow flies'. The picture of the 'green house', so precariously built on a hillside, tumbling down and shattering occurred to me in my mental eye.

How could this happen to a seasoned cyclist? When I set out to fix the bike tube, I discovered that my rubber cement had totally dried up. This was Sunday. Stores would be closed, right? *"No problema!"* said one of the attendants. "The convenience store across the street is open. They carry rubber cement." He was right. A little later, I rolled on into town and stopped at a supermarket, which luckily, happened to be open. A very Scandinavian looking fellow in front of the store admonished me in flawless English not to leave my bike unlocked. "How come you speak English so well?" I asked. "I am the local English teacher." Some of his students showed up eager to practice their language skills. Several of them were tall, blond and occasionally blue-eyed. One would expect to hear Swedish, German or French etc. But no, rapid Spanish with the typical Argentinean twist would come out of their mouths.

The streets in the south part of town were blocked. Large, noisy crowds had gathered there. Police officers on motor bikes, lights flashing and sirens howling were busily hurrying back and forth. What was going on? Great! A bike race! Hundreds of colorfully dressed cyclists approached at high speed, just like one would see on television reporting on the 'Tour de France'. I refer to fellow cyclists as 'brothers and sisters'. In that sense, motor-bikers, who are also two wheelers, are distant cousins to me. I like to tease them as 'cheaters' for using a motor instead of 'muscle-fuel'.

For a while, I biked through an agriculturally developed area. Then I was back in the heat of the desert again. There was a time when biking became mechanical, legs moving like the pistons of an engine. My mind slipped into a semi meditative state. This was one of those moments. There was nothing around to distract or interest me. The kilometers just went by hardly noticed. I was less conscious of the heat until I heard a very disturbing sound. Oh no, a spoke had broken on the rear wheel. This should not have happened for the wheel was new and I had been biking on well-maintained highways. I was almost afraid to look and see on which side the break had occurred. I had no tools to replace a spoke on the side of the chain. Fortunately, the problem was on the opposite, the 'good' side. That still presented a problem for I had left the pair of pliers which I use for a job like this at home. What could I do? For now, I adjusted the wheel so that I could ride with a minimum amount of friction on the forks. I was lucky that after a few kilometers I came upon a ramshackle ranch structure. There was a significant distance between the gate in the fence and the building. I had to scream at the top of my lungs hoping

South America: Into the land of gauchos

to be heard. I was about to give up when a fellow appeared. Good! The place was not too primitive not to have a pair of pliers. Now I discovered that all my six spokes I carried with me were too long. I took a chance by clipping a few millimeters off the threaded end. Fortunate again! I could make the nut fit to tighten the spoke firmly onto the wheel and continued riding.

Very much I welcomed the coolness of the night. The traffic was light. Soon the moon was shining on this quiet and peaceful world. Biking was fun again.

My first stop, next day, in Santa Isabel was a bike shop. The mechanic was not pleased with my overly long spokes. He did not have fitting ones either. He jumped on his motorbike and dashed to the only other bike store in town and returned with half a dozen of fitting spokes. One he used on my bike, the others he gave me as a present. My wheel perfectly adjusted; he refused payment for all his work.

I had hurried to reach town. To restore my energy, I stretched out on the lawn of a park and promptly dozed off. A well-meaning dog got me up rather quickly when he licked my face. In just a bit, I was back in the heat of the desert. Turning into a 'machine' did not work so well today. The heat got to me. I looked for shade where there was none. Then I got an idea. When it rains in these regions, it can do so quickly and heavily, as I was to find out a few days later. Ditches were maintained on both sides of the highway. To the extent that ranchers can get across in times of flooding, bridges had been built to connect their dirt roads with the highway. Through the bottom of them led concrete ducts about 1 m (3.3') in diameter. There was my shade! I crawled into one of them and found it cool and even felt a light draft. A little snooze and I felt so much better!

After 70 km (43 mi.), I needed another rest. When I saw the village of Puelen, a kilometer off the highway, I turned there. A boy thought he knew where a food store would be open and guided me there on his bike. Wrong! It seemed the youth and I were the only things alive in this sleepy community. Pang! Another broken spoke! Again, without any noticeable cause! Oh horror, this time it happened on the side of the chain. I was stuck. The next town was 40 km (25 mi.) away. "Is there bus service to and from this village?" I asked the boy. "Yes, sir there is, but we also have a bike shop right here." Now, that was a surprise. The mechanic also owned a grocery store, which he closed so he could fix my bike. An hour later I was riding again.

Chapter 9

Argentina 2 (2010)
Mighty storms, a cow, bees, police, apples, the Atlantic

Enjoying riding at night in the moonlight the land seemed less drab. Towards the Andes, I noticed flashes of lightning. Clouds were moving in. When I made camp, I put up the rain fly. I heard thunder far away and that was where the storm stayed: in the distance. The clouds also protected me from the heat for the first part of the following day.

Then, by midafternoon, I crossed the Colorado River. Of course, not the same named river flowing through the southwestern states of the USA. For several kilometers on both sides, orchards and fields were thriving. Immediately beyond, without any transition, the desert continued. That was where I headed for a while before the road turned close to the green belt next to the river again.

A change in the weather was brewing. The sky had rather quickly turned into a combination of colors ranging from intense orange to pink and purple. I had never seen anything so amazing and yet so strange. When I saw mighty dark clouds moving towards me from the south with an array of flashes of lightning, I knew something big was about to happen. The staff of the petrol station, where I sought refuge, was talking about an approaching *tornado*. Like an explosion a powerful gust of wind carrying blinding dust and dirt seemed to make the station shake. All sort of things flew through the air. When the tempest softened a little, the storm began. For an hour the rain was rather gentle but then it turned into a powerful crescendo. The station, like most, featured a convenience store including a section with tables and chairs where one could eat. That is where I hung out until the tempest slowed down.

Maybe it was not the best choice to continue biking after the rain had stopped. I could have inquired about a hotel and pedaled a few kilometers out of my way. Instead, I biked into a dark and wet world. Gradually the water ran off the highway and dry spots began to appear. After 20 km (12 mi.), I thought to have found a spot for the night. I branched off onto a small dirt road and got into a real messy situation. What, in this darkness, I had thought to be a patch of sand was the watery surface of a swamp. Too late! Both wheels had already sunk deeply into the mud. When I carried the bike back onto the pavement of the highway, it seemed Wilhelm had become twice as heavy. Mud had caked to the chain, the tires, the derailleur, everywhere and

South America: Into the land of gauchos

of course, on my sandals, socks and legs as well. Using a stick, I removed some of it so that I could ride again. How heavenly a cozy hotel room would be right now! Since everything around me was flooded, what I looked for was a rocky dirt road. Eventually I found just that and it became my 'bedroom'.

On the next day, the sun baked the mud solidly to the bike's frame and gave it a pitiful, reddish appearance. I had left the 'green belt' during my nightly escapade. There would be desert now until I reached the fertile crest along the Rio Negro 80 km (50 mi.) further on.

A cow had gotten outside the fence. While cattle are used to noisy vehicles driving by, a bike rider spooks them. The animal was running as if for her life along the fence when I approached. Only when she seemed totally exhausted, could I get past her. I wished, I had a way to alert the rancher or the authorities for fear an accident was about to happen. I had to leave the reporting to the folks traveling with cellphones. Wild honking behind me probably meant that the poor beast was already getting in the way of motorists.

Reaching the Rio Negro Valley was a delight. It was like entering a different world. While crossing the Rio Colorado earlier had been brief, here 'my' road followed the course of the river for the next 200 km (124 mi.). There was an abundance of fruit orchards. I wondered how there could possibly be a market for all the apples, pears, peaches, plums, grapes etc. grown there.

In the town of General Roca, I stopped at a large bike shop for some adjustments. My Wilhelm was still a sad sight. The owner must have taken pity on his appearance. He offered for me to wash him down with a high-pressure water hose. Afterwards, I was directed to dry the bike with a hot-air blower. The whole staff was quite taken by my appearance as a long-distance biker. Payment was refused and extra spokes and other spare parts were given me as a welcoming present.

When I inquired about the origin of the town's name, I learned that it was named after General Roca. "What made him famous?" I inquired. "He killed many Indians." So, you named your community after a murderer, but I only thought that. I didn't think that locals had yet advanced to accept all people as brothers and sisters, who we are to love.

Talking of killing, I could have potentially come close to my own death before reaching the town of Darwin, not from the guns of soldiers or bandits but the stings of bees. It was my great fortune or was it the intervention of my guardian angel again that I was warned just in time? A car heading towards me, stopped and flagged me down. The driver told me that a truck loaded with beehives had overturned and thousands of agitated bees were swarming about. As if to underline his warning a bee buzzed past us. I wore only my bike shorts, a T-shirt, a cap and sandals, not even socks. I dismounted, hoping to thumb a ride past the spot of danger. The traffic was light. I sat down to have a snack. Unsolicited, a van stopped, offering me a ride. Great! I shuddered at the thought what could have happened to me, had I biked on.

Most of the hives had fallen into a swamp. Men, fully covered with protective suits, were working in the water trying to salvage what could be saved. Swarms of bees all over!

Stopped by the police! Had I known why they would trouble me, I would have found a way to avoid their highway checkpoint outside the village of Pomona. "You cannot ride a bicycle in darkness! It is too dangerous!" "What? I am used to those dangers, but is it against the law?" I kept pressing the officers for an answer for I could not believe that such law existed. Frankly, I was annoyed, requested the commander's name and promised to make a report to the Embassy of Argentina, which would allow me to come forth with a solution far beyond this incidence. It was only 21:00 h when I, sort of under duress, pitched my tent a little way from the police station. I would have been good to bike for at least another 20 km (12 mi.) in the coolness of night. Being held back shattered my hopes to reach the Atlantic coast in daylight of the next day. After roughing it for 10 days, I looked forward to check into a nice hotel in celebration of reaching my destination, the coast and thus the end of this biking segment from the Pacific to the Atlantic.

Pomona was the last community before I reentered the dry pampa. When I continued my ride in the morning, I faced headwinds, poor road conditions and heat. It was a struggle to move on. For my entertainment and fun, I composed the letter in my mind that I had promised to write. It would sound something like this:

Embassy of the Republic of Argentina
Department of Tourism
1600 New Hampshire Ave. N.W.
Washington, D.C., 20009

Re: Tourism revenue expansion

Dear Sir/Madam,
I am an author and write books and articles about my multiple bike rides around the world which include three biking tours across your country. An

unfortunate experience I recently made in your state of Rio Negro propels me to make a recommendation that would not only attract substantial tourism revenues but also, in a major way, enhance safety for motorists and cyclists.

Concern:

At approx. 20:00 h on March 4th, 2010, I arrived at a police checkpoint in the community of Pomona about 22 km south of Choele Choel. Highway 250 here does not have any shoulder. To avoid the heat during the day, cyclists like me, prefer to ride into the night. Although my bicycle, similar to a motorbike, was properly equipped with a strong headlight and a red blinking light in the rear, officers not only stopped me from biking on, but would not even allow me to walk any further. I was told that it was "dangerous". I responded that as an experienced cyclist I am very aware of dangers and know how to handle them. I then asked the officer addressing me, whether there is actually a law disallowing biking at night (Incidentally, I had frequently seen local bikers in Argentina ride in darkness even without proper light fixtures). He would not answer my question and refused to give me his name after I repeatedly asked him for it. When the officer in charge appeared, he told me that it was indeed against the law to bike at night. He shared his name with me (attached) and was agreeable for me to bring this incident to your attention.

I cannot believe that such a law exists and think the officers involved were concerned about my safety which led them to overreact and to abuse their power. Needless to say, I was embarrassed. Pomona does not offer any hotel accommodations and I was forced to spend the night outdoors.

Solutions:

1. Simply providing your highways with a shoulder, ideally at least 1m wide and paved, as is already done on some highway segments, would keep cyclists out of confrontations and harm's way with motorists.

2. Since many motorists, in particular truck drivers, seem to be unaware that cyclists are legitimate traffic participants in streets and on roads, corresponding instructions via your driving education facilities would enhance the safety for all.

Benefits:

1. Economy: The number of cyclists in the world is rapidly expanding. If it becomes commonly known that the government of Argentina is providing safe bike lanes/paths, many more tourists would visit your beautiful country.

2. Ecology: Bicycle riding favorably addresses global concerns such as air and sound pollution, wasteful fossil fuel consumption and deteriorating health.

3. Optimal safety for cyclists and motorists.

I trust that my recommendations are of value to you and that you will initiate corresponding action to increase tourism revenues by addressing the safety of local and visiting cyclists and motorists alike. I have chosen English as the language of communication for I wish to directly share your response with my worldwide readership.
Sincerely,

Hans Frischeisen
Reno, NV, 89503

P.S: Colicheo Horacio T., OF Principal – F*6472, Policia de Rio Negro, was the officer telling me that biking and walking at night on Argentinean highways is "against the law". If he is misinformed, I request that you initiate corresponding correction.
(I actually sent above letter on 4/25/10 to the Argentinian embassy but never received a reply.)

Several times before I had been asked why I thought it to be advantageous to bike at night. Hence, I continued my entertainment as I turned into a 'biking machine' by recounting some of my observations. The major advantage, so applicable in hot regions, I already mentioned: It is cooler at night. Some others are: Normally lighter traffic prevails, winds typically die down, it allows me to add a few more kilometers/miles towards my destination, in exotic places my ethnicity is less obvious, my blinking red taillight makes my presence more obvious and a visit to the outdoor bathroom is less complicated. That was as far as I got. What else would you add to this list?

I had not counted on the fact that I would not come upon a single human habitation for the next 150 km (almost 100 miles). There was nothing but desert! I was not adequately prepared with food. Aside from my emergency ration of Power Bars, I had only one puny salami sandwich left and a little water. My good luck was with me again. After about 50 km (31 mi.) someone's misfortune became a lifesaving blessing for me. A truck, loaded with boxes of high-quality apples, destined for Holland, had flipped. Most of the shipment was lying in the desert. Men were loading the freight onto two other trucks. I was invited to take as many apples as I wanted. I could also refill my two bottles with water before I happily rode on.

I was now approaching the most southern point of my journey and it should have also been the coolest. It was not! By midafternoon, I was badly in need of a rest. No shade anywhere, just thorny little shrubs. To mark the entrance to someone's dirt road leading to their ranch far back in the 'bush', a huge, erect tire had been cemented on each side. That gave me an idea. I leaned the bike against one of them as to extend its length and spread my rainfly over both. By doing that, I created a small area of shade, where I crouched down in the dirt somewhat in a fetal position. I actually managed to sleep a little. That was all I needed. Eating another apple, I went on.

The sun had already sunk when I reached the top of a hill. And there, far below, it was: The Atlantic Ocean! Though to reach one of the hotels on the beach of the resort community of Las Grutas, I would have to bike another 27 km (17 mi.). No more biking for tonight! I was done for the day and decided in favor of following a little road beyond a gate through one of the ranch properties. Good choice, I thought, when I came upon a perfect place to camp: 500 m (1,650') away from the highway. The ground was level and sandy. Low hills surrounded me with an opening to the sea. I savored this special moment of wonderful silence and peace. The wind had died, it was pleasantly cool, and no mosquitoes were bothering me.

This was a compelling moment of reflection as the daylight faded and the distant nightlights of the community far below me came into view. I felt a deep gratitude for being alive and so richly blessed. I thanked God for allowing me to see and enjoy so much of His most precious gift to us: This beautiful planet. I thanked Him for allowing me to reach my destination safely and happily. Then I ate another apple and lastly prepared myself to enter the land of sweet dreams.

Next morning the coast was gone. Heavy fog lay over the land. For a change, it was almost cold when I set out to bike the last few kilometers. As anxious as I was to head for the beach, my first stop in Las Grutas was a supermarket. Living off apples, as delicious as they were, was just not satisfying enough to me. With a bag full of food, I rode the last few blocks to the beach. But where was the sea? All I saw was an unattractive wasteland. Ah, this was the peak of the low tide. Where I expected to see the ocean, the fog met the sea and the two became one and there was nothing but a dim gray.

A long row of brightly colored houses, restaurants, hotels and souvenir shops faced the street and promenade along a bluff. Presently, breakfast was my priority. For that, I made myself comfy on a bench. I had lots of time and munched leisurely. After that, I busied myself catching up writing my neglected diary. Typically, when I was biking, all sorts of ideas would pop into my head. I would tell myself, "You need to write that down tonight!" But when I went to bed, I was just too exhausted for any brain work.

Eventually, the sun lifted the fog. The sea was coming back. Sky and ocean turned blue. People showed up. In a while the empty wasteland which had become beach meanwhile was sprawling with vacationers. It was certainly noticeable that this country is 'blessed' with large families.

Now that the ocean had returned in all its glory, the sun's reflection created a golden path across the calm, deep blue water. My eyes followed out towards the horizon. Only three weeks ago, somewhere out there, Wombat and I passed on 'our' cruise ship through very rough seas. I thought of my beloved who was with me then. I missed her very much.

South America: Into the land of gauchos

Starting at the Pacific Ocean

What a pretty name for a seafood restaurant

Opposite: Chilean grapes are exported to the US.

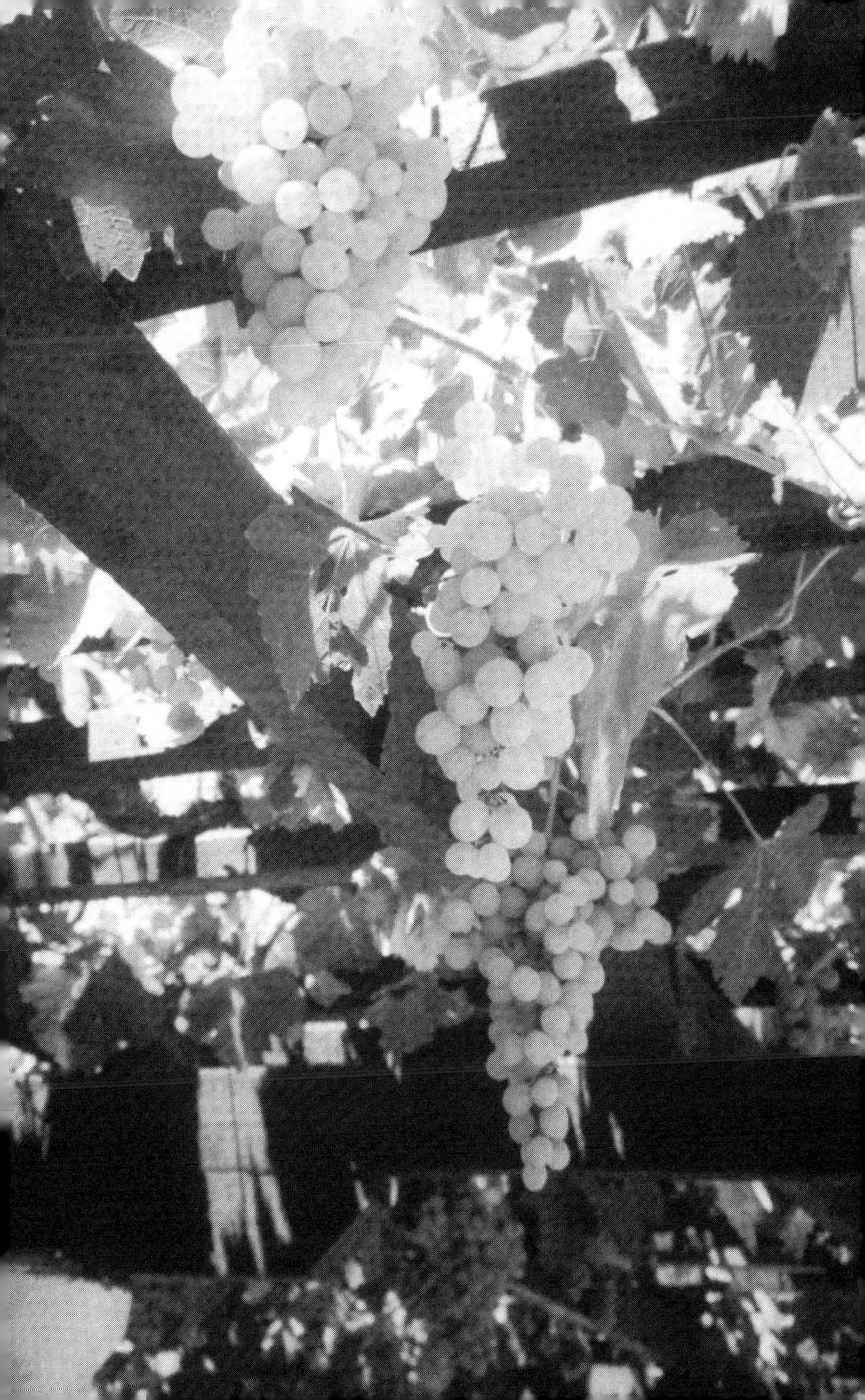

South America: Into the land of gauchos

Bike facilities in Santiago, Chile

Andean foothills

Leaving Chile – border post in the Andes

Entering Argentina

South America: Into the land of gauchos

Aconcagua at 6,962 m, the highest mountain in the Andes

Argentinian Desert

Lupins – flowers galore in Patagonia

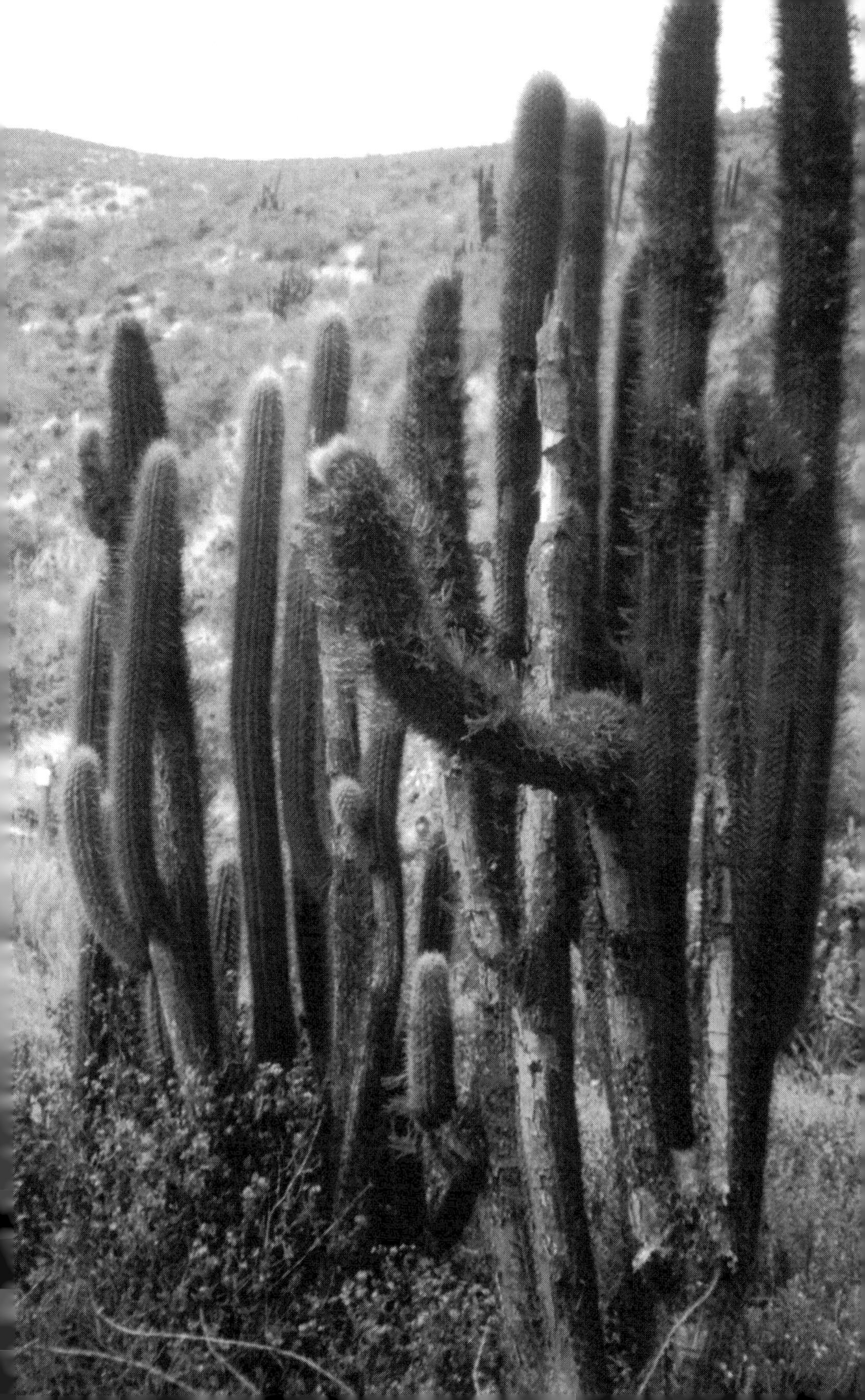

Pedaling, Paddling and Pedes 2

A smart energy source

Opposite: Cactus in bloom in Argentina

South America: Into the land of gauchos

Gaucho (cowboy) checking the cattle fence

Yucca, a staple food in South America

Chinese apples

South America: Into the land of gauchos

Hans' bedroom

Reaching the Atlantic Ocean – end of trip

A recent hike with my good friend Ragnar near Reno, NV.

Part II:

Biking Horizontally around the World through Countries of the Northern Hemisphere

IV. Europe
A view into European countries

Chapter 10

Through France and Switzerland (1995)
Losing Lisa, visiting Lourdes

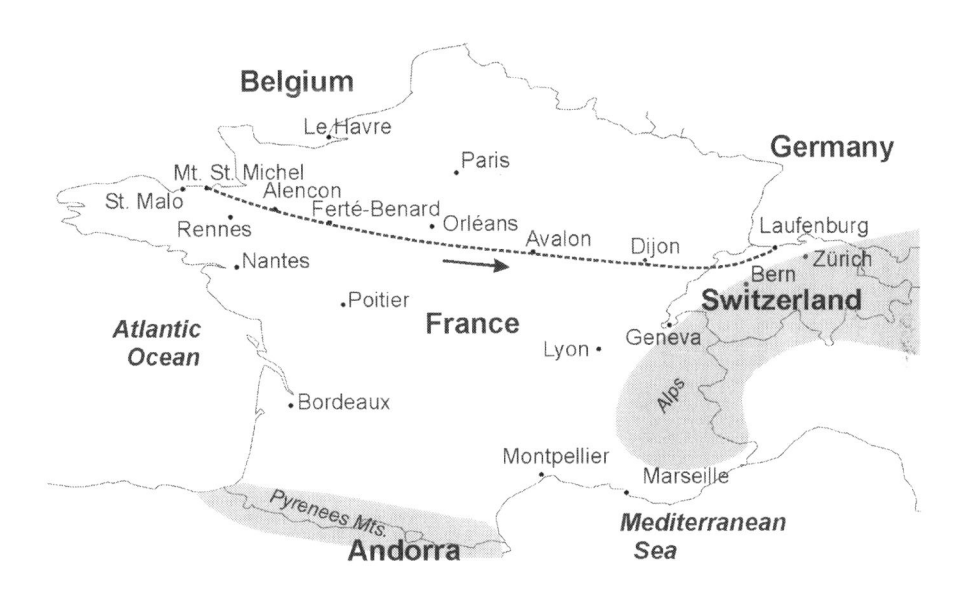

"Excusez monsieur, I am biking through your beautiful country and I'm having the time of my life. For this night, could I pitch my tent somewhere here?" Fluent in French, I asked that with a big smile directed at the farmer standing near his house. I had just ridden my bike up to him from the road where my friend, Lisa (not her real name), waited in our rental car. I then looked away from him toward the area where I hoped he would allow us to make camp. There must have been something catching as I turned my head to look, for he did the same. Then his eyes rested on a patch of grass next to a cherry tree. "How about over there?" and he pointed at the spot I already had in mind. "By the way, the cherries are ripe, so help yourself!" "Monsieur, the lady waiting in that little red car on the road over there is from America. She is traveling with me as my support person," I said. "That is no problem," I was assured. We had hardly put up our tent when the farmer returned with his wife. "Would you care to join us for a cup of tea?" they inquired. "We would be honored," I replied. Well, when we entered their home, we were first shown where we could wash up and later do our laundry. Then, we were guided to their dining area where there was more than tea, much more. Indeed, a generous dinner was served. Our contribution to all this was to share who we were, where we had come from, where we were headed, why we were doing this and what we had experienced so far. So, what was our story?

Lisa, originally trained as a nurse, was now a spiritual and herbal counselor in Mt. Shasta, California. We had met in Utah during a convention of Natures Sunshine Products, our favorite manufacturer of natural health remedies. We immediately liked each other and dated for a year, alternating visits to each other since I lived in Reno, Nevada. Then, I invited her to accompany me by rental car on a bike ride through Western Europe for my first segment of biking horizontally around the world.

On a beautiful, sunny morning in midsummer of 1995, we had arrived at the airport of Orly, outside of Paris. There we picked up a little red Peugeot rental car, which we immediately christened 'Poopsie'. Somehow, I managed to stow my partly disassembled bike inside this tiny vehicle and began to look for a solution to our jetlag. We checked into a little hotel and went for a snooze for a couple of hours. This was Lisa's first trip to Europe. So, of course, after a little rest, we had to do some sightseeing. We traveled by subway into the city center and did most of our touring from there on foot.

Was this for good luck what happened next? All tired out, we rested sitting at a sidewalk restaurant. Just then a pigeon's warm droppings landed right on my bare head, which was only sparingly adorned with hair. After an instant of surprise, I began to laugh about this humbling welcome to France.

Next morning, we drove to the Atlantic coast of the Bretagne Peninsula and marveled at the awe-inspiring rock formations known as 'Carnac'. Similar to the more famous Stonehenge culture in Great Briton, these were miraculously placed ages ago by Celtic tribes believed to have been the earliest humans in the area. Lisa, being very spiritually inclined, moved closer to the stones. I watched her hugging some rocks in a sort of meditative state and sensing their vibrations as if they were alive.

That night, we pitched our tent in a private campsite near the beach. I went for a luxurious swim in the Atlantic early in the morning. Lisa joined me shortly afterward for a stroll along the shore. We were almost alone to enjoy beautiful silence. Our peaceful reflections were suddenly jolted when we came upon sinister looking concrete blocks of Nazi fortifications left as reminders of World War II terror. They seemed just so much out of place here that we turned away not wishing to impact our tranquility with the ugliness of senseless carnage.

By midafternoon, we arrived at the spectacular site of Mt. St. Michel. Though the Eiffel Tower may be the most memorable impression of France for many, for art lovers it would most likely be the Louvre gallery or for others the nightlife of Paris. To me it was this fantastic, pyramid-shaped rock outcropping on the Atlantic coast. At times of high tides, so I've heard, it becomes an island that is almost as high as its diameter of .5 km (1,640'). A paved road of over .5 km in length connects Mt. St. Michel with the rather flat coast. When we arrived, we could drive right up next to the old city wall that surrounds the base of this fortification. We left Poopsie at a nearby parking lot and walked through the ancient gate and along the narrow streets of the community. Our path took us higher and higher until we reached the mightily fortified cathedral mount toward the top. A church spire stretched even higher yet into the sky.

It had been a very hot day. Refreshing winds coming from the ocean fanned us. It was wonderfully cool up there. "Look Lisa", I said, pointing westwards, "over there lies America", and jokingly I added, "If this was a day clear enough, we could see the Statue of Liberty." Its origin related right back here to France from where it had been made as a gift to the United States.

I could not imagine a more suitable location to begin my bike ride which was to eventually terminate at the Pacific coast of Russia. The sun set as I excitedly and jubilantly readied my bike for takeoff. Free of luggage, thanks to my companion driving Poopsie, I pedaled into the coolness of this glorious evening. Lisa followed me as I rode along. There was a Youth Hostel in the nearby community of Pontorson where we intended to spend the night. Unfortunately, it was fully booked. That, however, was not a problem for we were allowed to pitch our tent on their front lawn.

The nice weather held when we took off early on the next morning, so early that the songs from hundreds of birds were still in the air. The beauty of this trip was to choose the back country roads where tourists seldom or never would go. Besides that, it had several advantages: The traffic was lighter and it was relatively easy to find a site to camp either somewhere in the outdoors or on the grounds of a farm. Rarely did the distance between townships exceed 5 km (3.1 mi.). Mostly, Lisa would drive ahead and then wait for me near the sign posted to mark the entrance to a community. Waiving to her, I would ride ahead through a town. My friend, not yet trusting herself to drive in a foreign country, would at my rate of speed, slow down the vehicular traffic behind us. We got used to the wild honking and became the 'avantguard' of a noisy parade through these little villages and townships.

How about the common notion that the French do not like Americans? If anyone were to travel here with that disposition, it could become his or her experience, for negativity begets more negativity just as it would be true of the opposite. Thus, if you set out on a journey filled with kindness, joy and love, there will always be a corresponding echo. Because you brought your love with you, it is now present. Never were we refused hospitality. By

Europe: A view into European countries

avoiding large cities and typical tourist sites, we already reduced exposure to any possible frictions. Riding a bicycle has a distinct psychological advantage. People you meet often assume that you cannot afford costly means of transportation. They may also champion your sportsmanship or identify with your wanderlust. They will feel honored by your efforts to speak and learn their language and your respect for their customs and culture. This wealth of ready acceptance is not typically extended to those staying at fancy hotels and entertainment centers.

Amazing kindness and care were shown us on one occasion when Lisa and I lost track of each other. By that time, we had already traveled more than halfway across France. Everything had worked out extremely well so far. Maybe, because of that, we were a little less diligent about our rendezvous typically at the entrance into a community. On this occasion, as usual, Lisa had driven ahead. When I reached the town-limit sign marking the entry to the community of La Ferte St. Aubin, she was not there. While I waited for an hour, all sort of thoughts occurred to me. Might she have gone shopping? Not very likely! Lisa was not yet at ease without me. She did not speak the French language. Was there another entrance into town she may have chosen? Yes, about 500 m (1,650') back from where I was waiting, a street had branched off to lead into an industrial area. There was also a name-place-sign, but no Lisa either when I checked there. Had something happened to her? Did she perhaps ride on to the next community? She had an extra set of road maps with our anticipated route clearly marked on them.

It was getting late in the day. I had to decide on some action and biked on to the next village. She was not there either. An outdoor party was going on across the street from where I was waiting with growing concern. After 30 minutes, I knocked at my 'neighbors' gate within a thick hedge. For the sake of simplicity, I referred to Lisa as my wife. *"J'ai perdue ma femme!* (I've lost my wife!)" I said when someone appeared. The way I said it, it sounded as tragic as comical. These wonderful people immediately took me into their home and set about to help me. Lisa and I had agreed, should we lose each other, to contact the police to help us re-unite. My hosts now contacted various local police stations as well as the main office in the faraway city of Orleans. Incidentally, in most countries outside North America, like here in France, there was a charge for even local telephone calls.

Darkness had descended upon us. My hosts had meanwhile dismissed their guests. While we waited for some information from the police, I was served a sandwich and fruit. Finally, 90 minutes later, came the anticipated call with the good news that Lisa had been found. This smart little woman had located someone who spoke some English and informed the police of her location. And where was that? A campground in Ferte St. Aubin! The man of the house offered to take me there in his car while his wife stayed behind. Our tent was by far the smallest all around. It was easy to find, and soon Lisa and I were joyfully reunited. Next, we broke camp and with Poopsie followed our host back to the village of Menestreau. Now Lisa could give a full account of what had happened to her. Yes, she had waited for me at the town sign as we had agreed, except it was the sign at the industrial road entry. Then, when I was so obviously overdue, wondering whether something had happened to me, she had driven back to where we had been together last. While she was looking for me, I must have checked the place where she had been waiting only minutes prior to me getting there. So, we had missed each other.

Now we found out, why our hostess had stayed at home. The lady of the house had prepared one of those fancy, famous French dinners for us. No wonder the French word *"dinner"* was adopted into the English language. The feast, celebrating the event that 'my lost wife' was found, lasted deep into the night. We were then invited to sleep in one of their spare bedrooms. Of course, they would not let us depart in the morning until we had breakfast with them. So, what about "The French don't like Americans"? They even liked me, a German. Repeatedly, throughout history our two nations had been at war. It occurred to me, perhaps we should ignore our politicians, when they try to tell us who our enemies should be. Could it be that our problem is blind obedience, when disobedience may well be the best and only humane choice?

There was another time when we were exposed to exquisite French cuisine. It was dinnertime. We were hungry when we rode through the town of La Ferte Bernard. Instead of choosing one of the obvious roadside restaurants, we stopped to ask some locals standing in front of their home, where one could eat well. They jumped into their car and had us follow them. I was next on my bike and Lisa, driving Poopsie, at the rear of this little entourage, a noticeable procession through the narrow streets of this small town. Where did they lead us? We were far from the main thoroughfare and ended up in front of a private home. At least that was what it looked like from the outside. We would have never discovered this great place on our own. Nothing indicated externally that this was an eating establishment. We were ushered through the building into the backyard and placed at one of only five tables. What happened next was not just the serving of food. It was a feast. Only a master of the culinary art could do justice to describing what we were served. Voila! To begin with, there was a platter of fine fruit, followed by a most tasty French onion soup. The entree consisted of a spectacularly grilled trout with roasted potatoes and steamed vegetables. Incidentally, how many words could you detect in the last two sentences that also exist in the French language? I counted seven. I made it easy for you and underlined those I saw.

An "out of this world" piece of cake was served next and finally topped off with a fantastic assortment of cheeses. All this, at optimum levels of quantity and quality, was reasonably priced. Were we the first foreigners to have come here? Speaking English at our table, as we did, certainly drew some attention.

It remained unusually hot for the next few days. Thus, it was particularly inviting when on our fifth evening of this trek, we came upon a lake. How convenient that there was a campground right next to it. Even before we pitched our tent, we went for a swim and then spent a relaxing evening.

"How far is Lourdes from here?" Lisa asked me and then suggested that we visit this famous pilgrimage site. There, a poor, 14-year-old girl, named Bernadette, was said to have had a vision of the Virgin Mary. While Bernadette sought refuge in a cave, a spring sprung forth out of the rocks. Its water is said to have had curative powers ever since. Hence, believers afflicted with all sorts of maladies, pilgrimage there from all over the world to drink of this water. So did we, when we arrived and even filled a bottle with it to take home.

How did we get there? Lourdes was approximately 500 km (310 mi.) to the south at the foothills of the Pyrenees Mountains. In the next village on our route, we went to a farmhouse and asked whether we could leave my bike in their barn for a few days. "That's no problem," said the farmer and off we went, now by car, only. About halfway there we came through the town of Vichy, the source of the world-famous mineral water. It comes out of the ground naturally carbonated and is freely available to the public. We helped ourselves by filling all the containers we had with us.

It was an uplifting experience to be amid the throngs that came to Lourdes filled with awe and respect for divinity. Faith brought thousands together into a spiritual community. In that sense, we were all brothers and sisters. As active participants of the healing arts, Lisa and I closely related to the great awareness of God's presence here.

We spent the night in the campground of a village a little farther into the Pyrenees. Early on the next morning, we drove on into the mountains. The higher we got, the more often we passed bicyclists. Were they training for a biking event like the 'Tour de France'? In lofty heights, we met a young man from Belgium. His parents drove along in a support car. They had come here just for the thrill of the exercise in this most beautiful environment.

On top of a pass, only a weathered sign marked the border to Spain. The uniting process of Europe had accomplished the removal of border controls. Most member nations were in the process of converting to a common currency, the Euro. We had the sensation that countries were actually growing closer together. I thought of the Biblical passage: "and they shall beat their swords into plow shares, and their spears into pruning hooks. Nation shall not lift up sword against nation, neither shall they learn war anymore." Years ago, I had seen this quote from the Bible book of Isaiah (chapter 2, verse 4) imprinted at the base of the United Nations building in New York City. So, are we heading toward the fulfillment of this prophecy? Would not all of us love to see that happening? How about all of us being or becoming a part of this momentum?

We stopped to take pictures. A car with Spanish license plates came up from the French side and stopped as well. We started a conversation with a couple from Barcelona. "How did you like France?" I asked them in Spanish. We learned that it had not been a positive experience for them, yet it sounded so comical to us. They had just entered France for the first time in their lives only a couple of hours ago. Unable to speak any French, they were stunned when they realized that no one spoke their language. Feeling lost, they had promptly turned around and hurried back to the linguistic safety of home.

We spent a beautiful day on the Spanish side of the Pyrenees and then re-entered France through the little country of Andorra. By midafternoon on the next day, we reclaimed my bicycle, and I continued my ride. A few hours of rain next day brought a little cooling off. It did not last long, however. When we entered Switzerland by noon, the sun was again out in full force. This was the German speaking part of this little country known for its four official languages. Surrounded by European Union nations, it had elected not to join the alliance and maintains its own strong currency, the 'frank'. Might theirs be the truest form of democracy on earth? Typically, major issues are not decided by representatives but directly by the people in form of a plebiscite. When Lisa and I marveled about this, we regretted that back in the USA our representatives pay so little attention to the peoples' call for peace, natural healing alternatives and related health freedoms.

Lisa had envisioned ranges of snow-capped mountains and glaciers in Switzerland. Well, in this northern section of the country, it was just a little hillier than it had been in neighboring France. The closest we came on this trip to fulfilling Lisa's dream was later at the German/Austrian border. I climbed to the top of the Zugspitze, at 2,974 m (9,814'), Germany's highest mountain. Lisa traveled up to the top in a gondola. On this clear day, we met near the peak to be enthralled by the spectacular view over parts of the central Alps.

Back to the current bike ride: By noon on the next day, we reached the town of Laufenburg on the 'Old River Rhine'. Time for picture taking! Parts of the aging city walls and gates were still intact. We walked the narrow streets and marveled at structures centuries old.

Some folks believe that Swiss chocolate is the best in the world. It was also quite reasonable here. So, after our sightseeing excursion, we went shopping. We looked for gifts, for later today we would visit Mark, my youngest son now living with his mother in the resort community of Eggingen. With a lot of goodies, we rode across a bridge over the Rhine into my native Germany.

Chapter 11

Homeland Germany (1995)
Son Mark, my former wife, a basilica, Bad Wörishofen

The community on the German side of the Rhine was also called Laufenburg. It was time to celebrate our arrival in the country of my birth. We found a nice restaurant with a grand view of the Rhine and ate a belated lunch of trout. There had been some sections of bike routes in Switzerland, but here in Germany, I had the luxury of continuing my ride on a bike trail parallel to the highway. I no longer had to watch for vehicular traffic. It had been challenging when two trucks in France and Switzerland would pass each other right next to me on narrow roads. At such moments, when a vehicle came too close, I had to be ready to hit the ditch and several times felt forced to do so. Now, instead of with motorists, I had to share the trail with pedestrians and other cyclists, a much safer situation. Wide sidewalks, which would allow bike riding alongside foot traffic, would save bikers from potential harm from motorists. My pleadings to Washoe County authorities in Nevada to extend that sort of biking safety into the area where I live, have shown only marginal results. It is still a mystery to me why we, in the USA, continue to refuse to learn from what works so well in other countries.

Even though the only vehicle I had to watch for now was our Poopsie, Lisa and I had lost each other again, fortunately not for long. We reunited just before the long-expected meeting with two people who meant so much to me: Mark, my youngest son and his mother, my former wife. They lived in a newly constructed apartment building. Though their living quarters were small, the view from their balcony on the second floor made up for it. Meadows of juicy green grass immediately behind the building stretched over 100 m (330') uphill toward the edge of a dense pine forest. As we sat there, enjoying each other's company over dinner and taking in this fantastic view, several deer emerged from the forest.

Our joyful togetherness, albeit too short, was one of the highlights of this trip. On the next morning, all four of us left by car for the amazing Rhine Cascades near Schaffhausen, back in Switzerland. For a day, we all became tourists. Having spent delightful time sightseeing the magnificent and powerful Rhine Cascades with Mark and my former wife, we returned with them to their home, said a fond farewell and continued with my biking adventure heading east.

Would our approach of riding up to a farm asking for a spot to pitch our tent also work in Germany? This was my turf. I was not a novelty here, yet hospitality still prevailed. We were approaching Munich, our final destination. It was the last time to camp out. Alas, here in the state of Bavaria as well as in all of Switzerland, folks over 26 years of age were officially not permitted to stay at Youth Hostel facilities. It was hardly our youthful appearance that got us in, but rather the kindness of the management. Maybe, my lifelong membership of the organization helped. The following night we slept in a Youth Hostel in the town of Ottobeuren. The International Youth Hostel Federation represents over 60 member associations worldwide. These hostels are convenient room and board stopovers for the budget conscious. Our objective was to visit the basilica and Benedictine monastery in this community.

The Random House Dictionary defines 'basilica' as "one of the seven main churches of Rome or another Roman Catholic Church accorded the same religious privileges." We did not explore what these privileges were. Our privilege was to marvel at the extraordinary, truly breathtaking beauty of this structure, so enriched with colorful baroque sculptures and paintings. I had experienced it first in 1960 when, at the time of graduation for my class in naturopathy, we stopped here on a field trip. A monk had taken us on a tour then. He chanted for us to demonstrate the great acoustics. His lone voice filled the whole huge building. This time around, we were blessed to hear one of the best sounding organs in the world during a recital from the composer Johann Sebastian Bach.

Above the altar one would see a triangle as a symbol of the trinity concept of the divine. Surprisingly, in its center were the four Hebrew letters Yodh Vau He Vau (יהוה). These, known as the 'tetragrammaton', meaning four letters, refer to the name of God. In the Old Testament it appears over 6,000 times. A Catholic monk in the 13th century had translated it as 'Jehovah'. For fear of violating the 2nd of the Ten Commandments "Though shalt not take the name of LORD thy God in vain; for the LORD will not hold him guiltless that taketh his name in vain" (Exodus 20:7), Jews traditionally have substituted the tetragrammaton with Adonai for Lord or Elohim for God in plural form. Bible translators, notably the King James Version, followed the Jewish practice and substituted God's name with LORD spelled with capital letters. Some other translations like the American Standard Version and the New World Translation more accurately render God's Name as 'Jehovah' instead.

Now why did I find all this a noteworthy consideration in this grand basilica? Judaism like Islam strictly adheres to monotheism and so did early Christians, until mainstream Christianity in the 4th century adopted the trinity mystery. Here with the triangle and the tetragrammaton two major concepts of God came together. So often throughout history, rather than focusing on their common values, religions were fixated on their differences, frequently leading to violence even in the form of wars and other atrocities.

Our next stop was the town of Bad Wörishofen. 'Bad' in German has two meanings. It can simply mean 'bath' or as in this case, as a prefix, 'Bad' relates to hundreds of health resort communities throughout the country. Here, I continued my naturopathic training in 1960 at the 'Sebastian Kneipp Schule'. The college was named after the Catholic priest Father Sebastian Kneipp (1821-1897) a wonderfully wise man and true helper of mankind. History would probably never have noticed him were it not for a near-death experience propelling him onto a major path of healing. Hence, he became known as one of the fathers of the modality of naturopathy. As a theology student he had come down with tuberculosis. Medical doctors had given up hope for his survival. It was then that young Kneipp read about the curative effect of water. Having nothing to lose, he started to treat himself by alternating heat and cold water and applied hydro jets following certain regiments. He went as far as building a fire next to a frozen river, chopping a hole in the ice, daring a half bath and switching back from cold to heat. You

Europe: A view into European countries

can probably guess what happened. Right, he actually cured himself of this dreadful disease.

By the time he had helped to save the life of a fellow student from TB, the word of these healings began to spread far beyond this small community. People with all sorts of afflictions came for help. Over the remainder of his life, Father Kneipp expanded these wonderful water treatments, advanced into nutrition, exercise, the use of herbs and emphasized aspects of spiritual awareness. Though Father Kneipp primarily wanted to serve the poor, many of prominence, including Pope Leo XIII, came to be his patients. His papal connections most likely helped him to win a court battle against the strong opposition from the medical establishment. In fact, as time went on, many doctors in Europe and later in America became enthusiastic practitioners of these natural and effective healing disciplines.

In 1881, Father Kneipp had become a priest in Wörishofen, which in 1921 was so appropriately renamed Bad Wörishofen. When I lived, worked and studied here, my mode of transportation was riding a bicycle. I could not imagine a more appropriate way to revisit the sites of my student years, but on a bike. Though my ride had been an exciting physical, emotional and spiritual adventure thus far, I now experienced even greater health awareness and spiritual consciousness, almost as if stepping on to sacred grounds. The past had come alive! I was excited to make a visit to 'my' college, my place of work, hugging my employer of 35 years ago, walking the parks, showing Lisa the Kneipp Museum and sensing vibrating nostalgia. In the center of town stood the statue of Father Sebastian Kneipp, a selfless man who did not work for his own profit, but the welfare of the world and whose example would impact lives all over the globe as it has mine.

Europe was probably best known for health resorts and centers. These are communities dedicated to services of healing and wellness. In Germany alone there are hundreds of such health resort communities called *'Kurort'*. To put this into perspective, Germany is just a little larger than the state of Nevada. In the course of centuries, resorts have sprung up as people discovered the healing effects of thermal springs, forests, mountain and sea air, certain nutrition, therapies, etc. Thus, most of these communities are located in areas, blessed by nature like around Reno, Nevada. Germany's *Kurorts* have been planned by visionaries and boast parks, biking/hiking trails, imposed limitations upon vehicular traffic and pollution, cultural and artistic entertainment, schools and training facilities for corresponding practitioners and so much more and now attract health minded individuals from all over the world. Some of them, like world famous Baden Baden, were started by the Romans and have survived the Dark Middle Ages, two world wars and are still icons of health and financial successes.

Though in many cases insurance carriers, government and employers kick in, the expenses for treatments are at times privately financed. Most health facilities are housed in buildings probably best described as hotels or villas having a bit of the nature of a hospital in the sense that the staff includes doctors, nurses, various therapists, nutritionists etc. Physicians normally determine the health regiment for new arrivals and supervise their progress throughout their two to four-week stay. True, these treatment centers are elegant and costly, yet the collective benefits result in amazing health care cost avoidances, subsequent work-related increased productivity and constructive morale factors. Truly, the practice of prevention realizes enormous cost savings. For a moment, as it is often done, let us compare true health care with the maintenance of a car. If the latter is well taken care of, costly repairs and or dangerous breakdowns can be avoided.

Now may I invite you to come with me to visit an imaginary Mrs. Schultz, a bookkeeper and a mother of two in one of the industrial centers of the country? What you are about to hear from me is what I similarly experienced many times while working in Bad Wörishofen: For some time now, Mrs. Schultz has felt symptoms of nervous disorders. She sleeps poorly, gets easily irritated with her husband and at work, yells at the children, her productivity and her accuracy at her job have suffered. She is depressed and gets frequently sick. "I am glad you came, Mrs. Schulz," says her doctor, when at last, she pays him a visit, "Now, we can prevent the serious nervous breakdown you were heading for." As he talks, he writes her a prescription for a three-week stay in a plush mountain *Kurort*. "Not to worry", the doctor assures her, "it is all paid for by your insurance – your transportation, room and board and all your treatments." As if he read her mind the doctor continues: "Relax, Mrs. Schultz, you can still enjoy your four weeks of earned vacation with your family. This is considered time worked. So, you want to let your employer know where to send your paycheck while you are gone."

Mrs. Schulz begins to relax but is still wondering what exactly to expect. The doctor explains to her that she will be most likely wakened up early in the morning to congregate with others on a lawn still wet with dew for short exercises. He had noticed her cold feet, as a sign of poor blood circulation. "You will have burning hot feet in just a few minutes and your whole body will feel invigorated," he told her. At breakfast *"Muesli"* would dominate, often consisting of oats and raisins served with grated fruit, nuts, milk and honey. The therapies that now follow are individualized by in-house, medical doctors trained in naturopathy. The healing effects of daily treatments of therapeutic baths, partial or whole-body jets, herbal wrappings, massages, physical therapy and other specific exercises are truly amazing. Certainly, lunch and dinner are based on natural, wholesome foods. The afternoons leave room for choices such as sunbathing, swimming, biking or hiking on trails through the beautiful countryside, tennis, golf, cold water treading, football (soccer), tennis and other games. More relaxing walks after dinner, enjoying a concert or attending a presentation about the use of herbs or how to improve home gardening!

One could easily believe that our Mrs. Schultz already feels much better after the first day. Just imagine what she will be like when she returns home after three weeks of this treatment! At work, her performance and attitude are greatly improved. Can you hear the children say: "Mom is not yelling at us anymore!" She is preparing more wholesome food at home based on what she learned while healing. On weekends, she invites the family to a nature hike or a bike ride. Along with thousands of others similarly rejuvenated, she contributes to greater health consciousness in the country. Oh, yes, like the gaming industry, these health resorts churn a lot of money, but they differ in that they produce health and happiness.

What would have happened if Mrs. Schultz had not undergone this treatment? Would not the possible cost of a nervous breakdown, depression, disability etc. by far outweigh the expense of her resort visit, not to mention the loss to her employer due to marginal performance at work and discord at home? Better health and wellness awareness, improved work productivity and morale, balanced family life plus avoidance of enormous disease management expenses were the results. What works so well in Europe could work just as well in America! It has been my dream for many years to help to propel the Truckee Meadows, where I live, toward becoming a similar health resort community.

The next day we reached Munich, our destination, for now. Most of my family lives in this vicinity. We visited for a few days and then left Germany behind. We headed home where I began to plan my next biking adventure.

Chapter 12

Germany 2, Austria, Italy, Greece and Turkey (1996)
There is hope for mankind

SIBERIA! The very sound of the word runs shivers down our spines for our mental 'eyes' see gruesome things: Bitter cold, prison camps, forced labor, immense suffering, starvation and death. Yet, I found Siberia most enchanting and almost ideal for bike riding. Most of the roads were good, the traffic light, the landscape beautiful offering abundant camping alternatives and the people were wonderfully friendly and hospitable. Instead of imagined cold, the temperature reached 35º C (95º F) causing me to look for lakes and rivers to swim and to cool off.

Several of my friends with some Russian 'experience' had implored me with diverse warnings such as: "They will kill you for a bicycle tire. To ride a bike into former Soviet territory is provoking God. You will not even make it for 100 kilometers!" Addressing concerns such as these warnings absolutely had to be a part of my preparations. What if some of these warnings had substance? A little pepper spray can? Definitely! Beyond that I thought of camouflaging myself and my belongings. So, I painted my bike with off-white latex paint, all of it, including tires and the handlebar. For luggage, I

Europe: A view into European countries

had chosen a worn-out duffel bag which I stuffed into a burlap potato sack and string-tied it to my rear bicycle rack. My clothes matched this bum appearance, and the sun bleached them further into a ridiculous unattractive outfit. I blended in so well that when I later re-entered Russia from Kazakhstan, I, like locals, biked across the border of former Iron Curtain countries completely unnoticed. The border guards, equipped with automatic weapons, stood on the road when I biked up. Avoiding eye contact, I simply rode passed them. They never signaled me to stop to look at my documents.

Yet much more important to me appeared to be emotional/spiritual preparation. Love, joy and peace would be my gift to bring to wherever I was to go. They would be my protection. I do not recall a single moment that I did not get a positive response. Without fail, I was treated hospitably and kindly. No harm ever came to me on my three-month adventure but ironically, ten days before my departure date, my bicycle was stolen out of my garage at home in Reno, Nevada.

On my quest to traverse all continents by means of 'muscle fuel', I had biked the summer before from Mt. Saint Michel at the Atlantic coast of France into Munich and now returned to the latter to continue my trek across Europe, this time alone. There, the warnings increased and for the very love of life, I could not just ignore them. Europe does not only end at the Ural Mountains of Russia. Studying my map for a safe, route, I decided on Istanbul in Turkey, choosing an alternative to avoid the unrest in the Balkan Countries. And so, my journey continued.

On the 16th of May 1996, I left Munich heading south, laughingly riding into a rainy day. My first night, I spent at my sister's home in the community of Weilheim, about 30 km (19.5 mi.) south of Munich. With sunshine the following day, I experienced the Alps in full spring splendor: A fantastic display of wildflowers abundantly filling the rolling landscape and enriching my journey. I felt enormously blessed. In just one day, I crossed the mountains of Austria and began the descent into the fertile Po River Valley in Italy. Near Ravenna, I reached the Adriatic Sea and stayed along its romantic coast until Bari, almost at the 'heel' of the boot shaped Italian peninsula. On the ferry, crossing over to Igoumenitsa in Greece, I met two cyclists who were following Marco Polo's 'silk route' from Venice into China. Andreas from Switzerland had biked in Russia before. He told me what I wanted to hear, namely that the further east in Russia one gets, the more wonderful bicycling becomes. Subsequently, I began to formulate a new plan: After Istanbul, I would begin my Asia traversal from the lofty heights of the Urals, the mountain range that separates Europe from Asia.

I found the hills of northern Greece most challenging. Constant steep ups and downs and debilitating heat followed by miserable rainstorms! It was raining again when I arrived in the city of Thessaloniki, the modern name for Thessalonica. A Bible student may recognize the name for the church to which the apostle Paul wrote two known letters. One passage in the first epistle inspired me to envision a true Christian, not as wearing a military outfit, but as a person of peace trans-figuratively "putting on the breastplate of faith and love; and for a helmet, the hope of salvation." (1. Thessalonians 5:8) To me, the core of Christianity and other religions and their practice of loving kindness leaves no room for acts of violence. Twice in these letters the apostle Paul refers to God as the 'God of peace'. If Jesus were to live on earth today, I could not picture him in a uniform, a rifle over his shoulder, a hand grenade in his belt, shooting canons or dropping bombs from a plane. Hence, a true follower of Christ could not do so either. To anyone who reasons that love and violence are compatible, I would ask this question: "Which country's uniform would Jesus wear today? American, Russian, Chinese or maybe Congolese?"

These were some of the thoughts I entertained after I had moved into 'my suite' in Thessaloniki. It had still been raining heavily. No hotels were in sight; so, I chose a building in a state of raw construction for the night. With glorious sunshine next morning, I soon reached the Agaian Sea, a part of the Mediterranean. Staying mostly along the coast, I enjoyed fairly smooth riding, occasionally stopping for a swim. It was fairly easy to find a spot to camp on a beach for the nights. I would then, with fascination, look out on the sea, conscious of a wealth of historical events. Alexander the Great began his conquests from here which eventually would reach as far as India. In contrast, nearly four centuries later, the apostle Paul would send a message of peace to the church of Philippi he had founded in this area and later wrote to this congregation: "Grace be unto you and peace, from God our Father..." (Philippians 1:2).

Less than 1 km (.62 mi.) before I reached the Turkish border, I stopped to eat in a restaurant. "What is it like on the other side?" I asked the owner, who was well into his fifties. He had lived here all his life and never ventured into the land of his immediate neighbor. I sensed a strong apprehension toward the Turks. Was this based on ethnicity or religious differences or a political current? Would this be a remaining resentment from the defeat of the East Roman Empire in the year 1453 by the Ottoman Empire? Not until 1821, via a bloody uprising were the Greeks able to re-establish their independence.

I was still at the edge of Istanbul with a population exceeding fourteen million. When coasting down a hill at high speed, I heard a strange noise. The sound came from a sheep tied to a pole. I stopped and returned to find a ram

Europe: A view into European countries

in trouble of strangulation. It must have been circling around the pole it had been tied to until it was noisily gasping for air. There was no time to lose. I did not dare to approach the animal for fear I may be thought to be a thief. *"Merhaba"*, 'Hello' in Turkish, I yelled to some men nearby and motioned for them to hurry. Glad that I had alerted them, they freed the poor beast from certain death.

I found Istanbul to be the most fascinating of all cities I know. Here, Europe and Asia come together. The world of Islam overlaps the sphere of the Greek Orthodox Church. A narrow channel called the Bosporus connects the Mediterranean with the Black Sea. Formerly named Constantinople, it is located on a strategic peninsula. A mighty wall with intermittent watchtowers, built in the 4th century, to a large extent still surrounds the old city.

The plan I had meanwhile developed was to find transportation to Moscow, to catch a train to the Ural Mountains and then continue by bike into Siberia. Luckily, I could book a flight for departure in four days hence. Meanwhile, Wilhelm and I moved into a room of a small hotel in the center of the city. I had a lot of fun biking to sites of interest, here and there starting conversations with tourists, in particular, the pretty ones. On my last day, I sat on a bench in a park between the most beautiful Blue Mosque and an architectural masterpiece, the Hagia Sophia. The latter, a giant cathedral, originally built by the Byzantine Empire around 530 C.E., was converted to a Moslem Mosque, after the forces of Sultan Mehmet II invaded the city over 900 years later. Since 1935 it has served as a museum.

I was busy catching up on diary entries when I noticed locals, all formally dressed, heading for the nearby Sultan's palace surrounded by a tall wall. The gate to allow entry for visitors closed at 17:00 h. It was almost the hour of 18:00 now. I expected the throng to return shortly with obvious signs of disappointment, but they did not come back. That aroused my curiosity. Although, I wore my humble biking outfit, I decided to follow these well-dressed folks. How about that! The giant gate to the Topkapi Palace was open. A stream of people headed for and entered the Hagia Irenia, another mighty cathedral, the construction of which even predates the Hagia Sophia by 150 years. Ushers directed me to sit in a pew where I waited for things to happen.

What was going on here? Except for a few important words, I had not learned enough Turkish to make any inquiries. Suddenly the hushed voices fell silent all together. Men with beards and dressed in black had come upon the platform and began to chant. After some time, I identified them as Jewish cantors. They were followed by several performances of song, musical instruments and dance from various groups. A choir from the Greek Orthodox

Church appeared next. Strange were those tunes to me but pleasing. Although I could not understand the meaning of any of this, I sensed something great was happening. Armenian Apostolic Church members presented some musical performances after that. How remarkable if one appreciates the claim that early in the 20th century, Turkish forces were said to have massacred 2 million Armenians. The next performers were Maronite Catholics. Moslems made up the last group to present their musical favorites. Turkey is a Moslem nation and as such, represented Islam, the word meaning 'submission' (as to God). Obviously, they were the host of this grand evening. The facility certainly was theirs. It was nice that all was very respectfully orchestrated.

To me, however, this meant much more then functionality. This event was one of the highest emotional experiences of my life. I was deeply moved to see groups which throughout history were bitter enemies, were involved in incomprehensible violence and carnage toward each other, now got along like brothers and sisters. If the pursuit of art, music in this case, can peacefully unite us, can we not try that approach earth around? What I witnessed here inspired me to believe that **there is hope for mankind after all**.

Chapter 13

Turkey 2 (1999)
Lunch instead of prison, intestinal woes

Someone was singing in the darkness. The youthful male voice came closer. Not knowing Turkish, I could not make out a single word. I just lay there in the darkness of night in a patch of tall grass and enjoyed the serenade. What a wonderful voice, I thought. Was that a sad melody, a love song perhaps? Was he singing for his sweetheart? Had he lost her love? He paused now. That was good. I hoped not to be detected. I had traveled a long distance this day. It was late, and I did not want to move to another location.

I had arrived by plane on this 14th day of June of 1999 in Istanbul, Turkey. By midafternoon, I set out to continue my horizontal bike ride around the world. Anxious to get on with this adventure, I began to unbox and reassemble my bicycle right at the airport. Trouble! The derailleur was damaged. From my bike ride from Munich to Istanbul three years prior, I remembered that bike riding was not a prominent mode of traveling in this country. That in mind, made it appear miraculous when, out of busy crowds, a fellow emerged, stating in fluent German, that he owned a bike shop. Not only did he repair the problem right then but helped me with all adjustments and the mounting of my luggage. And thus began the experience of wonderful helpfulness and hospitality as I biked across this beautiful land of friendly people.

The stretch of 20 km (12.4 mi.) from the airport to the ferry pier, I chose along the Bosporus, the narrow channel that connects the Black Sea with the Mediterranean. After sitting over 33 hours on planes and in airports, it was an exhilarating sensation to jump on my bike to experience once more where East and West come together. Where Moslem mosques, Greek Orthodox, the Armenian Apostolic Churches and Jewish Synagogues co-exist. Ancient ruins stood next to modern skyscrapers, old-fashioned bazaars remained next to ultramodern supermarkets and department stores. People never seemed to tire out from moving about in large crowds while donkeys brayed into the traffic congestion.

As a welcome, a pleasantly cool breeze embraced me. There were people all along the seashore. Children played in the water. Next to them, men were casting for fish. Women pushed baby strollers. The good aroma of grilled fish filled the air and the sun shone on all these peaceful scenes. Then came the enormous, fortified wall, still largely intact, with huge watchtowers which surround the old city formerly known as Constantinople.

The sun was getting low by the time I reached the ferry. Along with large crowds, Wilhelm and I crossed over to Asia into the port of Üsküdar. This city appeared rather insignificant on my map, but as I pedaled into the evening, it just would not end. I rode on a divided highway long after the stars were out. Still, there were apartment buildings. Finally, a meadow and I hastened to make camp. Utterly exhausted from jet lag and effort, I was just falling asleep when I heard the beautiful singing mentioned afore. I have a 'hunter's sleep', meaning that I wake up easily and am quickly ready for action. Had I been discovered? My bicycle lay flat in the grass close to me. My bedding consisted of a poncho, Therm-a-Rest mattress and sleeping bag (under a space blanket when rainy or cold). Hence, I would not be easily visible in this high grass. The youth resumed singing but was more distant now and continued wandering away. The next voice I heard was the morning call for prayer so common in Moslem countries. From powerful loudspeakers mounted high on minarets (towers) of mosques, the voice of the muezzin five times daily, chanting in Arabic, is heard over large distances and often overlaps with the sound coming from other areal mosques. Although I would later often camp at remote country sites, these familiar sounds always reached me.

The next days presented a major challenge: Heat! I believe, if I had not fasted for two weeks and lost 9 kg (20 lbs.) just prior to this adventure, I could not have made it. Along the coast of the Mediterranean, I thought I would pass out. At least, I could dip into the sea and cool off for a little while! But then came the laborious assent into the mountains. Even though I pushed the bicycle, I had to rest every five minutes, drink water and look for shade. Traveling around the world was to be fun, adventure, sightseeing, meeting people and building endurance but not torture, as this was. Any more of this, I decided, and I would head home. Fortunately, the higher I ascended the cooler it became. It basically thereafter stayed more temperate for the remainder of my journey.

The policeman who stopped us spoke only Turkish, yet he made it very clear to me and my temporary companions that we were not to ride on the highway, not even on the side of it. We had to stay on the shoulder. That was a bummer, so Denise, Roger and I felt. The two had set out from their home in London three months ago and intended to bike all the way to India. Riding on the dirt next to the road was so torturous that shortly after the gendarme had gotten out of sight, we cautiously rode on the pavement again. If you have seen the movie 'Midnight Express' you can imagine how I felt when a few kilometers along, the same officer with flashing lights and a back-up cruiser stopped us. This did not look good. What would happen to us? But instead of prison and torture, we were invited for lunch. Now wasn't that a pleasant surprise! To make sure, we felt like honored guests, we were escorted by a patrol car with flashing lights in front of us, and one in our rear, as we now biked in the center of the highway into the next village.

Thus was the kindness and hospitality which I so frequently experienced as I continued my ride across this country. It was comforting to be among people with strong moral standards. Not once did I lock my bike, often leaving it unattended with luggage mounted, and nothing was ever taken, nor was I ever harmed or threatened.

A couple of hours later I was riding alone again. Just when an enormous downpour began to unload, I had reached the edge of a village. The building I dashed into for cover had potential. It was unfinished. On the ground floor, no one but the young owner was sitting in this utmost, simple and lonely restaurant. The second floor consisted only of the sidewalls and a roof. I had biked over 155 km (96 mi.) this day here in central Turkey. It was late. I was tired and I needed a dry place to sleep. As is customary, Emek offered me a cup of tea, a demitasse ever so strong, extremely sweet, hot and so typically Turkish. There was little potential for lively conversation. I don't speak but a few words of Turkish and my host knew even less of any of the languages I had learned. Yet somehow, we managed to communicate. I got his permission to 'move' in upstairs for the night.

It was drafty and miserably cold. I placed the bike in one of the door-less rooms. From odd boards and concrete blocks lying around, I improvised a door and 'built' a 'table' and a 'chair'. Now seated in the wind-protected

Pedaling, Paddling and Pedes 2

rear of my 'studio', I relaxed to reflect upon where I was and to enjoy the marvelous scenery. I felt a wonderful sensation as I sat there draped in my sleeping bag around me to stay warm and looked meditatively out over the land. The rain still came down heavily watering this valley which reminded me so much of the Alps. Lush green fields and pastures, wooded forests in the high regions and dark clouds above it all! Clusters of quaint villages with white walled and red roofed homes! There was one major difference: In lieu of churches, the minarets of mosques dominated this peaceful countryside. This was exclusive Moslem country and I felt welcome and safe here. "To you your religion and to me mine" is a statement of tolerance paraphrased from the Koran, the holy book of Islam. Interestingly, the name of Jesus appears on 108 occasions in these writings and their prophet Mohammed only 4 times.

Blue sky in the morning! Isn't the world most beautiful when the sun comes out after intensive rain? And so, I biked joyfully into a cleansed, sparkling world and on to the south shore of the smallest of the Seven Seas. The Black Sea was not black at all but heavenly blue. At great speed, I coasted down from high country through a narrow canyon. What a wonderful sensation! And then there she was, calm, huge and inviting, the sea. I headed right for the beach and went for a long, luxurious swim in clear, deep and refreshing water.

It was cooler here at sea level and rained occasionally, thus the hills to my right were always intensely green. Refreshed, I biked into Samsun, a very pleasant city and entered the bazaar. These enormously busy markets were divided into product and service sections. What a way to be in touch with the competition as your immediate neighbor! Here produce was sold, there fish, next meat, then there was a section for colorful and aromatic spices, followed by hardware. Now I was getting closer to the bike shops. Excellent, for I needed to have some adjustments made to my bike.

Since I own a center for natural healing, was it not amazing and even amusing, that of all places, the owner of an herb shop invited me in for a snack? In addition, he spoke English and was a fellow cyclist. What a coincidence! He showed me pictures of large groups of cyclists riding through Turkey. Where were they? I had only run into 4 bike riders in the entire country and all of them, like myself, had been visiting foreigners. He must have thought of me as an American for he had hamburgers ordered. Ironically, Americans are associated with hamburgers. Interestingly, the actual origin of this style of meat patties and the name stem from the German city of Hamburg.

Thankful and content, I resumed my ride along the coast, just a few meters above the sea, toward the country of Georgia still 550 km (341 mi.) further on. Biking along the shore was most enjoyable. Whenever I felt like it, I stopped for a swim. Watermelons, huge and ripe were offered for sale everywhere. There was one drawback, however, one had to buy a whole one and so I did. Regrettably, I ate more than my system could handle. The outcome was a troublesome diarrhea. Uncomfortable as it may be, it is the body's wise way of clearing out what it cannot use or what could be harmful.

Just beyond the city of Trabzon, it began to rain. I felt miserable with intestinal challenges. Fatigued and feeling feverish, I was approaching the state of not caring anymore. Hence, I did not use my usual precautions when I hurriedly sat up camp on a beach, rushed under my poncho and shortly after dozed off into jittery sleep. Approaching voices woke me. Men were speaking Turkish. My cover was lifted. The beam of a flashlight directed into my face prevented me from seeing the rude intruders. Police! Midnight Express again? Actually, they were rather nice and even helped me pack my stuff. It is not safe here, they pantomimed. I should find shelter in a hotel. I understood that there were four of them only 5 km (3.1 mi.) further on. One officer actually hugged me before I peddled drowsily into rain and darkness. It was really pouring now, and I was desperate for a way to find cover. Nothing! I had biked more than eight agonizing kilometers (5 mi.). Still nothing! Passing through a village, a three-story building in the final stage of construction caught my interest. No one in sight! I made a dash for the ground floor and 'moved in' for the rest of the night.

Air and earth seemed cleansed when I rode into beautiful sunshine the following morning. I felt much better now. A day and a half later I reached the country of Georgia where a new adventure was to begin.

Mont St. Michel at the Atlantic coast of France

Europe: A view into European countries

Here at the Atlantic began Hans' ride around the world

Fertile France

Camping with Lisa, my companion

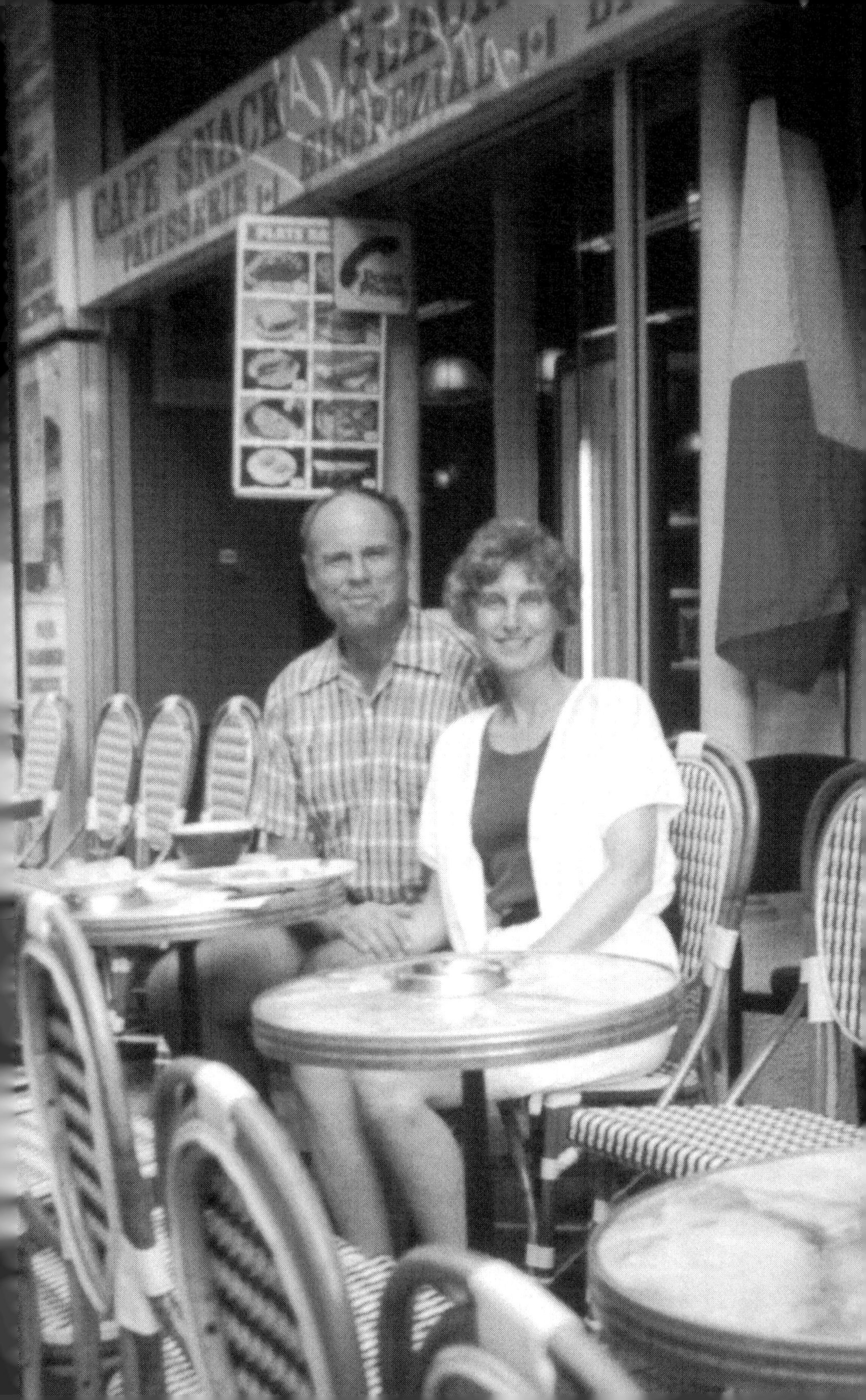
CAFE SNACK
PATISSERIE

Still grinding grain with wind power

Opposite: Dining with Lisa in a typical outdoor restaurant in France

Europe: A view into European countries

In the Pyrenees

Gorgeous Pyrenees

A typical Bavarian home

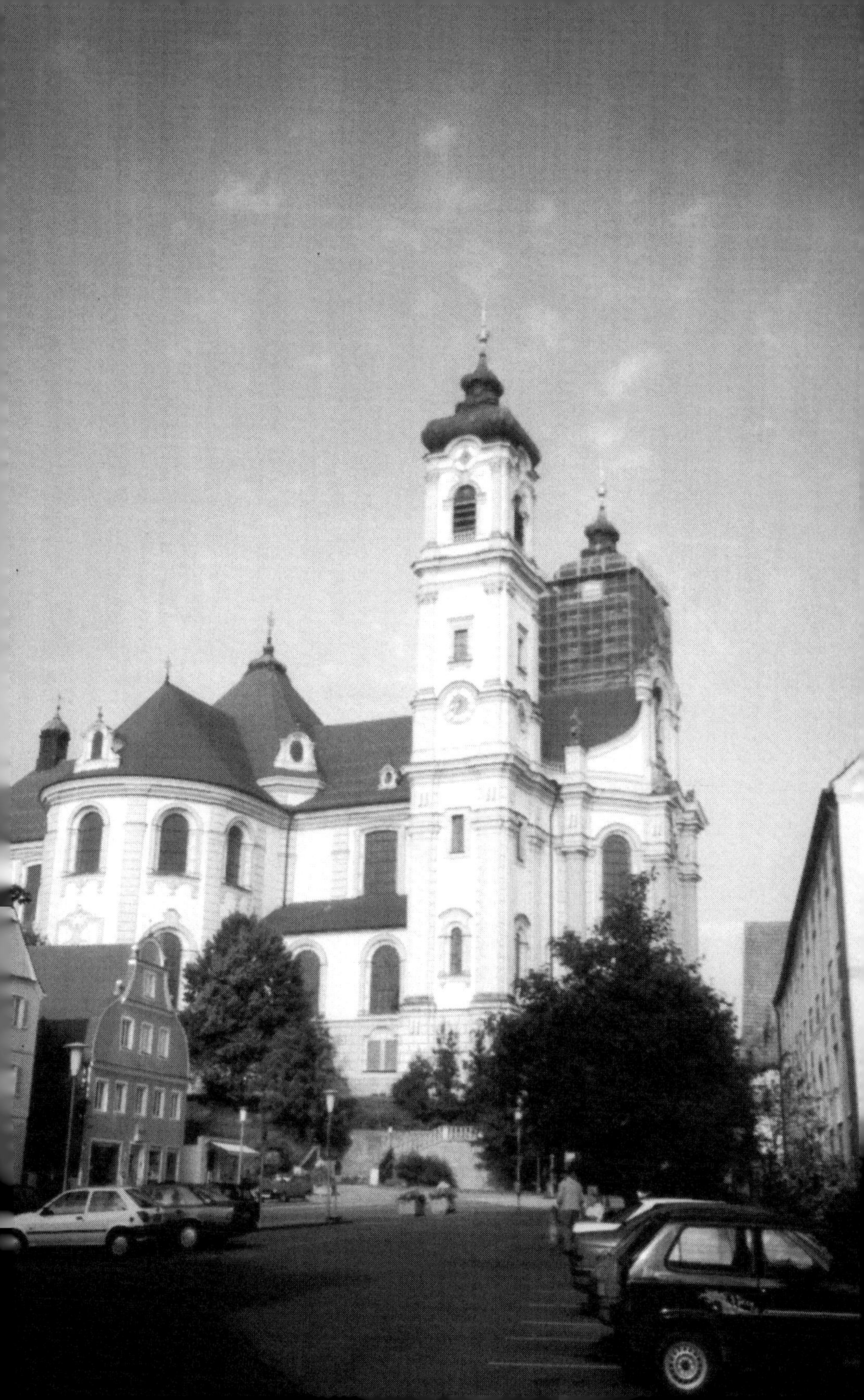

Pedaling, Paddling and Pedes 2

Basilica Ottobeuren in Germany

Opposite: Gorgeous Basilica Ottobeuren

Rentner radelt bis nach China

VON ALFRED SCHUBERT

Weilheim – Aufgrund der Länge der Strecke hat der gebürtige Ostpreuße, der 1951 nach Kanada und zwei Jahre später in die USA auswanderte, ist und seinen zweiten Wohnsitz in Weilheim hat, die Reise in zwei Abschnitte aufgeteilt.

76 Jahre alt und doch voller Tatendrang: Hans Frischeisen will mit dem Rad bis ans chinesische Meer.

MÜNCHNER MERKUR, GERMANY

Der Grenzgänger mit dem Kartoffelsack

So radelt ein Münchner um die Welt

„Etwas Einmaliges im Leben schaffen", beschreibt Hans Frischeisen die Motivation, die ihn zu einer Weltumradlung trieb. In sechs Abschnitten, jeweils ein paar Wochen pro Jahr, hat er seine Ost-West-Route abgestrampelt. Dieses Jahr vollendete er sie mit einer sechswöchigen, knapp 7000 Kilometer langen Tour: vom Uralgebirge über Sibirien und China bis Wladiwostok, etwa 150 Kilometer pro Tag.

Frischeisen bei seiner Ankunft in Qi Qihar, China. Foto-Repro: R. Kurzendörfer

Radler und Abenteurer Hans Frischeisen. Foto: rk

Mathias Ke...

Father Kneipp, a catholic priest, became one of the fathers of naturopathy

Opposite top article: Retiree bikes (from Munich) to China
Opposite lower article: Crossing borders with a potato sack

Treading ice cold water to increase blood circulation

Gelato, superior ice cream in Italy

By ferry crossing the Adria from Italy to Greece

Europe: A view into European countries

A Greek Orthodox church

A Greek Orthodox priest

Aqueduct in Kavala, Greece

Beautiful Blue Mosque in Istanbul, Turkey

Europe: A view into European countries

Turkish women in a park share their meal with me

Volgograd – sight of the WWII battle of Stalingrad with nearly 1,000,000 casualties

174

Ruins left as a war memorial

Europe: A view into European countries

Eternal flame to honor fallen Soviet soldiers in Volgograd

Opposite: Hans, as a German national, delivering a message of peace in *Pravda*, Russia's largest newspaper

УВЛЕЧЕНИЯ

Путешествие Ганса

пенсионер из американского штата Невада колесит по миру на велосипеде

Говорят, чудаки украшают мир. После знакомства с Гансом Фришейзеном, американцем немецкого происхождения, я лишний раз убедился в правильности этого утверждения. Вот уже на протяжении четырех лет он путешествует по свету, причем в одиночку и... на велосипеде.

Наша встреча со страстным путешественником состоялась в одной из семей, где г-н Фришейзен остановился на несколько дней на постой. В Волгоград он прибыл из Луганской области, что на Украине. Вместо запланированных пятнадцати минут мы беседовали с гостем около приезде домой, в Америку, серьезно займется изучением русского языка. Свои знания он продемонстрирует в письменном виде, прислав на редакцию по почте или Интернету весточку о себе...

Подружился г-н Фришейзен с двухколесной машиной в 1944 году. «Когда мне было три года, мама на день рождения подарила мне велосипед, — говорит Ганс. — Тогда-то я впервые сел на эту чудо-машину и познал все ее прелести. Но так как шла война, а жили мы тогда в Кенигсберге, пришлось оставить все имущество, в том числе и велосипед, и уехать в другую страну». Лишь спустя полстолетия Ганс вновь сел на велосипед и уже никогда с ним не расстается. Ведь для него велосипед — это не только средство передвижения, но и здоровье, только в России, но и в других странах. Однажды, путешествуя по Грузии, Ганс трижды в один день был ограблен неизвестными. У него утащили самое ценное: фотоаппарат, одежду, деньги... Правда, не все, а лишь малую часть, которую он оставляет на мелкие расходы. Основную же носит при себе в специально сшитом поясе.

Когда речь пошла об особенностях характера и гостеприимстве русских людей, Ганс заметил: «Русские очень гостеприимны, дружелюбны, ненавязчивы и с хорошими манерами. Среди них я чувствую себя легко и свободно». И неожиданно запел: «Веселая и грустная, всегда ты хороша, как наша песня русская, как русская душа». И хотя слова в произношении явно давались ему с трудом, Ганс не смущался. Закончив петь, рассмеялся от души.

Мы еще долго говорили о путешествиях, и Ганс вспоминал о своей семье: жене, которая вдохновляет его и поддерживает во всех начинаниях (она выпускает свою частную газету о здоровье), двух сыновьях, живущих самостоятельно в самом красивом штате Америки Оригоне, и об ирландском сеттере Ноке. «Они скучают по мне, — уверен Ганс, — и с нетерпением ждут моего возвращения домой. Ведь даже месяц разлуки — это для них чуть ли не вечность».

А проехал за эти четыре года неутомимый путешественник более 10000 км по дорогам Канады, Америки, Мексики, Гватемалы, Австрии, Франции, Италии, Германии, Швейцарии, Грузии, России... И повсюду у него остаются друзья, которых он очень любит и боготворит. Для него они все равны, несмотря даже на их профессию и материальное положение, будь то дворник или министр. Как говорит Ганс: «В этом бренном мире мы все ходим под одним Богом, а значит, грешны, счастливы и любимы». Сейчас он частый гость в компаниях своих друзей из Америки — двукратного чемпиона мира по велосипедному спорту Эдварда Раппа и трехкратного чемпиона мира по тому же виду спорта Грэга Ломанто. Однако путешествовать вместе им пока не доводилось, не позволяют частые соревнования. На Ганс надеется, что, возможно, это когда-нибудь произойдет.

На мой вопрос, чем, кроме путешествий по свету, Ганс занимается в жизни, он ответил: «Я являюсь владельцем оздоровительного центра "Вечное здоровье", где есть все: своя аптека, где продаются натуральные чаи, травы, комната для обучения йоге, медитации; четыре кабинета для лечащих врачей и дендрарий с фонтаном. И хотя я уже на пенсии, помогает справляться мне с работой мой менеджер. Он руководит самим процессом деятельности центра». Еще Ганс мечтает в скором времени открыть при центре секцию любителей велосипедного спорта, куда бы

Europe: A view into European countries

The Russian Kremlin, Moscow

St. Basil's Cathedral in central Moscow

V. Eurasia
Land of opportunities

Chapter 14

The country of Georgia (1999)
Three thefts, a broken pedal and George, my savior

Meeting wonderful people my heart again sang with joy. I will always remember the country of Georgia for three things. Its scenic beauty and lush vegetation stretching from the Black Sea into the Caucasus Mountains, being robbed three times in one day and finally, George.

Crossing the border coming from Turkey it appeared as if the 'Iron Curtain' had not been lifted yet from this former Soviet nation. There were ugly and depressing fortifications and security systems. Folks in and out of uniforms hung idly around, seemingly looking to take advantage of uninformed travelers. I had to clear several posts, present my tourist visa, complete forms and pay fees. When I thought to be all done, an enormously pot-bellied officer demanded $20 US extra. I tried to refuse. There was no superior to call on. He was it. When I finally handed him the note for 'police protection' it went right into his sweaty shirt pocket. I could easily envision a connection between funds thus collected and his big belly.

Finally, I was biking again. The impressive industriousness of Turkey had come to an abrupt halt. Poor roads, potholes, few vehicles and most of them old and dilapidated were my first impressions. Next there was the cattle. Cows in the fields, cows on the highway, cows in downtown Batumi, the country's third largest city! I arrived there in the evening and saw what I had sort of expected: Poverty, dirt, decay and apathy.

Though Georgians and Armenians are of the same racial background, share a lot of common culture, history and religion, they speak unrelated languages. They form an ethnic group completely different from any of their neighbors, which, in general, are either Turkmenian or Slavic descendants. I found them to be very handsome and graceful people. Almost everybody spoke Russian in addition to their native tongue. Eager to practice my Russian, I soon engaged in conversation, glad that it came back to me quickly. That helped a little to better comprehend what was going on around me.

Under Communism, unemployment virtually did not exist. It was sort of illegal. The State provided jobs. "Now we have a weak government," I was told. "Shevardnaze is a good man but a poor president". Some wanted a strong leader like a Stalin, who incidentally was Georgian, not Russian. I soon discerned that lack of infrastructure kept these people in a vicious cycle. Some felt, though they despised the Mafia, it was the best thing going to kindle the economy. "How could that be?" I wondered. Every street vendor, and they were numerous, every little and not so little entrepreneur was extorted to pay 'protection money'. Collection methods for non-compliance were brutal. This system of profiteering from people's proceeds might remind you of government entities enforcing payment of taxes, license fees in other, "more civil" countries. One could even argue, while governments often spend money wastefully, even immorally, the Mafia builds homes, businesses and entire industries, or so I was told.

I could not comprehend why the highway like the railroad tracks had not been built right along the sea, where traffic could flow evenly on level ground. Immediately beyond Batumi the road snaked into steep mountains. Buses, in particular, were a poor sight. I felt compassion for their sad condition and their whining and howling as they crept uphill, barely faster than me, and I was walking my bike now. The countryside was beautiful, even lusher than the Alps in Germany. Homes were dotted all over the area while dense forest grew in higher regions.

It was getting dark when I approached a pass. Menacing clouds and the late hour of day, I looked for a way to spend the night. I bought apricots from two teenagers next to the road. They invited me to their home to spend the night with them. Great timing! The dark clouds suddenly began to unload enormous amounts of moisture. It felt particularly cozy in this two-story brick building. Living quarters were on the ground floor, bedrooms upstairs. Spartan and old were the few furniture pieces. No running water! Burning nettles grew on the way to the dilapidated outhouse. The apricots reactivated my diarrhea. The warm hospitality, so proverbial for Georgia, dulled my usual caution. I did not, as is usually my habit, take my bicycle into 'my' bedroom. I even left some luggage on it.

How come my bicycle seat was lower when I took off next morning? Also, the pump was in a different location. Ah, I thought, the boy, seventeen years of age, went for a joy ride. Later I missed films, batteries and the chain lock. That was theft #1!

My hands firmly on the brakes, I cautiously coasted toward sea level again. I was just enjoying a stretch of even terrain when something terrible happened: A pedal broke off my bike. Yes, it simply broke off. A deep fear grabbed me. Would this be the end of my trip? I could not imagine any modern bicycles nor corresponding parts in the whole country. On top of my misery, it was raining again as I pushed my bike into the next community. The sight of a food store rekindled normal interests. I bought a long salami. Within 1 km (.62 mi.), I came upon an inviting restaurant. I was still battling with diarrhea. When I dashed to the toilet, theft #2 occurred. Upon my return my "colbassa" (salami) was gone. With a filling meal of baked fish and potatoes, I was much better prepared for such eventualities.

So, what was the best course of action with my bike? It would be easy to get my problem addressed in nearby Turkey. However, my visa for Georgia did not allow me a second entry. Return to Batumi seemed to be my best choice. If I could not find a solution there, I would catch a ferry to Sochi in Russia, 267 km (166 mi.) to the north. Maybe, I thought, my guardian angel was directing events. When I had received my visa from the Georgian government, I was sternly instructed not to travel along the coast. There had been a civil war. North of me began a rebel stronghold, known as Abkhazia, where I could have been robbed or even shot, so I was told. Yesterday, when I entered the country, these warnings were repeated. Okay, I got it; I was not to enter that "danger zone". So, was that why my pedal broke off? Was my guardian angel behind this?

I caught one of these dilapidated busses to head back to Batumi. Wilhelm III stood in the aisle. I sat nearby. Though there were several available seats, young men kept walking back and forth, each time stepping on Wilhelm's tires and spokes. I yelled as if their mistreating of my bike hurt me, for it did. They kept it up. Only later it occurred to me, their doing was their ploy to get me off my seat so they could have access to my wallet. Their trick worked. I got up to protect my dear friend, Wilhelm, from such abuse. As I leaned in a protective posture over my bike, a fellow squeezed himself past me from behind and my wallet changed ownership. Theft #3! I noticed the loss only after these villains had gotten off at the next bus stop. What to do? What was in my wallet? My thoughts raced. I was somewhat prepared for this eventuality. I purposely kept only a little cash in my wallet. In this case $12! The rest was hidden in pouches in my clothing.

I was a bit bewildered when I got off the bus in Batumi, pushing a useless bike, having been robbed three times and the day was not over yet. In fact, it was only midafternoon. There was an outdoor restaurant on the harbor dock as I strolled along in search of the ferry pier. Relaxing at a table over a drink sat two local men in semi-business attire. I approached them in Russian and they answered me in fluent English. I was instantly invited to join them for a beer and was made feel so welcome that I opened my heavy heart to them rather quickly. "No problem!" George kept assuring me with amazing confidence. Anyone with the name of George in Georgia must be a special person. Indeed, he and his friend, a marine officer, became my guardian angels.

After having heard my story, George got active on his cell phone. He arranged for a ride for me on the ferry two days later and reserved a room in

Eurasia: Land of opportunities

a hotel owned by friends where I would be safe. Later, I was to join them in a special restaurant for typically Georgian dishes. Despite my diarrhea, I managed to eat enormous portions of delicious dishes of grilled meats, baked fish, potatoes and a variety of delicacies. The more I ate, the more delighted my new friends became. Or was it the effect of wine and vodka they consumed? I had never experienced people seemingly so little affected by substantial amounts of alcohol. Well nourished, a long hot shower and a clean bed, the world seemed so much brighter.

As promised, George showed up next morning. We loaded Wilhelm into the trunk of his Mercedes and were off in search of possibilities. Finding the needed parts was surprisingly easy, as were good will and moral support. But what about tools or a way to remove the broken off crank! After about five places, we met with a big toolmaker and his enormous machine, impressively huge, but useless. Finally, with the help of a hacksaw blade, chisel and hammer, Wilhelm was rideable again, a process that had taken over 5 hours. My joy was great. What would I have done without my friends who took such wonderful care of me and continued to do so! They certainly made up for my previous disappointments.

With some time to spare, I strolled on my own through the city center. When I looked at some items at a flea-market, a lady moved herself next to me and whispered in English: "Be careful! The Mafia is watching you." Oops! My fanny pack had not been totally zipped up. Had someone already tried to get into it? I not only corrected the problem but also returned to the assumed safety of my hotel. I did not think being watched by the Mafia was a good thing.

George waived me off the next day when I left Batumi on the hydrofoil for Sochi in Russia. I suppose, it did not speak well of a country to report on three thefts in one day. Maybe, I could have avoided them. The high moral standards in Moslem Turkey had spoiled me to be less vigilant when I had entered Georgia. It was time to relax now on board of this hydrofoil as I watched the coastline of this beautiful, little country. The sun was smiling on lush green mountains which reached high into the sky, and I smiled back.

Chapter 15

Russia 1 (1999)
Black Sea to Ural Mountains, a pact with the wind, 'Stalingrad' and Pravda

It was almost midnight when I arrived in the resort community of Sochi in Russia. Because of my bicycle possibly blocking the passengers, Wilhelm and I were held back to be the last to get off the hydrofoil. The Russian authorities seemed to take a particularly favorable interest in foreign tourists of which I seemed to be the only one on board. Subsequently, I was the first to get out on the streets of this renowned beach resort. The blond immigration official had addressed me in fluent German and wished me a nice vacation as he gave my bicycle, laden with a burlap sack, a sort of peculiar look. Aren't all westerners rich? He must have thought this fellow (me) certainly does not look well-off. And that was by my own design. While biking in Turkey and Georgia, I had stood out as an obvious stranger by my appearance. That was no longer as obvious in Russia, meaning, I blended in better. I had repeatedly been warned of theft by folks who had traveled to Russia. Hence, I maintained my 'camouflage' described earlier, hoping to be mistaken for a farmer transporting potatoes. I never locked my bike, and nothing was ever stolen from it nor from me. On the contrary, I was frequently offered bits of food as a gift.

Modern music in the streets! Though it was late, everybody seemed to be up and about and particular young, wholesome looking folks. Oh, these wonderfully slim bodies lightly dressed in summer clothes - a picture of health and beauty! Imagine that, nobody appeared obese. I was surprised by the elegance of it all. Grand hotels, amusement parks, outdoor restaurants, streets lined with palm trees, beach front and the typical merry making of tourists everywhere. Though I did not fit into this picture, nobody seemed to notice me as I biked past it all.

It did not take me long to realize that the approach to road construction here was like that in Georgia. The railroad tracks ran next to the sea, the highway did not. It led a bit inland, in steep serpentines into the mountains heading up to the highest point and down again to the sea. And then to start all over again, a constant up and down; though very scenic, yet very laborious! For the stretch to Dzugba of 164 km (102 miles), a distance I would normally do in a good day, it took me three times that long. There were two other reasons for this delay: Leisurely stopovers on the beaches, cooling off in the water, resting and sleeping. The other reason was less pleasant: Diarrhea again! I just could not resist the ripe, juicy and wonderfully delicious apricots. Probably because I kept eating them, I did not get better. Then I indulged in cherries in all varieties from black to yellow, which didn't help either. Next there were my all-times favorites: huge raspberries and they did not help at all. Then I stopped drinking the local tab water and almost instantly got well again.

By that time, I was well beyond the Caucasus Mountains. When I had first turned inland, I headed up a pass of unusual beauty. This could have been in the Cascades of Oregon or Washington in the USA on a sunny day. Meadows and forests alternated. Flowers grew profusely. Along the highway folks sold honey, as well as all sorts of mushrooms and berries probably straight from the forests. Then there was the first *'Kvas'* cart on two wheels, with heavy insulating material, the outside painted bright yellow. *Kvas* is a very typical Russian drink made from fermented bread and served cool. That evening it became part of my dinner. Though it may sound romantic that I camped that night in a pear orchard, massive amounts of mosquitoes made sure that it wasn't pleasurable at all.

By now I had entered the fertile plains which surround the city of Krasnodar. It was about noon when I passed the outskirts of that well-sized community. A day later, near the city of Rostov, I crossed the river Don, so well sung about in Russian folk songs. All along, I managed to avoid the large cities, being not only perfectly content with country scenery, I was even fascinated by it. Huge fields of sunflowers, their heads like little suns, seemed to smile at me. The wheat and hay harvests were in full swing. Farmers in the fields waived for me to come and join them. Corn grew richly, the fields being separated by rows of trees. Occasionally there were emblems from the communist era indicating where a collective farm had been.

A mighty thunderstorm came down one late afternoon. I just so happened to be safely in one of those simple, little restaurants. The sky maintained such a menacing thrust that for the first time I stayed in a hotel for the night. It was very simple, relatively clean, and to my delight sported a shower room with hot/cold water. At $5 truly a bargain!

The next time I visited a village, I was deep into Russia, somewhere between the cities of Rostov and Volgograd. It is rare that highways directly passed through communities, as was typically the case in the rest of Europe. When I needed supplies, I had to go out of my way for them. On this morning it had rained heavily. The pavement ended at the entrance of a sleepy village. How long had time stood still here, enduring Zsarist and Communist regimes? Geese and ducks frolicked in puddles in the dirt road increasing the sound of their gaggle as I passed by and in turn, alarming the dogs. Distrustful, but from the safety behind primitive wooden fences, the latter noisily announced my arrival. Though there were flowers in the gardens, mostly vegetables and fruit trees grew there. The homes, in picturesque simplicity, barely exceeded 100 m² (900 sq. ft.) in size. In typical Russian style, they were mainly built from logs with colorfully painted window cutouts as a form of ornamentation.

A little girl ran barefoot up to me, then stopped short gazing at me the stranger in amazement. *"Gde magazin* (Where is the store)*?"* I asked. She pointed me in the right direction and my smile found an echo. All activities seemed to stop when I entered this utmost Spartan country shop. All I remember was one kind of cookies called *"Keks"*, some soft drinks and matchboxes. I asked for milk. *"Yest moloko?"* There were four *babushkas,* a term of endearment for women at the age of grandmothers. One of them had a mouth full of gold covered teeth that glistened when they met the sunlight. It was easy to tell that she was in charge of the village news as she walked me to one of the somewhat thirty homes and announced my request. An older fellow emerged with a large container of freshly hand milked milk and the family cup. This was not a time to question hygiene. I dug out my remaining bread and *colbassa* (sausage) and began to eat. My host kept bringing additional food items. All were strange to me, but good. Then, not only did he refuse payment, but insisted that I take an abundance of food along. When I parted the 'news anchor' lady blessed me with a final golden smile.

The further northeast I headed, the lonelier the roads became. The fields never seemed to end; communities were rare. The wind, actually a nasty headwind, was my constant companion. Traveling alone for hours and days spurs the imagination. So, I chose the wind as my conversational partner. I reminded 'him' that 'he' was supposed to blow from the west. Why had he not done that for several days in a row now? We were friends, mind you, and I repeatedly praised him for doing what he felt he had to do. Biking in a northeastern direction, I reasoned with him: If he were to come from the northeast again next morning that would be the sign I should travel with motorized transportation to faraway Siberia and bike back with his support in my back. Guess what? His answer was loud and clear. Thank you, my friend! Next morning when the wind blew twice as hard into my face, I got the message! From the nearby town of Morozovsk, I caught a bus to Volgograd 220 km (136 miles) further east. This city was formerly known as Stalingrad, Stalin's City.

I had heard a lot about the ferocious battle that took place there during 1942/43 between Soviet and Axis forces. I had read books and seen films related to this senseless carnage that cost almost 1 million lives. The outcome was not only a total victory for the Soviets but became the turning point in World War II in Europe. After the capitulation of the 6th German Army, Soviet forces, in a dramatic reversal of previous losses, routed Axis powers all the way back to Berlin, a stretch over 3,000 bloody kilometers (1,860 miles). Of the over 100,000 German soldiers who surrendered at Stalingrad, due to the hardship of imprisonment, only 6,000 would eventually return home.

It was early afternoon and miserably hot when I arrived at the railroad station, where I stopped to inquire about trains going to Miass in the far away Ural Mountains. Waiting in line, I became aware of an attractive couple standing behind me. "Excuse me, do you speak English?" I took a chance to inquire. To my surprise Vladimir was fluent in French and Zina, his pretty wife, spoke a little German. Their 22-year-old daughter had been to the state of Oregon and spoke English fluently. They wanted me to meet Tania at their home only five blocks away, right in the heart of the city, formerly known as the 'Red Square'. I was taken to one of these huge concrete apartment buildings, 12 stories high, so typical for the Communist era. The inner yard, the stairwell, the walls were run down, dirty and just ugly.

Was I in for a surprise when I entered the home of my hosts! Actually, the fine clothes they wore, could have prepared me somewhat: lovely furniture, expensive wood paneling almost everywhere, precious oriental carpets, luxurious drapes and curtains and tasteful, beautiful decorations throughout. Yet, most exciting for me at the moment were the air conditioning unit and the shower with hot water. I took my shoes off immediately and felt a bit ashamed about dirty Wilhelm. For safety reasons, I had carried him four flights up. He was now leaning against a magnificent bookcase. What a treat to be ushered into their bathroom. I was sweaty, dirty and smelly. Zina motioned for me to pass my soiled clothing out the door for her to launder them. This was absolutely heavenly.

There was something angelic about Tania, who welcomed me in almost flawless English. First a little shy, but warming up quickly to me, she was bright, thoughtful, kind, spiritual and overall, just a wonderful being. While I showered, a huge meal was being prepared for me. Where had all this fine food come from? It almost appeared as if I had been expected like an old-time friend. While I was indulging, a television station presented a segment of the 'Tour de France' bike race, narrated in English. Following this grand meal, I was made to lie down on the couch and Tania, a piano instructor, played her Tchaikovsky favorites until I fell asleep. This was 'Stalingrad'? While the sound of the word alone strikes terror in most German hearts for a place known as "hell", to this German (me) it was more like heaven.

While I had been resting, Tania had called her friend Lena, who also had spent some time in the USA. When she arrived, we enjoyed some quality ice cream. Then both beauties took me in their midst on a stroll along main street "Lenin Blvd." Inadvertently, our conversation got on to the topic of the battle that devastated Stalingrad. How much do young folks now living here actually know about it, I wondered? A lot, I found out. In lieu of some communist distortion, I received a very graceful answer when I asked: "In your opinion, why did the Germans lose?" "This war was full of mysteries" they shared with me. Indeed, a wise response, I thought.

Children were playing around the famous T34 tanks, the artillery pieces, mortars etc. which were lined up around the one large, shot up building left standing in ruins as a war memorial. Next to it was the huge Panorama Museum, unfortunately closed for the evening. On our way home, we stopped at the site of the only tree in the entire city that survived the shelling and bombing. Not a single building had remained intact. All of them were in ruins.

Apartments here, like theirs, were small. While I was offered a spacious bed in a well decorated bedroom, I wondered where my hosts would sleep. Maybe on the floor in another room? That would be typical Russian hospitality. During the next day my new friends took me sightseeing to war memorials, monuments and museums. At times we were so emotionally overcome, we just cried. The realization of immense sufferings, cruelty, heroism, stupidity and the senselessness of it all affected us deeply. In a huge underground hall, on top of a monument an eternal flame had been dedicated to the fallen. Two soldiers in immaculate uniforms paraded and saluted in respect of their dead comrades. I became aware of a familiar tune sounding from somewhere. It surprised me immensely that the composition *"Träumerei"* (Dreamings) from Robert Schumann, a German national, was played here. I looked at Zina. She just nodded and simply whispered the German word for friendship *"Freundschaft"*.

It was almost dark when the whole family on foot accompanied me to the train station. Why were they all carrying shopping bags? I later found out, that they contained food for my journey. Oh, these wonderfully thoughtful people! Zina had even brought freshly prepared cherry juice for me.

I had a concern about Wilhelm traveling along. My host, Vladimir, talked to one of the two sleeping car conductors. Promptly, the bike and I were assigned our own compartment. I stayed pretty much 'put' there until the train reached the Ural Mountains in the morning of the third day all along having a great time with all that good food, reading, writing, learning Russian and sleeping, of course.

Well rested and in the best of spirits, I arrived in the city of Miass, where three years prior I had begun my bike ride into Siberia to the city of Omsk, about 1,000 km (620 miles) to the east. Now I rode west. My old, good friend, the wind, was with me most of the way back to Volgograd, a distance of 1,600 km (992 miles). This was forest and mountain country of great beauty all around me. It began to rain and for the first time in weeks, after so much heat, I was actually cold. Toward night, I came upon a meadow where farmers had mowed grass around birch trees. There, hidden from the road, I spent the night under my poncho. The sound of raindrops on my cover put me fast asleep.

Sunshine and wild strawberries in the morning! While I ate breakfast in the forest, three timber wolves came as close as 50 m (165') up to me. "Hey, guys!" I said aloud, "You can watch, but neither I nor any of my food is available for your breakfast! Get your own!" As if they respected what I had said, they kept a safe distance.

The road had been good in the mountains, but now as I headed into flat country toward the cities of Ufa and on to Samara, it had become challenging. Local cyclists normally stay clear of the pavement. Not only was I not local, but I also was used to a traffic discipline that regards bike riders as traffic participants. I claimed my rights to .5 m (1.65') of pavement, often challenged by speeding motorists, anxious to pass another vehicle. At times, wildly gesticulating, I won. Occasionally, however, I had to yield to their superior power, by escaping to the soft shoulder or even into the ditch.

Frequently, it was easier to bike in the dirt next to the shoddy pavement than to negotiate the potholes in the pavement.

Heading south from the city of Saratov, I had to decide whether to ride either on the west or east side if the Volga River. Motorists and police officers I contacted had suggested the east side would be best suited for biking. Actually, that was a bad choice, as I was to find out 100 km (63 miles) further on. The condition of the 'pavement' was just horrible. I knew the Volga was nearby. Even though I saw glimpses of the mighty river here and there, the land was mostly arid. In the evening, I approached a little boy and a girl tending a campfire beyond a fence. I stopped for some water. Their grandfather, who had been child-sitting them, invited me to spend the night in his *'dacha'*. These are typical garden/weekend homes, normally found in clusters at the outskirts of cities.

I was led past well-kept gardens and fruit trees. While I was served baked fish on the porch, the children spread the word about me, the unusual visitor, in the neighborhood. Soon all sorts of folks came to see me, the spectacle. When I learned that a fellow in the group was the director of the Moscow Bolshoi Theater, my performance became even more alive. My host was actually a retired MIG fighter jet instructor. I just wished, he could have advanced to shoot down the aggressive mosquitoes, so numerous here at the shore of the Volga.

Unexpectedly the 'pavement' ended early afternoon on the next day. Bummer! I failed to see any humor in this. The sand was so soft and so deep that I actually had to carry my bike, with luggage of course, for the next 15 km (9.3 miles). It was hot. All traffic had stopped. I was worn out and famished. On the other side of the Volga, though not visible to me, was a paved highway I should have been riding on with all the "amenities" Russia offers. To me, the choice to turn was obvious. I retraced to Saratov, where I crossed the Volga over a bridge and reached Volgograd three days later.

When I showed up at my friends' apartment, they were just in the process of leaving. No matter how important their errands, they canceled them to welcome me back. Zina insisted upon preparing a meal for me.

In our multilingual conversations, I had shared that I was born in a part of Germany which changed hands after the Soviet invasion near the end of World War II. The province of East Prussia was divided up. The north fell to Lithuania, the south to Poland and the center became Russian. The latter is now known as the Kaliningrad Oblast (Region). It is separated from mainland Russia by Lithuania, Poland and Belarus, in a sort of way like parts of Canada lie between Alaska and the continental US. Somehow the idea came up for me to visit my place of birth. My visa for Russia allowed for a single entry only. Thus, flying was the obvious choice. Yes, why not return to where I had lived 60 years ago. None of my relatives and friends had been back there in all this time. Sad memories may have had something to do with that, for at the end of World War II all Germans had either been killed or deported to infamous Soviet gulags.

In the afternoon I booked a flight to Kaliningrad, which in my days was named *Königsberg*. I was to depart in two days. One thing remained to be done before my departure: I had to bike back to the town of Morozovsk. Remember? That was where I had made a pact with the wind. A distance of 220 km (136 miles) had to be covered. We both stuck to our agreement. My 'friend', the wind, blew nicely from the northeast again and pushed me back there in all but one day.

This time I returned to Volgograd by train. For the third time I was pampered Russian style by my hosts. My bike ride was complete now for the segment from Istanbul to the Ural Mountains, a distance over 4,200 km (2,604 miles). My joy over this accomplishment was coupled with the prospect of experiencing the place of my birth. Also, I felt so happy, safe and blessed to be with my wonderful host family. It filled me with great joy that I could do something in return for them. I took Wilhelm III, my faithful companion, and biked once more past the battlefield museum to a stretch of sunny Volga beach. Was it not ironic that I experienced so much bliss at the site of the most gruesome carnage in history? How extraordinarily privileged I was! Amidst laughing and screaming children and parents, I went for a swim. Then I gave Wilhelm a thorough bath. He almost sparkled like new when he became my present to my hosts. Just before I gifted Wilhelm, he and I, were to be immortalized in a picture and a full-page article in *'Pravda'* which translates into 'truth'. It is the largest newspaper of Russia. I felt deeply honored as a German national to serve as a messenger of peace, joy and health to the people of former Stalingrad.

Next morning, with deep nostalgic sentiments and joyfully excited anticipation, I flew to former East Prussia where my colorful life had begun.

Chapter 16

Russia 2 (1999)
A side trip to former Insterburg, my place of birth

East Prussia (*Ostpreußen* in German) was the most northeastern province of Germany. At the time of my birth in 1941, it measured 55,000 km² (21,236 mi.²). This entire region was only three times larger than Washoe County in Nevada. Four years later, my homeland had ceased to exist. The claim of its German origin dates back to the middle of the 13th century. At that time Duke Konrad I of Masovia, the center of Poland, invited the Teutonic Knights from Germany to expand the Roman Catholic faith into the area. The local Slavic and Baltic tribes were thus converted by means of 'fire and sword' and a monastic state was formed. By the year 1525, the area became a dukedom. Under Duke Albert, the population largely accepted the Lutheran denomination. In 1701, Frederic I was crowned 'king in Prussia' in the city of *Königsberg* (German for 'King's Mountain'). Since the formation of Germany in 1871, East Prussia maintained the status of a province. After World War II, the dictates of the strongmen of the Allies divided the province into three sections as I mentioned earlier. With that East Prussia ceased to be German and to no longer exist.

Over the course of years, I have visited all three areas. Former East Prussia was not on the path of my trek around the world. So, what compelled me to include it here? Several considerations: It is this area where my connection and love for bicycles began. Also, it is part of my and my family's history. And further, it allows me to honor my father by relating an amazing survival event.

Visiting the Kalingrad Oblast was one of the highlights of my Russian experience. The region averages a width of 90 km (56 mi.) of which I hiked one third. I biked through the Lithuanian section of former East Prussia and kayaked in the now Polish south. Above all, it provided me with the opportunity to highlight the horrors of war and to advance growing global peace consciousness. As a victim and refugee of war, along with promoting health and joy, peace is the foremost passion of my life.

Vladimir, my host, drove me to the airport of Volgograd in midsummer of 1999. Promptly I flew into Moscow's Domodedovo International Airport, where I changed planes for Kaliningrad. As if to welcome me home, I experienced two favorable events as the plane approached former East Prussia. First, the sky was cloudless and second, I

Eurasia: Land of opportunities

had a window seat. Being very familiar with the geography, I recognized the Memel River in the north of the province. Next, the plane flew over the *Kurische Haff*, a lagoon separating a long, narrow peninsula from the mainland. This narrow strip of dunes and forest was called *Kurische Nehrung* in German times. The plane now turned to the west offering me a grand view of the Baltic Sea, the second smallest of the Seven Seas. The plane continuing its' turn, we now flew over a section of the *Samland* peninsula and came down for a landing at the airport of the city now called Kaliningrad.

Events took place here involving my father that take us back to the early part of 1945. These were the final painful months of World War II in Europe. Since the late thirties my father, a native of Munich, had been stationed as an officer in the *Luftwaffe* (German Air Force) at the airfield of the city of *Insterburg,* now Chernyakhovsk. That is where he met my mother, where they married and where I was born. When my father sensed that the defeat of Germany was imminent, he had some of our possessions shipped to friends further west.

In October of 1944, 1.5 million Red Army troops, supported by thousands of tanks and airplanes began the invasion of Germany. My home state was entered first. The city of *Insterburg* was overrun. A while before that, as mentioned in the introduction, my mother had grabbed a few valuables, placed me on the rack of her bicycle and pedaled west. We were the fortunate ones. Tens of thousands of civilians perished shortly afterward. Hence, a bicycle most likely saved our lives and has ever since held an important part in my life. While the bulk of the Soviet war machine moved on west, toward Berlin, beginning in January 1945, a sizable force staged a siege of the 'Fortress *Königsberg'*.

My father had escaped the invasion of *Insterburg* into *Königsberg* and reported there to the German high command for military duty. This was an exceptionally harsh winter. With a group of unarmed, older men, my dad was assigned to dig defensive trenches in the frozen ground near the city's airport. A rather futile job considering the men had to even share shovels and pickaxes to work solidly frozen ground. "Over there at the edge of the forest I can see a bunch of soldiers. They are younger than we are. Why don't they help us?" my father, as a newcomer, asked the group. "Are you nuts? Those are the Russians in their tank and artillery positions. They are encircling the city and could hit us any moment." My father got the picture. "So, we are here to stop an attack with our bare hands?" Of course, he had no interest to serve as cannon fodder or to freeze to death.

Over on the tarmac of the airport, he noticed a lone *'Ju 52'*, a German military transport plane. Actually, it was the last German aircraft in East

Prussia. Something did not seem right to my dad. The *Ju 52* was well within firing range of the Soviets. Why did it not move? Maybe here was a chance to survive. He walked over to investigate. A desperate pilot told him that the engines would not start in this low temperature. *"Das werden wir gleich haben"*, said my father in his Bavarian dialect, meaning that he would get the problem resolved quickly. Repairing and maintaining airplane engines was my father's specialty. In fact, he held an engineering degree in this field. There was no time to waste. The hostile canons could blast any moment. I remember so well the face dad made when he explained how he got the engines started and revved up. It must have been one of the most exciting as well as scary moments of his life.

The plane was overcrowded with women and children of officers, who would rescue their own first. "Now let's take off", my father told the captain. "I cannot", said he, "I have to wait for a signal from the tower". My father had kept a small pistol on himself. He grabbed it now, held it against the head of the captain and said, "Here is your permission for takeoff!" The captain was only too happy to oblige. Now, he had a good reason and excuse. Actually, both could have been shot over taking such liberties. The two befriended each other while in flight. When they landed a little further west, they went their separate ways to avoid knowing of each other's whereabouts. It probably helped that at this time, the retreating German military was in a state of utter chaos and confusion.

And that is how the last German plane got out of East Prussia. Father related this heroic event occasionally to us, my mother, brother, sister and me. We had asked him repeatedly to jot it down. Alas, he was not much of a writer and so it never happened. Therefore, I feel honored to do it for him on this occasion, now that he is gone.

On April 6th the Soviets launched their final attack. The senseless carnage lasted three days. The proud city of *Königsberg* died. The 200,000 remaining defenders and civilians were either killed or deported into the Gulag. Why? Why all this totally needless violence? Was it because people obeyed two ruthless rulers? Was this not the wrong kind of obedience? I later thought of a quote by American historian and author Howard Zinn: "Civil disobedience is not our problem. Our problem is civil obedience. Our problem is that numbers of people all over the world have obeyed the dictates of the leaders of their government and have gone to war. Millions have been killed because of this obedience…" Was President John F. Kennedy not right in 1961 when he said: "All wars result from stupidity!"

I took a good look at the airport when I got off the plane. So, this was where my father took charge of things. I could well imagine that very little

Eurasia: Land of opportunities

had changed since 1945. There stood the gray terminal tower. I visualized where the *Ju 52* was parked and where it took off from. Was it on the same runway where I had just landed?

I left my knapsack at the baggage counter and took off with only my fanny pack. Next, I caught one of the minibuses taking passengers into town. Most of the farmhouses we passed seemed untouched for the last 60 years. Some were still marked by bullet holes. Typically for northern Germany, houses were built with reddish colored bricks as if to last forever. While in the northern section of East Prussia allotted to Lithuania and Poland to the south, reconstruction resembled East Prussian architecture, it was not the case in the area around former *Königsberg*. The few remaining German era buildings were flanked by unattractive, Soviet-style concrete blocks.

I wanted to see *Insterburg*, the city where I was born. From the central terminal, I caught a bus for the 90 km (56 mi.) ride to my former hometown. Again, I could marvel about how time had stood still over so many years. This was fertile land, once considered the 'breadbasket' of Germany. Every tenth loaf in the country was said to have come from *Ostpreußen*. Now, the region is agriculturally unproductive and has to rely on imports.

My exuberant anticipation grew as I neared the place of my origin. Would I find the house where we used to live? The street was named after the famous World War I aviation ace Max Immelmann. The house number was 50.

The bus was already passing the edge of town. The huge building near the center must have been the schoolhouse. Though *Insterburg* was the second largest city in the province, in contrast to *Königsberg*, little had been destroyed. The two major churches caught my attention. I visited both. The larger one of the two, St. Michaels Cathedral, originally Lutheran, was now used for Russian Orthodox services. The smaller one became a Roman Catholic Church. I had brought a picture of the church where I was baptized showing it located beyond a bridge over the Angerapp River. When I asked some folks in the street, I was told that it was burned down.

During this conversation, I also learned about a hotel frequented by German visitors. It had two names. One in Russian, one in German, both meaning the same, namely "At the Bear's" (*'Zum Bären'* in German). Glad that I headed there, I would have loved to stay for the evening, chatting with visiting fellow East Prussians in our distinct regional dialect, listening to their stories, sharing mine and partake in singing once local songs. A whole busload had arrived and, unfortunately for me, the establishment was booked full. To comfort me, the innkeeper presented me with something of great value: A copy of the city map of prewar *Insterburg*. Within seconds, I had located 'my' *Immelmannstraße* (street) on it. That propelled me into action like: Wait! I will be right over!

And there it was, the row of two-story apartment buildings just a little older looking than I remembered them. Now, where would number 50 be? The Russians had not only renamed the street a long time ago but had also renumbered the houses. I walked the whole length of the former *Immelmannstraße* in the direction of the airport, where my father had been stationed. Since I looked closely at every building I passed, I most certainly had seen 'our' house. I was satisfied with that as I watched the goings-on in the neighborhood. Grownups returned from errands and strolls. Children played in the yards just as I had so long ago. I sensed a spirit of peace and tranquility over the land and town and hoped that it may last forever. Seeing everyone as belonging to the human family, it does not matter as much, what nationality may be claimed but rather that respect for freedom and human dignity prevails.

And now, let's return to the Russian mainland.

Chapter 17

Russia 3 (1996)
Ural Mountains to Omsk, Volga Germans,
an illegal border crossing, ice cream

In midsummer of the year 1996, I flew from Istanbul into Moscow. A few days later, I took a train to the city of Miass in the Ural Mountains, where my Asian biking adventure began.

"Sprechen sie deutsch (Do you speak German)*?"* a lady asked me in excellent German, while I was assembling my bike on a platform at the railroad station. "Please give me a call when you come to Chelabinsk." And with that she handed me her business card. I later learned Tatjana was one of several million 'Volga Germans'. Who were they and how did they get here? During the reigns of Catherine the Great and Peter the Great in the eighteenth century, folks from central Germany, in particular, were invited into southern regions of Russia and the Ukraine. The intent was for them to introduce and teach western style agriculture. In return they were given land to own.

So, at the time when immigrants from Europe came to the Americas and pioneered the land and developed flourishing communities, others did so heading east into tsarist Russia. German remained the predominant language in those thriving villages and townships. Since in the beginning, they did not speak the language of the land, Russians called them 'deaf' (*njemjets*) and that term became the Russian word for German and still is. Despite this 'hearing problem' these often-called Volga Germans over the next 300 years did very well for Russia, and peaceful relations with their hosts prevailed. When that changed between 1870 and 1919, over 100,000 Volga Germans emigrated to the US and Canada. Some of their better-known descendants are the bandleader Lawrence Welk, singer John Denver, actress Angie Dickinson, former US Senator Tom Daschle...a long list. Things changed dramatically when World War II broke out. Stalin, probably fearing a link-up between these Volga Germans and the advancing Axis forces, confiscated their properties and freighted them in boxcars to Siberia and Kazakhstan. Without land and suffering vicious political persecution, a time of severe hardship began of the kind so typical for this country. To survive, they became a part of Soviet society. Tatjana is head of a law firm which primarily represents ethnic Germans seeking repatriation.

What a way to start, I reflected as I began my ride into seemingly endless Siberian birch forests. Flowers grew everywhere on the eastern slopes of the Ural Mountain range. After 100 km (62 miles), I entered the forested plains known as the *'taiga'*. The landscape remained basically flat for the next 1,000 km (620 miles). Occasionally there were fields and meadows. The soil seemed fertile, but no one appeared to really work the land. It seemed to me that time had stood still in the sleepy villages I passed through now and then. I never felt any sensation of danger. Whenever I met people, they were extremely friendly, helpful and almost embarrassingly hospitable despite their so common poverty. Or was it because of it?

It was getting hot late one morning. When I came upon a pond surrounded by bushes, I decided to go for a swim. To my surprise, I heard music in this vast empty land. I moved on to investigate its source. There, on the grass of a clearing were about a dozen Russians spread out for a picnic. Mountains of interesting food had been placed on a large blanket. Friendly eyes examined me, the approaching stranger. I asked for drinking water and after filling my bottle, I was motioned to have a seat with them, in front of a huge plate that meanwhile had been filled for me. None of this food had come from supermarkets. It could not have; there were none. The taste reflected that everything was home grown and naturally prepared. So well I remember the scrumptious deviled eggs, sliced cucumbers, green beans, marinated herring, boiled potatoes, wonderfully dark, solid rye bread and a host of other delicacies, several totally unknown to me. The timing was right. I was famished and the more I ate, the more I seemed to please my hosts, who sat around me beaming friendliness and hospitality as more food kept coming my way.

Today was Sunday. Here, as in many parts of the world a festive spirit was maintained. All, in particular the children, were neatly dressed. One muscular lady wore a baseball cap marked 'California'. I pointed at it and said, "We are neighbors", since my present home state, Nevada, borders California. We all laughed. Our communications were not only limited to the few words I knew in Russian. Flowers speak volumes! I scored highly when I picked a few bouquets in the surrounding meadows and presented them to the ladies.

We ate sitting on the edge of the blankets on the ground. No one spoke any English. So, my Russian had to do which was hardly adequate for a basic conversation, but certainly not for a political discussion. National elections were just around the corner. There were some communists in the group. They were unhappy to face another defeat but respected the democratic process. My contribution was to encourage growing and advancing beyond political, national, ethnic, religious or any differences, toward justice, peace and freedom. Everyone seemed to agree. When I left, it was like parting from old friends.

Back on my bike, I had ample time to reflect upon this heart-warming experience. It occurred to me that what I had encountered here was so typical of people everywhere around the globe, this desire for justice, peace and freedom. So why is what all of us want so elusive? Maybe we just don't want it strongly enough, for if we did, I believe, we could overcome the demands of those _we_ empowered into political and religious positions. Then, "what if they called for war and no one came?" leaving the politically invented problems for the politicians to straighten up and to fix the messes they caused by themselves. In order to execute such a forward-thinking idea, I wish to submit that we all raise our voices more forcefully and persistently for peace everywhere!

Toward evening, I approached a lonely shish kebab stand. There were few customers. Seeing me approach they stepped into my path, made me stop and motioned for me to eat with them. How wonderful these people were and how unaffected by tourism!

In Chelabinsk, a city with a population exceeding 2 million, I became the guest of Tatjana. I had arrived at her home late in the evening the day we met. The timing could not have been better. It had begun to rain and had turned cold. Spending the night under my poncho, no matter how miserable, would have still been a luxurious experience compared to the immense suffering so often associated with Siberia. Tatjana insisted that I stay for the night at her warm, cozy apartment. She had heated water on her stove and while I bathed, she prepared a big dinner. I had wanted to leave early in the morning. Tatjana objected. She won. I was low on rubles, the Russian currency. Today, being a holiday, the banks were closed. "So why don't you stay? I'll show you around and introduce you to my friends. Besides, several of them are cyclists and can help you prepare for the road ahead", she effectively reasoned. She was an attorney after all. Tatjana made a few phone calls and provided me with a list of contacts, mostly Volga Germans, on my route. In addition to this helpful information, I was wined and dined royally and shown points of interest, my reward for not leaving prematurely. One of the churches we visited is said to be the only one in all of Russia to have an organ.

It had been raining almost all day, even heavily at times. The next morning the sun was laughing again. I entered a bank to exchange American Express Travelers Checks for rubles. "Yes, we can do that, except we have never done this before. Bear with us! We have manuals and will figure it out," pretty tellers told me. Meanwhile there was entertainment, tea, curious eyes and big smiles. This could have been the first time I didn't mind waiting for two hours for them to 'figure things out'.

Well rested and with money in my pockets, I said goodbye to Tatjana and continued my ride east. Just a short distance outside the city, I came close to a nuclear power plant, looking run-down and foreboding. I thought of the radioactive disaster in Chernobyl and automatically biked a little faster to get beyond this area. Back in forested land, I just began to feel good, when I was startled by wild honking coming from behind me. My hostess' friends, all males this time, had come to say once more a fond goodbye in Russian style. So, they lined up to kiss me. Not really an experience I cherished, but when in Russia you do as the Russians do. I hugged each one back as he kissed me first on one cheek and then the other; but frankly, it felt strange.

For some reason the forests were seldom plagued with thick underbrush. Hence, it was fairly convenient to walk into them, was it not for swarms of mosquitoes. The vast majority of trees were birches. I loved these trees with spotted white bark on crooked trunks, but apparently so did the little bloodsuckers. Near the city of Kurgan, I came upon a forest of firs. A pleasant change, in particular, since there were fewer mosquitoes. In lieu of visiting the city, I hung out there for a couple of hours enjoying a little snooze following a picnic lunch. I would be remiss if I did not mention the wonderful nights I spent sleeping and dreaming under charming birch trees in this vast, enchanting land. I felt good, so good I just wanted to go on and on.

The rationale (or lack of) behind determining borderlines between cities, counties, states/provinces and countries has always puzzled me. How does or did these political processes occur? An even deeper question to me is: Why must there be national borders? Are there any benefits to these areas of control? Are they not more likely to divide people, cause distrust and the negativity of nationalism that so often has led people to barbaric acts against those on the other side of the border? The famous author Dr. Deepak Chopra refers to these divisions as "tribalism", which we need to overcome to arrive at universal peace.

Well, here now was the border to Kazakhstan. I stopped and duly had my passport checked. A few minutes later I rode on. Nothing changed: Russian people, language, architecture etc. I even used Russian rubles. So, why was there a border? I biked about 80 km and was about to re-enter Russia. This time, I decided to have a little fun. My camouflage of keeping my knapsack covered in a potato sack, the use of an old bicycle ridiculously painted with off-white latex and my corresponding bum attire, hardly discerned me from the appearance of the locals. At the border stood several uniformed men holding automatic weapons. I rode toward them at a leisurely pace avoiding eye contact, passed them and rode on across a border which not too long ago was part of countries beyond the Iron Curtain. I expected someone to call out *"stoi!"* (stop!), but no such thing happened.

Around noon, a couple of days later, I arrived at the edge of Omsk, a city with a population of 1.3 million. It was hot and humid. How could I find Eduard Rapp, another Volga German and, incidentally, twice bicycle racing world champion back in the seventies. Tatjana had provided me with his phone number. Now I needed a phone to give him a call. When I came upon what looked like an office to a factory, I tried my luck. That was a good move. I was instantly treated like a celebrity, entertained with questions and served tea. I was asked to relax in an air-conditioned room. Friendly office workers reached Eduard for me. Fortunately, he spoke a little German and offered to come and pick me and Wilhelm up in his station wagon.

Eduard drove me first to his place of work. He was the director of the Omsk Sports Club. I was introduced to several young athletic enthusiasts and learned of Eduard's scope of activities. A little later he took me to his home, a small apartment in a large concrete block building so typical for the Soviet era. I met his pretty Russian wife Nina and their son Kostya, 13 years of age. I believe that Russian hospitality is unmatched. To the Rapp family, though I had arrived totally unannounced, there was no question that I would stay with them. Already in his forties, Eduard was still active in area biking races. He is a modest person and without a trace of arrogance showed me various medals and trophies he had won in his younger years.

Kostya was on school vacations. For the next day, he was assigned to show me around the city. We did this by riding our bicycles. With the blend of his knowledge of German and my Russian, we got along marvelously. I trust that Russian ice cream was made from natural ingredients. My young friend had a great liking for it, and I had the money to enable him to indulge. The afternoon we spent on the beach of the Irtysh River which runs through the city and a few thousand kilometers further north joins the mighty Ob River. It was hot. A swim in the river was rather refreshing.

I would have loved to stay on, but the time had come to meet with fellow UNR Russian language students for a four-week class in Moscow. So, the family saw me off the next morning at the railway station when I parted for Moscow. My bicycle stayed behind with Eduard and so did my pledge to be back some day to continue this great Siberian adventure.

Chapter 18

Russia 4 (Siberia, 2001)
From Omsk to Irkutsk, Mormons, a bike problem

It was purely coincidental that I landed in Yekaterinburg on the 9th of May (2001) which is one of the great national holidays in Russia. It commemorates the victory of the Red Army over the Axis (NAZI) powers and the end of World War II in Europe. In this senseless slaughter, the Soviet Union took by far the highest losses. In his book "Inferno, the World at War, 1939-1945", Max Hastings shares their astounding number of casualties as high as 26 million.

Eduard Rapp, my contact in the city of Omsk, had alerted friends in Yekaterinburg to pick me up at the airport in their '*machine*', the Russian word for car. The ongoing festivities as we rode through the city were similar to our 4th of July celebrations, except much, much more alcohol, mainly vodka, flowed here. So, I was glad when we safely reached the railroad station. The communications with Olga and Sasha were rather limited. I needed a bit more time and practice to revive my knowledge of Russian. However, my hosts made it clear to me that they wanted me to stay with them for a while, a totally unexpected surprise.

Yekaterinburg is located in the foothills on the east side of the Ural Mountains. Already from the air, I had seen that this was a very scenic region, somewhat a bit like Reno, Nevada, flanking the Sierra Nevada range. With such cheerful companions and beautiful landscape, it was a tempting thought to stay a few days. I, however, was eager to start my bike ride. In addition, Eduard and his family in Omsk expected me by midmorning on the next day. You might remember, the Rapp family had been my host three years prior when I had biked from these mountains deeper into Siberia. This time my trip was to take me on the long way all across Siberia to the city of Vladivostok on the Pacific coast.

Eduard had registered an official invitation for me with the authorities. This sort of document was needed to obtain a tourist visa for the Russian Federation. I had tried really hard to have my visa extended for dual entry. Thus far in vain! Shortly after my arrival in Omsk, Eduard went with me to corresponding government offices to try again. No success here nor in other Siberian cities where I pursued it on my own later. Why was such a dual entry permit so important to me? One needs to know and appreciate the geography of the region to understand my concern. A few hundred kilometers beyond

Pedaling, Paddling and Pedes 2

the city of Chita in eastern Siberia, the Armur River serves as the border with China, which though in general flows east, makes a giant bow northward. Several thousand kilometers further on, the Armur leaves the border and heads in northeasterly direction toward the Pacific Ocean. The train tracks of the famous Trans-Siberian Railroad make a similar big turn along this northern extension of China. To bike following this big bow had two distinct drawbacks: First, it was about 1000 km (620 mi.) longer and second, even worse, there were no roads. Imagine that, no connecting roads.

Obtaining a visa for the direct route through China on excellent, paved highways was surprisingly easy. However, to reach Vladivostok, my destination on the Pacific, I would have to reenter Russia and that is why I needed a dual entry visa. Since it was not to be, as you will read on, you will see how I managed to bike all the way to Vladivostok without sacrificing as much as a single kilometer.

My three days stay in Omsk was very delightful. Eduard, Russia's great cyclist, took me to the bike club he had been directing for so many years. One evening, I accompanied him and his son Kostya to attend a German class at the local Goethe Institute, an organization to promote German culture and language. Incidentally, Johann Wolfgang von Goethe is commonly considered Germany's most prominent poet. The school, named after him, issued their own newsletter. Subsequently, I was invited to be interviewed for a major article. I received a copy at home a few weeks later.

During the following day, I went grocery shopping with Nina, Eduard's wife to stock up on victuals for my forthcoming trip. And then I was ready for departure. It was already afternoon when Eduard accompanied me on his racing bike for the first 10 km. We parted, and I was alone in Siberia, totally alone in a bleak, world. Though the snow had melted, spring was not quite ready.

Cold, overcast and gloomy was the world around me. In a hollow among trees, I found a little protection for the night against a biting wind. I had not brought a tent along on this trip. So, what would I do in real inclement weather? I had an oversized plastic rain poncho which I could wear while biking but also crawl under when sleeping on the ground, as was the case now.

Glorious sunshine in the morning illuminated my frost covered surroundings of still barren birch tree forest. Occasionally, I passed plowed fields. After a while, I stopped at the edge of forest facing east toward the sun, a place offering me a little protection from westerly winds. This was the warmest spot I could find anywhere. I sat down in the grass and for my breakfast munched on some of the food I had brought along. This would become my standard practice whenever I felt hungry for there was nothing else than the enormous expanse of forest, namely the 'taiga'. In this sheltered spot there were already some timid blades of green in the midst of brown and gray grass. Look here! A few flowers were brave enough to spring forth. With this as an inspiration, I continued biking, singing German springtime songs as if to hurry up the arrival of a warmer season. I was so filled with joyful exuberance, I even kept on singing out loud when I biked through an occasional village in this "sleeping land". That is what the word Siberia literally means in the language of the Tatars.

Thomas Dudley was a chiropractic physician in Carson City, Nevada, at this time. In my endeavors to connect and network with area health professionals, I had called on Dr. Dudley's office and learned that his father was the 'President' of the Mormon Church for most of Siberia. His office was located in Novosibirsk, the largest city in this Asian part of Russia. I had tried to announce my approach by e-mail but as it turned out, he never received my messages. Nevertheless, I was welcomed like an old friend into their apartment overlooking the city center. While LDS missionaries are not allowed to have visitors in their homes, this rule did not apply in the position of a mission president. Thus, I became his and his wife's guest for the night in the heart of Novosibirsk.

So how are the Mormon Church and other denominations doing in the post-Soviet Union era? Having been starved of religious freedom for so long, it seemed that many Russians have developed an enormous interest for, in particular, denominations originating in the United States: The Seventh Day Adventists, Jehovah's Witnesses, Baptists and several others often referred to as fundamentalists. To the consternation and loss of the Russian Orthodox Church these faiths enjoy rapid growth.

So, to be among Mormons with their strong moral standards and family orientation was indeed refreshing, as was the opportunity to converse in English. How kind, 'Sister' Dudley had prepared some food for me to take along the following morning. Something else was given me that later proved to be very valuable: The address of a Mormon couple from Idaho, now living in the city of Krasnoyarsk, the next larger city on my route. Their name was Lutz. They were not actually missionaries but seemed to fulfill a function of supporting them. One activity 'Sister' Lutz delighted in was baking cookies for the Mormon 'elders'. Of course, I was later given the opportunity to sample some of these baked delights.

As enjoyable as the stay with the Dudley's had been, I was happy to be back to bike riding through the rapidly awakening spring in the Siberian wilderness. Almost overnight, nature had turned the world green. Out of the ground, flowers shot up profusely. With rising temperatures and expanding daylight the mosquitoes came as well, and did they ever show up in huge numbers. In daytime, another awfully disturbing pest was the horseflies. Were they just waiting for me when I was about to ascend a hill, knowing that I had to slow down? By now it was warm enough for me to wear shorts and T-shirt. I guess the horseflies really liked that. So, how did I combat these attacks? At times it literally appeared that 100 or more would buzz around me, ready to strike. When I anticipated their presence, dressing up helped. Mostly it was too late for that. Then all I could do was to wildly brandish all moveable parts of my body madly back and forth. What a sight I must have been for anyone passing by. At one time when I struck out, I hit three of these critters. Oh, were they ever aggressive! Even when I picked up speed riding downhill, they pursued me. Fortunately, they were not always present.

I was now in the heart of Siberia and just loved it. Was this the land I had heard such horror stories about from German soldiers who as POW were incarcerated somewhere in this huge, empty land? All I saw was beauty and all I experienced was peace, kindness and boundless hospitality.

Besides being rare, eateries along the road were rather austere. Since I kept a supply of bread and sausage with me, when I ate at one of these small, simple restaurants, I mostly ordered soups. Not only were they rather readily available, they also were nutritious and delicious. I think best known is probably *'borsht'* which is also my favorite. I love red beets and they make up a major part of the stock. Added to that are chunks of beef, cabbage, carrots, potatoes and onions. Another soup, very similar, was called *'Shchi'*. It differs mainly in that cabbage is the primary component. I liked these two soups since they were served warm. A glob of what I thought was sour cream floated on top. It was referred to as *'smetana'*. When it was hot, I liked *'okroshka'*, a soup which was served cold. The word is a derivative of 'crumbles' meaning the stock is cobbled together from cold leftovers, cucumber, meats, radishes, green onions and eggs.

A young lady accompanied me to my bicycle as I left one of these little restaurants. Had she taken a liking to me or was she just a loving soul? A bit shy, she handed me a chunk of bacon and raw onions. Was it smoked or cured in some other fashion? Naturally, it was very greasy. Eaten along with dark rye bread, it was actually quite good. This too was part of my Siberian experience. By me eating only small slices at a time, the bacon lasted a whole week.

The days had gotten long, meaning the hours of darkness were shorter. One memorable night stuck in my mind. As usual I had bedded down among birch trees, growing far apart. There was almost no underbrush in this forest.

Eurasia: Land of opportunities

The wonderful sensation of this wide openness was touching me. The sun was approaching the horizon. Its golden light shone upon the leaves above me. It was absolutely quiet. Though many of my outdoor nights were similar, something powerful grabbed me this time advancing me into a meditative state. I experienced a deep sense of gratitude and euphoric joy. I felt so very blessed to be in the heart of Siberia, that I had followed my intuition to bike here and that I had the health, strength, endurance and financial means to fulfill my dream to visit this enchanted land and meet its wonderful people. Was this the spirit of pronoia, the mindset that there is a lot of love for me in the world? If so, I would believe it to be the most valuable mental/spiritual component of trekking anywhere.

Talking of traveling, the traffic was very light. I never saw a single license plate other than of Russian registration. What did not really fit in here where vehicles with steering wheels on the right side. Most of them were Toyotas. A thriving business had developed to import used vehicles from Japan, where left-hand traffic is the rule. I imagine, they were considerably more affordable than Russian or other European automobiles.

The weather changed. Toward the evening it rained heavily. I was poorly prepared for this sort of downpour and far away from any community. My poncho could not even prevent me from getting thoroughly soaked while biking. This was no fun to spend a night. I had no choice but to make the best of it and began to sing and hoped that it would soon be over. It was not. As usual, I walked with Wilhelm into the forest, spread my poncho out over wet grass and ground and managed to somehow crawl underneath and into my sleeping bag. This night was awfully long and miserably wet.

In Germany we have a saying that a bad situation comes seldom alone. My best and only way, I thought, to deal with all this wetness was to just keep pedaling along by the next morning. "Bang!" What now? Where had this ugly sound come from? At times, a pebble would noisily escape from under a tire. I hoped that was it. It wasn't. I stopped and checked the spokes. Yes, one was broken on the side of the derailleur. Bad news! To fix that it would take special tools which I did not have along.

In the middle of the following day, I broke a second spoke on the rear wheel. Here I was with a broken-down bike a second night in pouring rain and nightfall was upon me. Indeed, a challenging moment! Can you see it was high time to sing? Did I catch myself looking longingly at airplanes landing and taking off at a nearby airport? Oh, yes, there were times when I wished for more comfort. This was definitely one of those moments.

There was a layer of moss in a patch of evergreens where I bedded down for the night under my poncho in my still wet sleeping bag. It rained all night long and continued when I took off next morning. Water had collected on the road and shoulders. Should I dare to ride with broken spokes? The wobbly ride was a much lesser concern than having more spokes break on me. I had only 30 km (18.6 mi.) into the city of Krasnoyarsk. As cautiously as I could, I rode on. That did not protect me from getting shower-like loads of water and grime splashed over me every time a vehicle passed.

I hoped, I was not overly abusive when I stopped at a roadside restaurant and spread some of my wet clothes and the poncho over chairs to dry. Fortunately, the place was empty. The owner's curiosity about the 'on-goings' of this stranger must have been greater than his annoyance.

By midmorning, I crossed a bridge over the mighty Yenisey River. From the mountains of Mongolia and southern Siberia it flows all the way to the Arctic Ocean. What might it be like to travel by kayak from here to the open sea? Of course, at this time I had no idea that I would someday do exactly that. Today, with rain and low hanging clouds, the river was gray, wind-whipped and hence totally uninviting. But that did not discourage me from dreaming. Tomorrow, it will be totally different, said the optimist in me. Pictures of my kayak adventure from central Canada to the Arctic Ocean became alive in my mind.

Enough dreaming! I had to concentrate on finding the Lutzes, the couple of elderly Mormons, I had mentioned earlier. When I had called them from the outskirts of the city, I received a hearty invitation and directions to their home. I imagined what a shock it must have been for them to move from a typical American home into this most unattractive, drab hump of concrete thrown into the shape of a rectangular apartment building. Yet none of this shock was noticeable with these cheerful folks. They had come here so serve the Lord. Then no sacrifice was too big. Their third story apartment was very space limited. It became even more so when I brought my bike up and spread my stuff out to dry.

Nevertheless, unperturbed we engaged in delightful conversation. 'Sister' Lutz served her popular cookies so much appreciated by the two area Mormon 'elders'. It was through them that I connected with Vladimir, who spoke English fairly well. I thought he was the director of a bike club. He came with his *'machine'*, again the Russian term for car. In it, we transported Wilhelm to a sport complex which featured a section for bike repairs. Where were the tools? There was only a handful of the most primitive set of them. "No worries!" Vladimir remained very encouraging when I must have looked a bit doubtful. A stout Buryat woman fixed my bike in no time at all and then refused payment.

Buryats are one of the indigenous, Mongolic tribes inhabiting central

Siberia. I found them to be very gentle, cheerful and friendly people. Now, that more religious freedom was flourishing in the land, many returned to a blend of shamanistic rites and Buddhist traditions and practices. The invasion of the white man, in this case Russians, was fairly recent and somewhat coincided with the timing of the conquest of the Americas by Europeans.

The weather cleared up. By the time the sun was shining again, I was chauffeured back to the Lutz's with whom I spent an enjoyable evening. They truly lived a way that became an inspiration to me to make the best of any situation. When I left them next morning, it was with a bag of 'Sister' Lutz's famous cookies. Even more enriching was the experience of a heart-warming human encounter. Ever more joyfully, I rode on, glad to be back in the forests of my 'Beloved Siberia'. The latter, incidentally, is the translated title of a wonderful German book I read when I was a young man. At the time, when World War I broke out, the author was just completing his study of medicine in Kiel, Germany. And, incidentally, this was the same university where I began my studies in the field of naturopathy. The doctor was from Estonia, one of the small Baltic nations often dragged into the conflicts of their two larger neighbors, Russia and Germany. While visiting Russia as a non-combatant, the author caused the suspicion of the authorities. He was arrested, tried and banned to a German prisoner of war camp in Siberia.

This could have been a terrible predicament, yet he was able to turn his situation into a wonderfully enriching experience. In the beginning, he was assigned to tend to the medical needs of his fellow inmates only. He soon was asked to treat staff members and their families. Moscow and 'Papa Tsar' were far away. Rules were lax prior to communism. Eventually the doctor was dispatched to extend his services to local villages. Over time, he became a traveling doctor covering wide areas of the land. Russians are very thankful people. In response for his house calls, the doctor was well compensated with food, and fur and pelts for clothing which he could share with fellow prisoners. He fell so much in love with this enchanting land, its wonderfully hospitable people, the countryside with its forests, rivers and mountains that when the war ended, he was not eager to return home. I fully understood, for I felt such great attachment to this land that I wondered whether I might have lived here in a previous life.

Winter had been long in Siberia this year. When I had left the Ural Mountains only a few daring plants had showed some green. All that changed quickly as I biked toward and across the central Siberian plains. Within two weeks, winter's gray had transformed into a lush green landscape. Profusely growing flowers delighted my heart and inspired me to sing out loud. Life was just wonderful riding through these endless seeming forests of birch and occasional pine. The road was good. Here and there I would pass through a sleepy village with friendly, hospitable people. Sometimes I would inquire about milk and be given it fresh, raw and cool. Seldom would a farmer, though so very poor, accept payment. To honor a visitor with a gift and to engage in conversation seemed far more important than monetary compensation to them.

Three days later, on a sunny afternoon, I arrived in the city of Irkutsk. The clear waters of the Angara River flowed swiftly and forcefully when I crossed over a bridge. I continued on its eastern flank into the city. For now, I passed some exceptionally beautiful churches which I would later visit. I was hoping for a hot shower which I so badly needed. I checked into a relatively pricey hotel in the downtown area. Cold water was all there was for body and laundry. The bike shop I visited next morning did not differ much from any we have at home, except, so I was told, it was the only one in all of Siberia, an area larger than the entire USA. Wilhelm got a minor tune up. Of course, I could not know that a few days later, help from this store would save me from terminating my trip.

I took my time to visit some of the churches, I had passed before. At the turn of the previous century there were 40 churches in Irkutsk making the city the 'Spiritual Flower' of Siberia. All of them were Russian Orthodox except for one Roman Catholic Church. The most impressive, I thought, was the Epiphany Cathedral. It certainly was also the largest followed by the Savior Church. I wondered, why they fascinated me so much. Was it their physical beauty or just because their architecture was so different? In my life I have visited many churches in different parts of the world. I have found those in the German state of Bavaria to be the most exquisite. Could there be a kinship to the churches in Russia? Both typically are kept in white exterior and feature onion-shaped domes. A major difference is that there are no organs and no pews. Those attending services will have to remain standing. The lack of musical instrumentation is richly compensated by fantastic chorus performances.

So, are these churches the major tourist attraction or would it be a boat excursion on the Angara River to Lake Baikal, the jewel of Siberia? Both are outstanding. The Angara flows rather swiftly through Irkutsk. I stopped at a restaurant their terraces overlooking the close by river. It would be great to experience its wildness by kayak, I thought. Alas, first Lake Baikal was upstream and second, I was here on a bicycle. So, I would approach the lake by riding to it. 'Okay then, Hans', I told myself, 'let us get going and pedal to famous Lake Baikal.'

Only later did I find out that four fellow adventurers from the west were in the area. Two fellows from Australia and two from Canada were rowing by boat from near the source of the Yenisey River to the Arctic Ocean. They rested a few days in Irkutsk. Had I known of their presence, I would have loved to meet with them for kayaking this, the 5th longest river by kayak was a growing dream within me. One of these daring souls, Ben Kozel, wrote the book "Five Months in a Leaky Boat". I delighted reading of his Siberian experience. The dominating perception of Siberia as a wasteland devoid of charm and beauty, already on very shaky ground before my arrival, had been utterly shattered during recent months, to the point where the notion of life in Siberia, became rather appealing. Never had I encountered a land that made me feel so alive. Never had I met a people so spontaneous in the approach to living, people who were so warm and welcoming towards total strangers, people who did not think twice before sharing the little they had, and expected, nor demanded, anything in return.

Now that was to be my experience while biking through this "sleeping" land and even more so, when I, eight years later kayaked on this very Yenisey River. (See my Book 1 'Pedaling, Paddling and Pedes').

Chapter 19

Russia 5, Siberia (2001)
Irkutsk to Vladivostok, Lake Baikal, Buryats

One more time I crossed the Angara, which rushes out of Lake Baikal only 60 km (37 mi.) to the east from Irkutsk. The highway, however, did not follow its course, but headed into heavily forested mountains. Though this meant more effort, scenic beauty coupled with blue skies and sunshine compensated for it. For the first time in Russia, I ran into other cyclists. They were returning to Irkutsk as I headed out. I wondered whether the impact of the bike shop raised the consciousness for biking or was it the other way around? How often have I heard people around Reno, NV, say that they would like to ride a bike in the area if it were not so dangerous! If authorities in the Truckee Meadows would listen and actively pursue the construction of biking facilities, I am certain, a wholesome biking subculture would be the outcome.

As so often, I camped out in the forest for a long, peaceful night. Next morning there was a breathtaking view in store for me, the reward for laboring up to lofty heights. It came as a full surprise. I had just biked around a curve when suddenly, far below me, I saw the seventh largest, freshwater lake in the world glistening in the morning sun. It is said that because of its enormous depth, it contains more water than the lakes Superior, Huron, Michigan, Ontario and Erie combined. Surrounded by mountains and forests, I had heard Lake Baikal being compared to Lake Tahoe, probably because of their clarity. Jubilantly singing, I coasted down to its shores, biked through a lumber town on its western edge and continued on my way to the community of Baikalsk.

By now, it was the middle of June when I rode along the lakes serene shores which resonated with the deep peace over land and lake. Incidentally, the Russian word for earth *"mir"* also means 'peace'. Thus, I had no premonition that I would be 'beaten' this very day. By midafternoon a car, driving in my direction passed me slowly, too slowly for my comfort. About 100 m (330') ahead, it made a U-turn, coming back slowly on the opposite side. The male driver and a woman next to him seemed to eye me intently. Bandits? Trouble? I looked for a way to escape! Steep slopes on both sides of the road! No other soul anywhere! This did not look good. Fifty meters (165') behind me, they turned again, approaching me now from my rear. My only "weapon" was a tiny pepper spray canister meant to hold off dogs chasing me on occasion, good, pure, hot, cayenne pepper, excellent for respiratory, circulatory and digestive disorders. Remember! I am in the herbal business. I

Eurasia: Land of opportunities

fingered it into position and was ready for action. Now driving next to me at my pace, a woman through an open window tried to address me in English. "What?" It did not work. She switched to Russian sitting next to the male driver. Though I did not understand a lot, her face told me, this was not a holdup. She smiled and I understood something like "bicycle club" and saw bicycles inside their car. That did it. We pulled over and in short became friends.

They were driving the support vehicle for seven cyclists including one woman. They had left Irkutsk over 100 km (62 miles) back early in the morning. As we were talking, one by one, they all passed us. Would I join them in Baikalsk at their hotel for dinner and enjoy a sauna bath with them? Right on! I was eager for warm human contact, food and a badly needed thorough cleaning. They offered to transport my luggage, trading it for a huge sandwich and departed.

Then it hit me. Had I been overly trusting? Had I possibly been conned? What if I didn't find them? No, I did not really worry. No one but genuine athletes with corresponding ethics would ride through truly challenging mountain terrain covering enormous distances in just a few hours. Besides, my passport and money were still with me. It was a delight to bike without my "potato sack". In short, I finished the 20 km (12.4 miles) into Baikalsk. Igor, one of the cyclists, had positioned himself at the highway to catch and escort me to their lodging quarters. He was a medical doctor. When I learned that he treated his patients with acupuncture and herbs, I instantly liked him even more.

A while after dinner, we headed for the sauna bath. Today was "Men only!" When I attended naturopathic classes in Germany, we learned that most meaningful after a thorough sweat is the instant cool off. The sauna room consisted of the typical three-layered rows of wooden benches with heated rocks in one corner. Ice cold water just coming down from nearby snow-capped mountains was running into and filled a basin in an adjacent room. The idea is that heat expands our tissues and the cold contracts them again, resulting in therapeutic exercises of blood vessels. Blood is rushed to the periphery of our body to cope with either cold or heat resulting in increased blood circulation to carry oxygen and nutrients into our cells. It is believed that the artificially, slightly raised body temperature helps to fight disease-producing microorganisms and the profuse sweating causes the body to expel toxins and wastes. Today though, I was not there for therapeutic considerations as much as I just wanted to be clean and to enjoy the fun and camaraderie of my fellow sportsmen. They had brought freshly cut birch twigs. To increase blood flow to our body's surface, we began to hit each other with these, hence, my earlier comment of being 'beaten' on this day. Then we ate little dried fish from the nearby lake, joked, laughed and acted as if we had always been friends. Then came the vodka, and we had ourselves a little party, all this in the heart of Siberia.

The good weather held as I continued eastward along the lake next morning. Around noon, I stopped at a pebble beach for lunch. Nearby, on a driftwood tree trunk sat three youths. Instantly they invited me to join their meal of dark bread, cheese, kielbasa (sausage) and onions. Such is Russian hospitality! I took my shoes off and waded into the lake. Though the air temperature was close to 30° C (90°F), the water was much colder than Lake Tahoe in June, but just as clear. There was another major difference. Years ago, I had kayaked along the shores of Lake Tahoe and came upon housing developments just about everywhere. Here, aside from a few isolated, far apart villages, nature had remained untouched.

For a while, the road followed the shore to eventually turn away from the lake. Two days later, I arrived in the town of Ulan-Ude for the first of four times. In the center of the city, formerly known as the Red Square, stood a giant monument, a replica of Lenin's head. I wondered how much life had changed since the fall of communism! I believe, the further away one got from Moscow, the less it had affected local communities. While in former Soviet 'republics' south of Siberia like Turkmenistan, Uzbekistan, Kyrgyzstan, Tajikistan and Kazakhstan Islam flourished, here, in particular, among the Buryats, Buddhism, in part, was making a comeback.

Back in Novosibirsk, Mormon president Dudley had offered to have some of my extra baggage shipped to Mormon missionaries in the city of Ulan-Ude. When I arrived in that city, I reclaimed my belongings from these two 'elders', both Americans. They appeared rather reserved to me. Oh well, maybe that was due to church directives as well. If not, I would hope that some of the warm friendliness of neighboring Siberians would rub off onto them.

What was I to do with the stuff in the box which I did not need? Most of it was warm clothes, and it was now much too hot for any of them. They would only burden me. Could I trust the Russian mailing system to have it shipped back to Reno? My decision to try the postal service turned into a rather entertaining event. Maybe mine was the first shipment from here to the USA. I had to fill out Russian forms printed in Cyrillic letters while I responded and wrote in our familiar Latin alphabet. Following that, the cardboard box was stuffed into a linen bag provided by the post office. Next, it was literally hand sewn shut and sealed with wax. Now the ship-to-address was written on the bag. A clerk with a big smile had guided me through this process which took nearly 30 minutes. Good news! The parcel actually made it intact all the way to Reno.

It was at the post office, when I experienced a surprise: An elder Buryat fellow addressed me in fluent German. Years ago, he had studied in Germany and Switzerland. He expressed high esteem for central European culture. He promptly invited me to be his guest at his home. We drove there in his car. It surprised me that a man so intelligent and highly educated would live in such primitive environs. The toilet worried me most. I just hoped that neither constipation nor diarrhea would keep him or his wife for long in that ramshackle outhouse when the winter temperature would drop to -40° C (-50°F). Now in summer, it was surrounded by a miserable stench that only the plentiful flies could enjoy. The next trepidation were the mosquitos in the shed where he and his native wife lived. Just before I had met Igor, he had been shopping in a grocery. Nina was now busy preparing dinner with the fresh meat he had bought. I appreciated that these folks were good eaters and served me a well-sized meal.

Leaving Ulan-Ude the next day was a true pleasure. A strong wind at my back moved me along swiftly. At the top of a hill, I stumbled upon money spread all over the highway. I stopped to examine the shiny metal pieces. These were not the Russian coins I was familiar with. Maybe they were from neighboring Mongolia? I could not determine it for the coins were deeply baked unto the asphalt. Later I learned that tossing out coins at mountain passes is part of the Buryats' belief to assure a safe journey.

I encountered serious trouble on my second day. My derailleur broke rendering my bike inoperable. What a disheartening experience! What could I do? Luckily, I was close to a train station and caught a train heading back west. Unfortunately, it did not take me back to Ulan-Ude, at least not yet. The train stopped for the night in a small community. There would not be a hotel for sure. I just knew it. So, I did not even ask for one. After getting my bearings, I walked Wilhelm following a trail into some section of forest looking for a site to camp. To avoid curious visitors, I did not wish to be seen and tried to keep out of sight of young couples strolling about. This was 'lovers' lane'. Amorous behavior went on deep into the night.

Would there be a way to get my bike repaired I wondered when I arrived in Ulan-Ude by the next day? An event a little later made me believe that it might be possible. Meanwhile, I had studied my maps for the best option to reach my destination, the Pacific Ocean. Knowing that at some point beyond the city of Chita the road through Siberia would end, I looked for better options. I had read of die-hard cyclists who had biked next to the tracks of the Trans-Siberian Railroad across mosquito infested swamps. Not only would that be extremely miserable but also an enormous detour. So, what if I, instead of east, headed south from Ulan-Ude toward Mongolia first and then on to China? There was a Mongolian consulate in Ulan-Ude. When I stood there in line for a visa an oriental lady addressed me in excellent English. I shared my predicament with my bicycle with her. "No problem!" she declared confidently, "our mechanics can fix anything." With my Mongolian visa stamped in my passport, the lady and her companion drove Wilhelm and me to their vodka distilling plant. Well, I hoped my bike was the first and last thing their mechanics could not fix. They tried so hard, yet in vain. I saw no other alternative but to return to the bike shop in Irkutsk.

It was actually quite pleasant to catch a sleeping car of the night-train and to wake up in Irkutsk in the morning. At the railway station, speaking German to each other, were two young fellows attempting to buy train tickets. When I heard of their concern and confusion, I offered help. They had come to travel around Lake Baikal and were the only foreign tourists I met in all of Siberia. With my limited Russian and my biking experiences, I appeared like a Siberian tour guide to them. Few people here spoke English and fewer yet knew German.

I was fortunate at the bike shop. The proper derailleur was on hand. Within the hour Wilhelm was rideable again. Filling out the time before I caught a night-train back to Ulan-Ude, I set out to see some more of the colorful churches. Oops! In the middle of a major street, I barely avoided a manhole, left open without cover. Neither was there a warning sign. Locals must know about this hole in the ground and just navigate around it. Well, that is one way of addressing the problem.

I ran into some complications when I set out the next day to bike toward Mongolia: Heat had melted the asphalt, making riding extremely miserable. So, it got hot in Siberia? The temperature had climbed over 40º C (105º F). What would it be like to cross the road-less Gobi, the second largest desert on earth? More heat yet and enormous distances between water sources? The closer I came to the border the more I worried. Then, on the second day, I could already see Mongolia glimmering with heat, I abruptly turned around. I was biking here to have fun, not to suffer and to risk my life. Maybe, I reasoned, I could enter China further east instead. Of course, I had no idea when I reached the border town of Kyakhta, that 5 years later at a much cooler time of the year, I would look at this community from the Mongolian side. To escape the heat, I caught a bus to travel back to Ulan-Ude, arriving there in the evening for the fourth and last time.

I preferred to stay in the main hotel located at the central square. From my room, I could look right onto the scalp of Lenin's huge head bust, a nice landing spot for the crows leaving their droppings behind, which I thought, he so well deserved. Crows were so plentiful through Siberia and Russia in general that I thought they could be declared the national bird.

A train took me back next morning to the little station where I had originally interrupted my ride when the bike's derailleur had broken down. Now I was back in earnest to do what I love most: Biking. It was a little cooler here. There was plenty of shade as the highway snaked through the *taiga*. Again, taiga is the term for the belt of forest between the treeless tundra in the north and the mountain ranges to the south. Some of the world's largest rivers carry their snow melt all the way to the Arctic Ocean. These majestic rivers reminded me of my kayak trip on the Mackenzie from central Canada to the Arctic Ocean. It is the second longest river in North America. What would it be like to kayak on one of the mighty Siberian streams? That thought began to grow with me. As I rode on now, I began to work on a plan.

Ouch! Stop dreaming and pay attention! Abruptly the pavement had ended. The ongoing dirt road was horribly rocky and dusty. Fortunately, the traffic was light. There had been no indication either on my maps or via road signs of this lack of construction or for how long it would be going on. It did not really matter, did it? There was only one choice: to continue pedaling. Collectively, these occasional stretches of dirt road did not exceed 100 km (62 mi.). The further east I rode, the more I had the sensation of approaching the end of the world.

Ethnic Russian and indigenous tribesmen lived side by side in the little villages I passed through. Lack of hygiene had made my first encounter with Buryats a little challenging. Now, I was about to have a very different experience. I was biking a long stretch through grassy plains and was ravenously hungry when I came upon a neat, tastefully decorated restaurant far away from any community. Both, the inside and outside were clean. Even the toilet was passable, a real rarity in these regions. Cheerful Buryat youths, seemingly the owners, greeted me. Presently, I was their only guest and got all their attention and lots of it. Young women, pretty and nicely dressed, were my audience while I consumed great quantities of tasty food. There was a lot of giggling and laughing going on and even more so, when I tried to pay, as if that was something terribly funny. Needless to say, they refused any money I offered. I cannot imagine this ever happening at McDonald's in our part of the world.

A day later, I entered, what was either a store or a restaurant or maybe both. I was told that last year another foreign cyclist had passed here. He had made an entry in English into a sort of logbook. A biker struck the owners/managers as more sensational than the occasional vehicle drivers stopping by. I asked for milk. If I had known that they didn't have any, I would have asked for something else to drink. In this case, ethnic Russians were running the store. They asked me to sit down for a moment. Only later I learned that someone meanwhile had dashed into the nearby village to get some milk for me. As if that wasn't enough, anything I showed an interest in, was given me without possibility of payment.

A light rain sprinkled the world with moisture. On meadows, Holsteins were grazing, a familiar sight to me. I grew up in a region in Germany called 'Holstein' and where this kind of cattle was rather common. On the opposite side of the road, a policeman was busy stopping vehicles for a check-up. Since I was sort of a novelty, his curiosity got a hold of him. He hand-signaled me to stop. Though I knew exactly what he wanted, I waved back at him, shouted out a greeting and biked on. He blew a whistle and yelled after me. I looked around as if he meant someone else and kept riding on. A few minutes later, he charged after me in his little police car, pulled right in front of me and made me stop. *"Vashe passport* (your passport)*!"* he barked at me. He looked like a native of the land. I wondered whether his reddish face was an ethnic feature or whether he was simply angry. His tirade went on a little while, but when he noticed that I did not understand, nor did I want to, he gave up and let me go on. Actually, I had fun with this little diversion from long hours of monotonous biking.

It was already late in the evening when I reached the outskirts of the community of Chita. The rain had stopped. Rather than entering the city, I camped on a hill which offered a view, as I understood, over Siberia's most historic city. It was founded as a penal outpost in the eighteenth century by Russian nobility, known as the *'Octobrists'*, caught in a revolt against the autocratic rule of the czar. Here something outstanding happened. Though I could envision aristocrats to be spoiled brats, the wives of these convicted men chose to accompany their husbands into banishment of no return. Thus, they founded Chita and made it a self-sufficient community. They built homes, workshops, a school, church and a hospital. For folks accustomed to work, in particular farmers, it would have been fairly easy to carve out a life here. There was plenty of space, undisturbed soil, plenty of water and sunshine, wood for construction and heating. However, these men and women were not used to manual labor. They became an example of how fast one can adapt when one is forced to, for they developed a remarkably functional community. Though there were other waves of immigration, many here trace their origins back to these *Octobrists*.

I met one of these descendants. Great, he spoke English very well having lived in Australia for a while. That was very valuable to me, for very few spoke a language I know. I invited him to join me in a Chinese restaurant. He was a schoolteacher. I became an eager student for the story of his life. We visited a museum complex existing of original homes and a church built by these convicts. So, that was how the "East was Won"! When I later continued my bike ride, I pictured myself living in those days and imagined what I would have done.

Before I headed south toward China, I stopped at the appropriate government agency in hopes of still acquiring a dual entry permit for Russia. I was surprised to find an official speaking German rather fluently. She was eager to practice her language skill and used this opportunity seemingly to show off in front of her colleagues. Alas, though she was determined to help me, she could not. The laws did not allow it.

By now my Russian language skills had improved to the extent that I could carry on a simple conversation. It made me feel good when a policeman at the outskirts of Chita stopped to talk to me. There had been a car accident. He was redirecting the little traffic there was. Foreigners did not come here often, particularly not on bicycles. Our conversation stayed on a personal note. How did I like Russia and those kinds of considerations? With a pronoic disposition it is easy to answer in most positive terms. In parting, he wished me well on my journey.

A dish known as 'shashlik' appeared to be very popular. It is a Turkish form of shish kebab. The word means 'skewer' and relates to pieces of meat, fish or vegetable being grilled on a little metal rod. At the outskirts of Chita around noon, I stopped at an upscale restaurant and was served generous portions of mutton. By now I had lost almost 4 kg (8.8 lbs.) of body weight. Might that explain that my stomach had shrunk? Well, I made good use for the leftovers later at dinner time.

Toward evening, threatening clouds were building up, the forerunners of two events: first a wonderful cooling off which I took advantage of by riding much faster. With the wind in my back, this was fun! The next event was less enjoyable. Flashes of lightening were building up in the distance. As the storm moved closer, or I toward it, there was plenty of time to prepare for it, but how? I wanted to find a place where I would not be visible from the road. That took some doing. These here were steppes which are the grasslands bordering the Gobi Desert. Finally, there, in the distance a stand of small trees! Would I get there before this forthcoming deluge? Somewhere I had come upon a large sheet of plastic, which I used to supplement my poncho. The ends I tied to the trunk of two trees just far enough apart to create a roof. From branches I cut sticks to use as spikes attempting to tie down the sheet on the two sides. That was all I thought I could do. Was it enough? I crawled into my 'house' and tried to sleep. I did not get far when 'all hell broke loose'. First, strong gusts of wind attacked my 'home'. Great, it withstood the onslaught. Then a real tempest of hail came down. My abode still prevailed. Now the thunderstorm was forcefully over me. Did it decide to stay there? As if it was not enough, a dose of shower-like rain hit 'my roof'. I did not sleep much that night but stayed fairly dry. After the first anxious moments, lying in my sleeping bag, I actually began to feel cozy.

I woke up to glorious sunshine and a cleansed world. It turned more desert like as I rode on. What was this? There were some strange looking pipes sticking out of mounds of sand. All of them were pointing toward China. When I came closer, I realized that those were the barrels of tanks; hundreds of them partly covered with sand. No people in sight! So, where were the crews? I did not want to display any noticeable interest in military hardware of the former Soviet Union, but I was curious. Why were all these tanks spread over a wide area stuck in the earth? Would that not make them highly immobile? Why were there no people around? There was a tank close to the highway. I dared to approach it a little. Abandoned and decaying. Then I realized they were all like that. Decades ago, during a time of tensions with China, the Soviets must have positioned this entire armor in case of an attack. Fortunately, no confrontation ever happened. All the tanks had simply been left behind.

Zabaykalsk was a dirty, drab and poor community. I arrived in this border town in early afternoon. Suddenly, there was a cluster of new, modern buildings in radiant colors, but that was already Manzouli on the Chinese side. Here I would for the last time attempt to find a way to reenter Russia once I left it. The folks at the Russian border post were very friendly. They offered me tea and produced an officer who spoke English. Even the commander in charge showed up. Yet the answer was, *"njet"* (no) with a smile and *"isvenitje"* (sorry). They would not allow me to reenter Russia if I was to leave it now.

It was really not a surprise to me that my plan "A" did not work. For quite a while I had considered a back-up alternative. I headed to the railroad station in town and caught a train back to Chita. This ride became one of the most miserable I ever experienced on account of sweltering heat. No air conditioning! The windows could not be opened. No way to cool off or to escape into sleep! There was only suffering! Fortunately, by the time the train reached Chita in the morning, the weather had changed. It rained for the next two days.

So, what was the alternative plan? I would catch a train to Vladivostok, my destination on the Pacific coast of Russia, enter China from there and bike to Manzouli, which I had just seen across the border. By doing

Eurasia: Land of opportunities

that, I would complete my horizontal bike ride across Europe and Asia.

It was a wonderful sensation to travel by train in the comfort of a dry, cozy sleeping car and watch the rain drench the world all around.

On the second morning, arriving in the town of Birobidzhan, I woke up and peeked out of the window. The name of the station was written in Hebrew letters. Had I really woken up or was I still dreaming? No, this was real. Facing suppression and even persecution in many parts of Russia, Jews had withdrawn to this remote location and had established their own community. With the dissolution of the USSR, travel and emigration restrictions had eased. Many had left for other countries as well as Israel. Typically, today in the community of Eilat on the Red Sea coast of Israel, I witnessed that Russian is spoken almost as commonly as Hebrew.

Early on my third day, I arrived in Vladivostok. This city, so far from Moscow, was the last holdout of Imperial Russia against forces of the Bolshevik revolution. Also known as "White Russians", their militias held out from 1917 until 1920, when they were totally routed as shown in the movie "Dr. Zhivago". Following this event, the evolving Soviet Union made this city a naval center. For a long time, it was off-limits to all foreigners. Visitors often refer to the city as the 'San Francisco of Russia'. I did not notice a great resemblance. Well, there was one as I got off the train: fog.

A former colleague of mine, when I was a sales representative for IBM, had come here while on a cruise. She had maintained e-mail contact with her English-speaking tour guide. I had used her address to announce my visit and after a corresponding phone call headed to her family's home. Here I experienced another demonstration of exceptional Russian hospitality. I had hardly arrived when Olga's mother placed all imaginable delicacies on their dining table and encouraged me to eat. After this scrumptious meal, Olga became my personal tour guide. We began with a walk to the top of a hill that offered a view over parts of the city, in particular, the bay. In the harbor, a few outdated battleships were anchored, appearing old and 'tired'. Was that what was hidden so long from the world? We took a cable car to lower levels of Vladivostok and walked along a street with prominent buildings dating back to times of Czarist Russia.

Every city in the country seemed to have a plaza formerly referred to as the 'Red Square'. Here we toured a bazaar rich with products from all over the world. I thought of it as tragic that foreign goods were more obvious than Russian-made products. Why would one rather buy a chicken, for instance, that had traveled all the way from France over one locally raised? On top of it, a local chicken would less likely be contaminated with hormones, vaccines or chemicals.

Olga confused me, when she complained that the federal government from Moscow was neglecting this region, known as the Primorsky Krai. I, on the other hand, perceived such enormous potential here that I thought it should be the other way around, meaning it could thrive and prosper on its own. The ocean could support a major fishing industry and the favorable climate would allow meaningful agriculture and forestry. Tourism could flourish and trade could be developed with nearby Korea, Japan and China.

When I continued my bike ride next day, I kept wondering why all this fertile land was practically unused. The villages were in a state of decay with folks roaming about with seemingly nothing to do. If years of communism had destroyed initiative, which I could understand, why was it so very different in nearby China as I was to find out two days later?

How could I compensate Olga for her help? Money, a gift or something else? After I talked to her a little, I decided to invite her to the nicest restaurant in town. I think that did it. We then returned by trolley car to her home where I picked up my bike and rode to the nearest beach.

A special moment had arrived. This was the end of 'Eurasia' for me. I had begun my bike ride by touching the waters of the Atlantic Ocean in France and was now wading into the waves of the Pacific. The place I had chosen for this symbolic act was a beach front amusement park. I walked with Wilhelm into the water never minding what the people around me thought. How could they possibly know what I had accomplished or was about to accomplish? All I had left to do now was to bike to Manzouli in China and be totally done.

When I left my hotel next morning, it was a beautiful sunny day. I headed north. Now I saw a different Russia: Newly constructed businesses and upscale homes, playground of the rich. Was this the work of the Russian Mafia I had often heard about? I thought of George's comments in Georgia that the Mafia had done more to build a business infrastructure than the government. Whatever, something was truly happening here. The opposite was true as I headed into the countryside - a sad state of affairs. In one of the drab villages, I came through, I asked a man for directions. He promptly invited me to his home for a generous lunch. Inadvertently, the conversation centered on the local economy. So, why was this great land dormant? As is so often the case, the government got all the blame. I have a problem accepting that unless the powers put in charge, prevent and castigate their subjects for working and that was hardly the case.

By midafternoon, I reached the border. Alas, only Russian and Chinese nationals were allowed to cross here. So, I had to head to a far-away border crossing, which I reached by the next morning. More limitations! The border only opened for certain hours. Lucky me, there was a good restaurant nearby where I enjoyed an excellent breakfast. When the border finally opened, I was told, I was not allowed to ride my bike to the Chinese border control 5 km further on. I had to travel in a vehicle. There was no other choice but to accept a ride on a bus for $15. My experiences with border crossings during the last two days had made me dislike them even more. Soon I was to find out what the Chinese formalities were like.

'Dosvidanje Rossiya!' (Goodbye Russia!).

Chapter 20

China 1: Suifenhe to Harbin (2001)
High work ethics, police headquarters, turnpikes

I was a bit apprehensive as the bus, which took me across the so called 'no-mans-land', approached China. I had heard that the Chinese authorities did not allow tourists to bring their own bicycles into the country. Would I have to give mine up and buy a new one in Suifenhe, the first nearby town? Two armed men in neat uniforms entered the bus at the first control point. My fellow travelers called out that I was from America. I had not expected their immediate reaction. They walked up to me, shook my hand and laughingly welcomed me to their country in halting English. Well now, that was a good start.

A little further on, we came upon a large, modern border facility. The processing was rather amusing to me. My fellow travelers were Russian 'merchants'. They would buy cheap goods at Chinese markets and sell them, at a profit of course, back in Russia. They came here often and knew their way around. I soon noticed the frustration the orderly Chinese officials seemed to have with them. This unruly bunch was more involved in gay chatter and could not care less about Chinese regulations. One official, who I believed to be an officer on account of his more colorful uniform, was so annoyed he yelled at the group to stand in line and physically pushed them. He was so young and so dutiful and those were my first impressions of China. To my great relief no one questioned me about my bicycle.

An hour later the bus took off for the border town of Suifenhe. A well-meaning Russian lady took me under her wings and showed me where I could change dollars into the Chinese currency known as 'yuan'. Then I was off biking again and soon rode through the countryside. How different everything here was, though not topographically. The hills, the valley and the river continued just as in Russia. Everything else was different. Every square centimeter of land seemed to be cultivated. Men, women, young and old were out there working the fields with hoes, rakes, spades shovels and all other sorts of tools. Horses, donkeys and cattle were used to pull plows. At times, I even saw men, like beasts, dragging a plow. There was also machinery in use from handheld rototillers to most sophisticated tractors. No grassland was wasted on livestock. When they were not working, cattle were allowed to graze on the narrow grassy strips next to roads and between fields.

So, what was grown here? A lot of rice, of course, as well as onions, carrots and various sorts of other vegetables! All were well tended. Even the highway was diligently taken care of. Every couple of kilometers, I saw a young woman, dressed in a bright orange coverall. A part of her function was to pluck out weeds growing between concrete slabs. Precision work!

In Russia, I had sort of blended in and passed as a local. For my optimum safety that was the plan. Remember my simple and used bicycle? I had painted it a dirty white, and my luggage was stuffed into a potato sack. My clothing almost matched this pathetic appearance and maybe that is why not even the most destitute thief would lower himself to steal from me. In China, however, this camouflage did not work at all. People openly stared at me in amazement – wide eyes, open mouths. I would grin, waive and/or give the 'thumbs-up' sign, so popular here. There was always a positive response. Non-Orientals were very rare this far north in China.

Communications were somewhat a challenge. No one knew English. My Chinese was limited to "hello" and "thank you". Very useful was a little phrasebook I had brought along. When I wanted to order a certain dish in a restaurant, I simply pointed to an English term in my booklet. I could also inquire about prices that way. The hospitality, however, was such that payment was often refused. For two reasons that would never happen to me for example at McDonald's in Reno or elsewhere: 1. They are not that generous and 2. For reasons of health, I would hardly ever eat at their restaurants.

Most confusing were road signs in Chinese symbols to me. When I asked for directions reading from my road map, even though I pronounced geographical terms in any imaginable way, I was never understood. When I thought someone wanted to know where I was from, no one would understand when I said 'America' or 'San Francisco' or the like. Obviously, they must have their own words and corresponding pronunciation for them.

The highway I traveled on was in immaculate condition. It bypassed villages at a little distance, but never went through them. When I got hungry, I entered one in search of food. When I saw some folks in the street, I pointed to my mouth and made a chewing motion. Subsequently, I was directed to a store. That part was easy. But now, that I was in a tiny grocery, I was at a loss. What were these items? I did not find bread, cheese or anything we are accustomed to. Ah, there was something familiar: eggs. Yes, they were already boiled. The lady running the business noticed my dilemma. She simply pointed to a few items. All I needed was the courage to try them. Eventually, I extended my knowledge of all those strange things by tasting them and watching other people eat. The villages were very simple, even outright austere. Normally only dirt roads led to them. The houses were built of adobe, their roofs covered with red tiles. The cities, however, held some surprises.

My first night I spent in a little roadside hotel. Curious children gathered around me when I ate at the downstairs restaurant. Some knew a couple of words in English and were eager to share their vocabulary. The only toilet was an outhouse. But then what could I expect at a price of $4 per night?

By noon of the next day, I fled into a little restaurant when a thunderstorm was about to hit me. The owner had three lovely daughters in their late teens and early twenties. I was sixty years old. The attention shown me was overwhelming. Was there anything beyond hospitality and kindness? As a newcomer to this country, I wondered about that. It took me a while to appreciate how genuine the generosity was. After a hearty meal, that I was not allowed to pay for, I was ushered to a bed. Then one of the smiling beauties covered me with a blanket.

The next night I slept at the edge of an elevated field from where I could watch 'field hands' work until darkness. No matter how early I was up and out on the road, there were always some folks already working the fields. I called them 'field hands' instead of farmers, because with the latter I associate ownership of the land in some form. In a communist society, which to me is a form of state capitalism, there is typically no individual ownership other than by the government. Hence, I saw these field workers as actual state employees.

In the years 1969 and 1970, I lived, worked and studied in a similar environment in Israel, known as a 'kibbutz'. There, a group of like-minded people leased land from the government and worked it as they saw fit. The proceeds went into a common fund, which was used to cover the needs of the community. *'Ein Harod Meuchad'* was the name of the kibbutz where I stayed for 6 months. With a population of around 800, it was one of the larger ones. An elected board functioned as a decision-making body primarily as what crops to grow, when, where and by whom. This committee also set rules and enforced them. It may have decided on adding manufacturing facilities, tourist attractions, health services, schools, childcare, entertainment and sport centers, a swimming pool, cafeteria, commissary etc. Most impressive to me was that from the proceeds also homes were built, eventually for all their members. The administration would also decide who would be sent for some specialty training and education and pay for it.

After my graduation from my Hebrew class, known as *'Ulpan'*, I inquired about my options to return to this kibbutz with my car, which I had hoped to bring from my home in Germany. "You are welcome to return", I was told, "your car, however, will become property of the community." Hmm!

Eurasia: Land of opportunities

I didn't think so! I had worked hard to afford this car, I felt I deserved it and wanted to keep it and thus departed from the concept of socialism. The beauty in Israel was that one had choices beyond the kibbutzim (plural for kibbutz).

After riding a whole week, I encountered the first other Caucasian, a Canadian. "Stay clear of the police", he had warned me, "they are quick to throw you in jail and will fine you heavily." Too late for the warning! Totally innocent, I had already gotten into the 'lion's den' and had an absolutely wonderful time. It had happened on my third day in China. Looking for a hotel, there was a beautiful new one right next to the highway, so I thought. Invitingly, it was surrounded by well-kept, park-like gardens.

When I reached the entrance, a man in uniform approached me. Oh, excellent, a security guard, I surmised. Not knowing Chinese, I motioned the gesture of sleeping to him. The fellow stared at me with growing expressions of surprise, signaled for me to wait and walked inside. Through a window I saw people eat. Oh, it dawned on me maybe that this may also be a restaurant. But why are they all wearing uniforms? Also, the folks arriving now wore official looking attire. I switched my sign language to the motion of eating by pointing to my mouth. More stares. Oh no, this was not a restaurant either, this was the police headquarters. Hmm! I was motioned to follow the group inside.

Was I in trouble? What was I getting into? There was a beautiful wood paneled room reserved for high-ranking officers, I supposed. Someone brought a dish with water; another handed me soap and a towel. Time to wash up! All along there had been smiles and other signs of welcome. My audience was growing. I was now ushered into a huge kitchen. It was as if I had come to inspect the place and everyone seemed anxious for a favorable outcome. Favorable it was, but mostly for me. Whatever I looked at with seeming interest was prepared for me. I stuck to the food I thought I knew; yet several were not what I thought they were. I was then returned to the 'officers' quarters. Besides being brought food continuously, I was left alone to eat. Though I am a good eater and was famished, I could hardly eat one fifth of what was placed in front of me.

When I had reached my absolute limits, I pulled my wallet out, but payment was energetically refused. Well, there I was alone in a beautiful room with a mountain of exquisite food provided by amazingly friendly and hospitable people, who as communists are our political 'enemies'. Hmmm!

In parting, I wondered whether it would be permissible to take a picture of some of my hosts. I pointed at them and my camera. To my surprise the group moved into a posing position. What might be the equivalent to saying "cheese" here? Anyhow, I handed my Nikon to one of the 'comrades', put one arm around one of the cute policewomen, and we both smiled into my camera.

I was geographically so far from home yet was made to feel so close. An enormous joy filled me about what I was doing: Biking around the world and having a wonderful time seeing the land, meeting the people, touching their lives and having theirs touch mine. This was the last stretch of my global bike ride that had taken me from the Atlantic coast of France, through Switzerland, Germany, Austria, Italy, Greece, Turkey, Georgia, all of Russia, the USA and now into China. In my pronoic disposition, I always felt safe and welcome. Often it seemed the poorer the people appeared, the friendlier and more hospitable they were.

Who in China owned the houses people lived in? I never found out. Since the country is gradually allowing more capitalistic practices, the ownership situation may undergo changes as time goes on. Another question I could not answer was what was happening to the one-child-per-family rule. I assumed that it was relaxed for I met families, though rare, with more than one child.

I consider school bussing one of the great follies of our society, for it robs our children of the opportunity to walk, skate or bike to and from their school. It creates a totally unnecessary expense, wastes fossil fuel and causes pollution. Here mothers would typically transport their smaller child on the rack of their bicycle to kindergarten or elementary school until they were grown enough to get there on their own. To ensure biking safety, most cities maintain bike paths separate from the streets. It is just beyond me, why back home in the richest country on earth, our governments are either too stingy or lack the vision to build meaningful biking facilities. Could it be that the strong arms of the car and oil industries are behind this?

I hit a snag later on my third day. I had just biked through the city of Mudanjiang when I noticed a toll booth ahead. 'My' road had turned into a turnpike. Would I be allowed to ride on it? I decided to play dumb, something that comes easy to me. Uniformed, armed men stormed out of their booth when I attempted to bypass them, running and yelling after me. Obviously, I could not go on. What now? This stretch of freeway was only 30 km (18.6 mi.) long. I joined the officials in their air-conditioned booth and pulled out my map. They showed me an alternate route, a dirt road through mountains and a detour of 200 km (124 miles). Not a good choice! No one spoke English. It probably would not have helped my situation anyhow. I grabbed a piece of paper and drew a picture showing a bike on top of a vehicle and handed it to them. They got the message and eagerly negotiated a ride for Wilhelm and me with one of the next arriving vehicles.

Three days later, just a few kilometers short of the city of Acheng, I ran into a similar situation. When I was dropped off, I found myself on a dirt road at the outskirts of the city. This could not possibly be the highway to Harbin, the capital of Manchuria, the most northern region of China. Thick, dark clouds hung so low that I feared they would unload any moment. It was already evening. My major fear was, where and how would I spend the night? There were houses everywhere ruling out camping. Even if I would have found a field, the thought of lying out there in the rain was absolutely horrid. If I only could find a hotel! It was hopeless. I could not possibly expect to find one in this poor, residential neighborhood.

I was pushing my bike up a steep road expecting the downpour at any moment. Oh, if only one of these people walking here could speak English to help and direct me where to go. The driver of a car must have sensed my dilemma. He stopped and a God-sent teenage girl got out. She spoke English surprisingly well. While she pointed me into the right direction, she mentioned that a Canadian was staying at a nearby hotel. What? A hotel? Nearby? Where? She walked with me two blocks and there it was, a three-star hotel. At the counter this girl helped me to ask for the Canadian. The manager showed up instead. Promptly he comped me for dinner, a room for the night and even breakfast. He spoke some English. "Would you prefer beer or wine with your dinner? Would you like to have it delivered to your room?" Wow! Before I indulged in a lavish dinner, I took Wilhelm up to 'my' room. Just then with enormous ferocity, the thunderstorm unleashed. Only 15 minutes earlier I was faced with the prospect of the most miserable night of my life. Now I found myself in a safe and dry place wondering why so many wonderful things happen to me. Was this not pronoia?

A little later the Canadian showed up in 'my' room. He was here on a teaching assignment. This was the fellow, I had mentioned earlier, who warned me about the police. It was his birthday, and his Chinese friends were throwing a party for him.

It rained most of the night. When I was ready for departure in the morning, the earth was washed clean, and the sun shone brightly over the land. China was turning out to be a great experience. When I reached Harbin, a city with a population of over 4 million, I was in luck again. This time it was to watch a tremendous spectacle. A sort of parade was going on. Different groups of men and women dressed in colorful, traditional garb promenaded through the streets. Musical bands moved right along. When the throng reached a large square, all sorts of dances were performed.

Chapter 21

China 2: From Harbin to Manzouli (2001)
A fancy dinner, getting lost, a haircut

A little north of Harbin, like yesterday, the highway became a turnpike. To catch a ride with a vehicle was even easier here. One of the toll booth officials spoke a little English. He negotiated a ride for Wilhelm and me with a car driver who had stopped to pay his toll fee. When I was left to bike again, I was at the outskirts of the city of Daquing.

Oil had been recently discovered here, making it the newest and richest city of Manchuria, so I was told. New concepts, which I perceived as extremely progressive, had been implemented in the planning and construction of this city. Apartment buildings in bright colors reflected a cheerful playfulness, reminding me of Disneyland. Large, well-cultivated parks, flower patches, playgrounds and various forms of landscaping enriched the neighborhoods. Most impressive, revealing future vision, was the layout of the streets. Wide strips of greenery enhanced with flower arrangements, bushes and trees divided the sets of two traffic lanes from each other as well as an 8 m (26.4') wide bike lane and an equally wide pedestrian sidewalk on each side. What a wonderful way to keep motorists, cyclists and pedestrians apart for the safety and convenience of all! Green landscaping then continued toward and around the buildings. All this was truly picture-book-like. It was a pleasure to bike here, not only due to the convenience and safety, but also here was understanding and respect for the needs of cyclists put into action. So, how was it possible that with all these great biking paths, I broke a spoke? While I had it fixed at a sidewalk repair shop, how convenient, I checked into a hotel just across the street.

Having had the experience three times now that the highway turned into a turnpike, I was not anxious to choose major routes. As modern, even futuristic, as some cities appeared, the villages along backcountry roads were still very laidback and primitive. Nevertheless, television antennas were seldom missing. In one village, I stopped to look for something to eat. All I found was a very small grocery store, barely large enough for two people to stand in it. Again, the only items I recognized were eggs. Somehow, I managed to convey to the saleslady that I wished to eat two of them. Would you believe, she boiled them for me on an electric burner? And then she accompanied her act of loving kindness with a big smile as I ate.

On one hot afternoon, I had taken my T-shirt off, I was struggling with the soft asphalt surface of the road. When I approached a village, I noticed two Land Rovers had stopped there. Ten Caucasians had gotten out of the vehicles to take pictures of village life and each other. They were just as astonished to see me, a half-naked white man, as I was to meet them here. These, besides the earlier encounter with a Canadian, were the only other white folks I came across on my bike ride through China. "Do you speak English?" I approached them. The couple from New Zealand obviously did. The eight others were on a visit from Holland. All spoke some English and/or German. Great! The New Zealanders were running a milk processing plant previously owned by 'Bordens'. The Dutch folks were agricultural professionals. I shared a little of my bike ride adventures. When they left in their air-conditioned cars, I set out for the city of Qiqihar, hopeful to reach the two million community by evening. I did, but differently than I had planned.

Hardly 10 minutes had passed when one of the Land Rovers returned with an invitation to join this group for the night. Wow! Phil Thompson and his wife lived permanently in a nice house on the fenced and guarded compound of the milk processing plant. There were several other homes, in this case for the guests from Holland. I stayed with the Thompsons in the nicest and biggest of the buildings. Just a while prior, I had been exposed to the heat, grime and the hardship of the road and now I felt so pampered taking a refreshing shower in a most luxurious bathroom covered with brightly colored marble tiles. It was larger than my bedroom at home. Now I had to ready myself as much as possible to be presentable having been invited to accompany my hosts to a formal dinner.

Half an hour later all of us 'palefaces' took off for Qiqihar, 30 km (18.6 miles) further on. We headed for a first-class hotel within the heart of the city. Located on the 22nd floor was a fancy, rotating restaurant where we dined. Way below us, beyond the flower covered square, I observed two train stations namely the original old Russian terminal, now inactive, and the new modern Chinese station teeming with activity.

Course after course of exotic dishes were served while beer speeded up the merrymaking. There was a lot of interest in my bike stories. I had fun relating them. What a contrast this event was to my usually austere life on the road.

When I left the Thompsons in the morning, Phil had drawn me a map showing a shortcut through an area he had never visited. Hmm! That could mean trouble and it did. In this region there were only two bridges across the Nen Jiang River. By taking the first one I got on the wrong road but did not realize it for quite a while. I kept biking even when I could no longer find the towns I was passing through on my map. To make matters worse, the highway ended abruptly. I came upon a long stretch of freeway construction. There must have been signs somewhere redirecting the traffic, in Chinese, of course. First, I thought this would only be for a short distance. Wrong! It went on all day long. In part I rode on the dirt, graders and bulldozers were traveling on. No fun! In sections concrete slabs had been poured and were covered with straw. I biked on them too. An additional great challenge in all this was the heat and humidity. Many times, I pushed Wilhelm and even carried him. Literally tens of thousands of laborers were at work here. Just like in the fields, they worked with everything available to them. Prominent were the infamous three-wheelers and wheelbarrows. The former appeared to be a combination of a motorbike in the front and a pick-up loading area in the back. Most of the workers, however, had no more than a shovel. Often the handle was nothing but the crude trunk of a slender tree.

Their approach here was to work the entire length of the freeway in one pass. Thus, brigades of workers each worked a section. Not enough of that, they worked throughout the night as well. I know for certain for I witnessed it, having gotten stuck and spending the night sleeping in a stand of nearby trees.

On occasion there were villages where I could buy some food. In the morning of my second day in the midst of this road construction, I stopped in a village restaurant for breakfast. The cuisine was excellent, the information as to my whereabouts was not. Around noon I entered a larger town. I could not just go on without finding out where I was and where I was heading, could I? But how would I resolve my dilemma? Don't they teach English in high schools? Assuming that, I looked for a large building which I thought could be a school. I found one. The adjacent schoolyard confirmed it. I entered and kept speaking English to everyone I met. Had there ever been a white person in this so remote community, I wondered since my appearance was such a sensational event? Teachers left their classes and flocked around me and escorted me to the principal's office. And yes, there were English teachers. I spread my road map out on a table. With their help, I could identify my location and where I needed to go. I had strayed at least 80 km (50 miles) off the correct path. Two of the teachers, ever so helpful, escorted me on their bicycles out of town. It was such a relief to me to know where I was going and to get away from the tiresome freeway construction site.

Since my departure from Reno, over seven weeks had passed. I was overdue for a haircut and a beard trim. Of course, I was a sensation when I entered a barbershop in one of the towns I came through. I had to admire the courage of the young lady who, instead of running away, set out to attack my mane. A misunderstanding was all too easy to happen, and it did. I had shown her by leaving a 1 cm (.4") gap between thumb and index finger how much I wanted my hair to be shortened. She, however, interpreted that as how much length of hair I wanted to be left on my scalp. This disaster included my beard. Only natural hair growth could, over time, resolve the problem.

At one point, I wanted to exchange more money. Someone in the bank I had entered spoke some English. "So, can I now sign my travelers' checks?" I asked the lady at the counter. She and others there were horrified that I wanted to sign and write on what they must have thought to be money. I did not deem it worth my trouble of trying to explain. Leaving the premise seemed to be my best and only alternative.

China is of similar size as the USA but has four times the population. In addition, there are large regions of desert namely 28% and 58 % of the country is mountainous. Thus, the inhabitable areas are densely populated. Normally, villages were never more than 10 km (6.2 mi.) apart. That was rather convenient for I always had a nearby source of food and drink. I had come to rely on this geographical advantage in lieu of carrying my own supplies. At noontime one day, it was hot, and I was thirsty and hungry, yet no village would come up. Hour after hour passed! My energy sank, my misery increased. Should I stay in the shade of a tree, rest, preserve and hopefully regain some strength until it would be cooler? Or should I use what I had left in me to speed up my salvation and bike on? Glad that I decided on the latter! It would enrich my life with the greatest experience of unimaginable trust.

By midafternoon, I finally arrived in a little village. Totally bushed, I entered a small family restaurant and just sat there for a few minutes to cool off and to catch my breath. After a while, as usual, I used my phrasebook to order some food. The young couple, the apparent owners of the establishment, must have become aware of my distress. Though we could not communicate by means of language, we did it via demeanor. They rushed food and drink to me. Then, when I had eaten, something unusual happened. They directed me into their bedroom and motioned for me to sleep there. That, in itself, was very trusting toward me a total stranger and foreigner, the kind they probably had never seen before.

But what was even more trusting was the fact that their little daughter of about 2 years of age was lying naked asleep on their bed. This could not be right! Had they not heard of 'weirdos' or did they not exist in this country? My hosts left the room and shut the door. What was I to do? Cautiously I lay down next to the toddler. What, if she woke up and saw this bearded, tall stranger so close to her. Would it not give her a shock for life? No, I could not risk this. I looked at her cute, innocent face for a while, an innocence so badly needed in this world. Then I quietly left the room. I thanked my hosts. As was so often the case, they refused payment. Though so very poor, the joy of giving was theirs. The joy of experiencing unbelievable trust was mine.

The stretch of 300 km (186 miles) from here to the Russian border consisted of grassland. Trees grew only where they had been planted in towns which were far apart. This was Mongol country, known as 'Inner Mongolia', the latter term meaning it was located within China's present national borders. I wondered whether the grass was always as green, or would it turn brown as summer progressed? Though the country was slightly hilly, there was little to block the view. Here was a herd of cattle. I stopped to watch them. A mighty bull probably thought that I was interested in one of the ladies in his harem. He left the group and started to trot toward me, increasing his speed. I swung back on my bike and fled. Triumphantly, he stopped his pursuit, now that he had shown his 'ladies' what kind of boss he was.

I remembered having learned that the predecessors of the horse came from the steppes of Mongolia. It appeared that meanwhile the local horses had reached a state of perfection. Here and there, I marveled at their beauty. As if to show me their horses or to impress me with their riding skills, herdsmen would gallop up to me and wave in form of a salute. Those herding sheep were less dashing, maybe rather a bit 'sheepish'.

My first night in the steppes was a rather creepy experience. Near a town, I had come upon a stand of evergreens I thought would be ideal to serve as my bedroom where I would be undisturbed. Well, not quite. Ants! I fought back. They kept coming. The only solution when you are so heavily outnumbered is flight. When I collected my stuff to move away, I discovered that I had made camp next to an anthill. Some of the ants must have liked my company. They moved right along with me to my new location.

When biking in this mostly treeless landscape, I was visible from afar. One morning, after I had biked about 25 km (15.5 miles), I came upon a group of three yurts. These are circular, normally brightly colored tents used by nomadic Mongol tribes as they herd their livestock over the grassy plains. When I approached, a fellow, dressed in customary colorful garb, stepped into my path to stop me. He then pointed at his mouth. Ah, time for chow. I was motioned to enter one of the tents and to sit on one of the tiny stools. Boxes standing on their side served as shelves. In the center, a young, rosy cheeked woman cheerfully got a fire going burning cattle dung in a small cast-iron stove. Soon she fried generous slices of meat. The neighbors showed up. Did they smell the food or were they curious to take a look at this strange cyclist? Probably both! Meanwhile, noisy, laughter filled conversation went on, in Mongolian, of course. Glances in my direction told me that some of their

Eurasia: Land of opportunities

chatter must have been about me. What a strange sight I must have been to them. Traveling on a bicycle? Did I not know that a real man rides a horse? Two more fellows arrived on horseback, dressed in similar colorful clothing. We all had spiced chunks of meat for breakfast and that was fine with me. Payment was energetically refused and that was not fine with me. I would rather have contributed something to these poor folks, though poor only in a worldly sense. I wondered how they make it through the severe winters in these tents. No firewood, no coal, no oil nor natural gas, just dung to burn! There were piles of it stocked next to the corral.

I had only biked a couple of hours when a similar situation repeated itself. I was 'held up' again and forced to eat. There was no way for me to get across to these wonderful people that I was already replete and literally so. I had to 'stuff' some more. Did they not know that the size of our stomach is only as big as one of our fists? The present scenario reminded me of a scene in the movie 'Dancing with Wolves', when after a successful buffalo hunt, the Indians wanted their white companion to eat and eat and then eat some more. Incidentally, they too lived in tents, were nomads and are said to be ethnically related to the Mongols.

On the next day, I came upon a group of yurts which functioned as a restaurant, except I was not allowed to pay there either. Along with large portions of meat, I was served *koumiss*, an alcoholic drink made from fermented horse milk. After I had my fill, I was ushered to one of the yurts and was left alone to sleep there, though it was only midafternoon.

The next night was my last one in this wide-open country with its friendly, hospitable people. I had biked for hours in darkness hoping to reach a community with a hotel. I reached a town but found no hotel. At the outskirts, I slept on the grassy plains. While Mongols dominated the steppes, Han-Chinese by far outnumbered them in urban areas. This was also the case in Manzhouli, which I reached by the next day. I looked across the border into Russia where I had been only 10 days earlier. Here was gaiety, industriousness and wealth. On the other side lies Zabaykalsk, a pitiful community in a state of decay! Yes, there was a tremendous difference between these two people, and I loved them both.

My horizontal bike ride from the Atlantic coast of France to the Pacific coast of Russia was now complete. My goal achieved, would this be the end of my exotic biking trips? No, not yet. At an age of 60, I was much too young to quit. As my exuberance and euphoria grew upon reaching my destination, I already in my mind began to outline the continuation of my earlier kayak/bike ride from the Arctic Ocean to the Antarctic Ocean. With other words, a ride around the world once more but this time vertically.

Prior to my departure, I had several stubborn health concerns that even experienced physicians of natural healing found challenging. All these infirmities totally disappeared during my trek. I guess if I were a doctor, I would prescribe bike riding to almost all my patients. Yet there is so much more beyond restoring health and becoming physically fit. Think of the enrichment of your life through adventure, excitement and fun, the great learning about our world, its people, landscapes, cities, cultures and art, making new friends, plus the awesome discovery that there is a wonderful world out there to be discovered.

On the next train, Wilhelm and I traveled back to Qiqihar. There I sat in the train with a feeling of joy so strong I could have hugged everyone. Fortunately, there was a young man who knew English with whom I could share my story. Once more I experienced amazing Oriental hospitality. He was traveling back to rejoin his wife and little boy in Qiqihar. When we reached our destination, he took me to his uncle's restaurant. While I dined in style, Lee made arrangements for me to be interviewed and photographed by a local newspaper. When he and his little family accompanied me back to the railroad station, it provided me the greatest pleasure to leave my bike with them as a gift. To me, it was a token response for all the generosity I had experienced in this hospitable land. Yet it was not the end of it.

The train to Beijing was very modern, clean and fast. I shared my sleeping compartment with a lady and her 11-year-old daughter who was studying English and kept feeding me bananas. In the morning, the two invited me to have breakfast with them in the dining car.

Why Beijing now? My return flight home was to take off from there in three days. Behaving like an ordinary tourist for that timeframe, I visited the Great Wall, Tiananmen Square and the Forbidden City. Thus, I came to finish this great bike adventure by experiencing some extraordinary highlights.

Summary: What a wonderful trip this had been. It took me close to 9 weeks to ride almost 5,000 km (3,100 miles). Not once did I experience danger or harm. To the contrary, I felt welcome wherever I went and was treated with an astounding amount of generous hospitality and loving kindness. Besides the obvious benefits of biking, like ecology, health and endurance building, education, adventure, making friends is the economy. Between leaving and returning Reno, I spent a total of $770 US and that even included buying some gifts for friends and employees. Besides hoping to inspire folks to ride bicycles, I think my most valuable contribution is to further understanding among people, peace and joy and to foster the spirit of pronoia wherever I go.

Eurasia: Land of opportunities

A Siberian highway through the taiga (forest region)

A flat in the Ural Mountains

Pedaling, Paddling and Pedes 2

Countless birch trees, a source of Xylitol, a natural sweetener

Kvas, a drink from slightly fermented bread

239

Eurasia: Land of opportunities

My hosts for a breakfast buffet

Opposite: Russian sweethearts

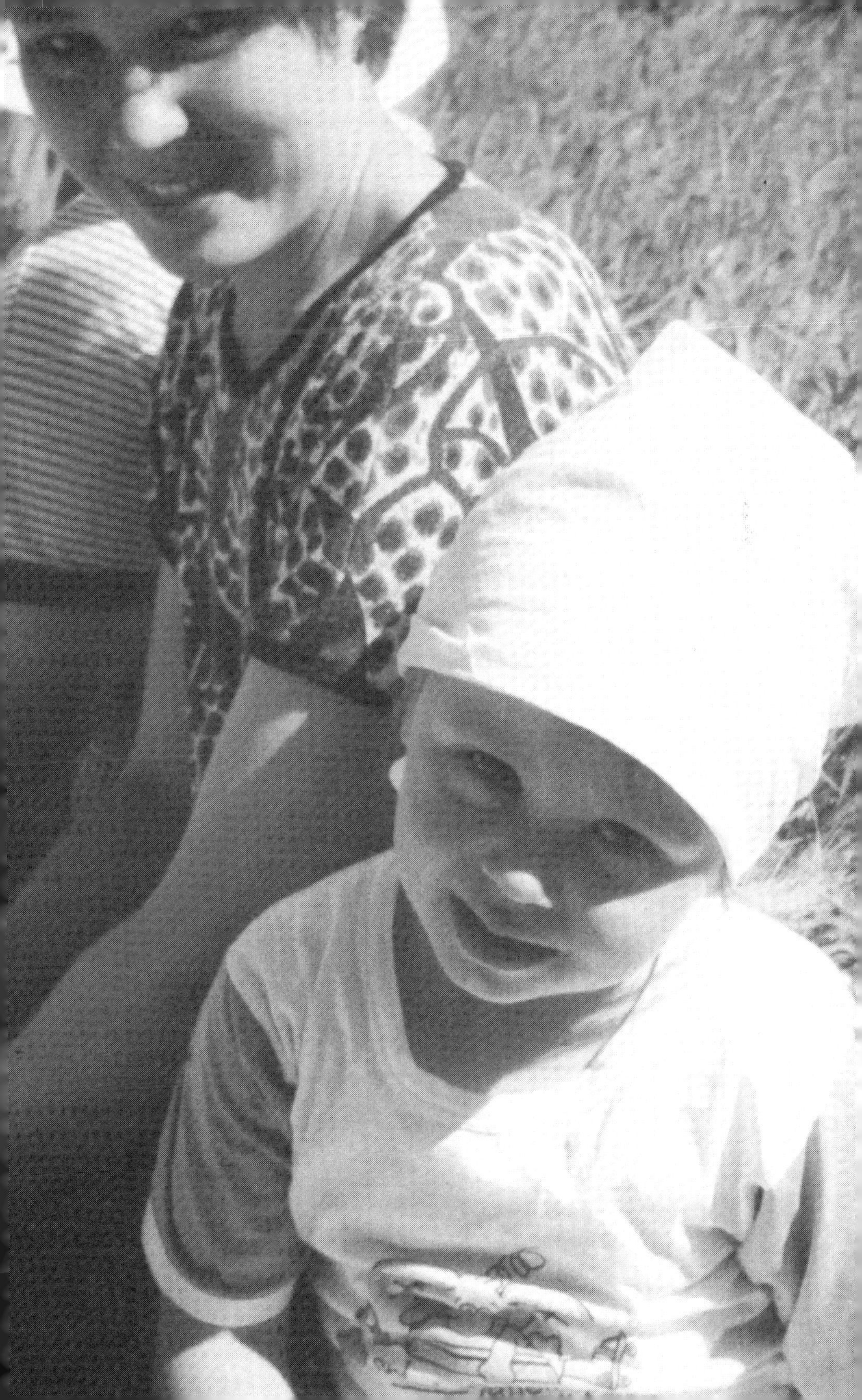

As if time has stood still

Freshly picked mushrooms in the forest – for sale

Eduard Rapp, twice world bike racing champion with son Konstantin

Meeting a biking brother

Mormon missionaries in Ulan-Ude

Lenin monument in the city of Ulan-Ude

Traveling with a potato sack as camouflage

Lake Baikal, the deepest in the world

中国旅游报

CHINA TOURISM NEWS

7/12/2000

中国旅游协会主办　　　　　　　　　国内统一刊号：CN11-0013（代号：
2000年8月11日 星期五 第2665期　　　网址：http://www.ctnews.com

前沿人物

让生命精彩一次

——访骑车环游世界的美国旅游者汉斯·福利斯齐森

□ 本报记者 李冰

汉斯在齐齐哈尔火车站前

对于探险家、流浪者，我总怕有种莫起敬的分儿了，因为他们惊人般的毅力和体力令人望尘莫及，让我不解的是，他们为什么选择这种一种方式来证明自己？不久前，我有幸采访了一位骑自行车环游世界的老外，与他的谈话使我觉得不可及的领域——探险旅游。

初见汉斯（Hans Frischeisen）时，他给我的印象是一个再普通不过的老外帮包游客了。他上身穿一件蓝色T-shirt，鼓鼓囊囊的挂在身上，下面破旧的咖

大号旅游鞋已分辨不出原来的颜色，伴身上背着一为物件就是那个不大但严整的已半磨旧泡过的旅行包。

汉斯的身材虽也很高大，一副运动员的体魄，皮肤已被酒成深黑色，但很健康。他的声音洪亮，极富感染力。"你好！"听见面时，他字正腔圆地用中文跟我打招呼，并伸出有力的大手与我握握，让人无法抗拒地的热情。在中国之行中，"你好"、"谢谢"、"再见"是他说得最流利的汉语，使用得频率极高。

汉斯是美籍德国人，在第三届满了40年，曾从事一家庙店的片一

齐森，我已退休，今年60岁这让我的岁月有了保障吗。他要在任的晚年生活中实现两个计划：就是骑自行车纵贯横向环绕地球。然后再沿着纵度环绕行地球。此次来中国，是已第一次的最后一站，途经美国、法国、德国（奥大利）希腊、土耳其、格鲁吉亚、俄罗斯，最后到达中国黑龙江齐齐哈尔，行程23000公里。

以下是记者与汉斯的对话。

为什么会有这个骑车环游世界的想法？

"在美国，许多退了休的人无所事事，在家看电视，喝啤酒，就这发福、生产。55%以上的美国人都大腹便便，我不愿意看到这样的生活出现在我身上，我希望生活丰富健康向上的。

美国革命时期最著名的总统本杰明·富兰克林在被人问到是否害怕死亡时说过这样一句话，'当我做了我要做的事以后我就不再害怕死亡'。这句话给我触动很大，一直激励着我，我很喜欢骑自行车，比较喜欢旅游，于是我决定在晚年骑车环游世界，然后写一本书，告诉人们这是一个既经济又

他使你大开眼界，让你的生活变得积极、健康。"

骑车环球旅游这类探险运动是否需要人们具有运动员的身体素质？

"健康的身体素质确实能够保证充足的体力，但如果你身体不好，也不是不可以去尝试。要知道我今年60岁，在大多数人眼里，人们为我不适合环球旅游。我没为同意的关键就是要你对自己有认识。如果你认为这种方式会给你带来欢乐，能够体现你生命的价值，那你就认真、不要听太多的所谓的'善意'，好多了，它会让你对旅行，其实时自行车是一种对身体有益的运动方式，还会让你变得更强壮、更年轻。

探险旅游需要做好哪些准备？

"你在出发之前需要做好充分的准备，包括心理、生理和其它各种必要的准备。比如你要设计最佳的行程计划和路线，以保证你有时间和体力，去点能经历坦的公路上骑车，你要挑选最精良最耐用的旅途工具和用品，以保证你的旅途质量；你要准备充足的钱，并适度分散地放在你随身的地方，如

带，内裤里，以保证你在走投无路的情况下有能力返家。一但因为这些都是很容易解决的环节，重要的是你要抱有良好的心态，带着一份发自内心的、快乐的好的心情上路，为自己，也……"

旅途中遇到意想不到的事时该怎么办？

"在你的旅途中，你会发现不再像一般旅游者那样可以飞机、可以住高级宾馆，只钱，你可以不需要别人的帮助作为背包游者，你会很多预想不到的麻烦，比如机械…你经常会需要当地帮助，所以，你要用你的真诚感染别人，你的态度就赠给对方的一份礼物。我在法国这中感受特别强烈，法国人生、特别是对我很热情，当他用带笑容真诚地用法语问候好了，他们就会很亲切地助你。在环球旅游中，语言沟通，我基本能用七个国语言进行简单交流，只可以太唯，只会说'你好'、'再见'。不过中国人很友善们的帮助是无私的，让我动。

"另外，快乐的心情对…

Pedaling, Paddling and Pedes 2

My Chinese welcome committee

Biking does not harm our planet

Opposite: Hans presenting a message of peace in a Beijing newspaper

Cultivating every square inch

A street bike service for broken spokes

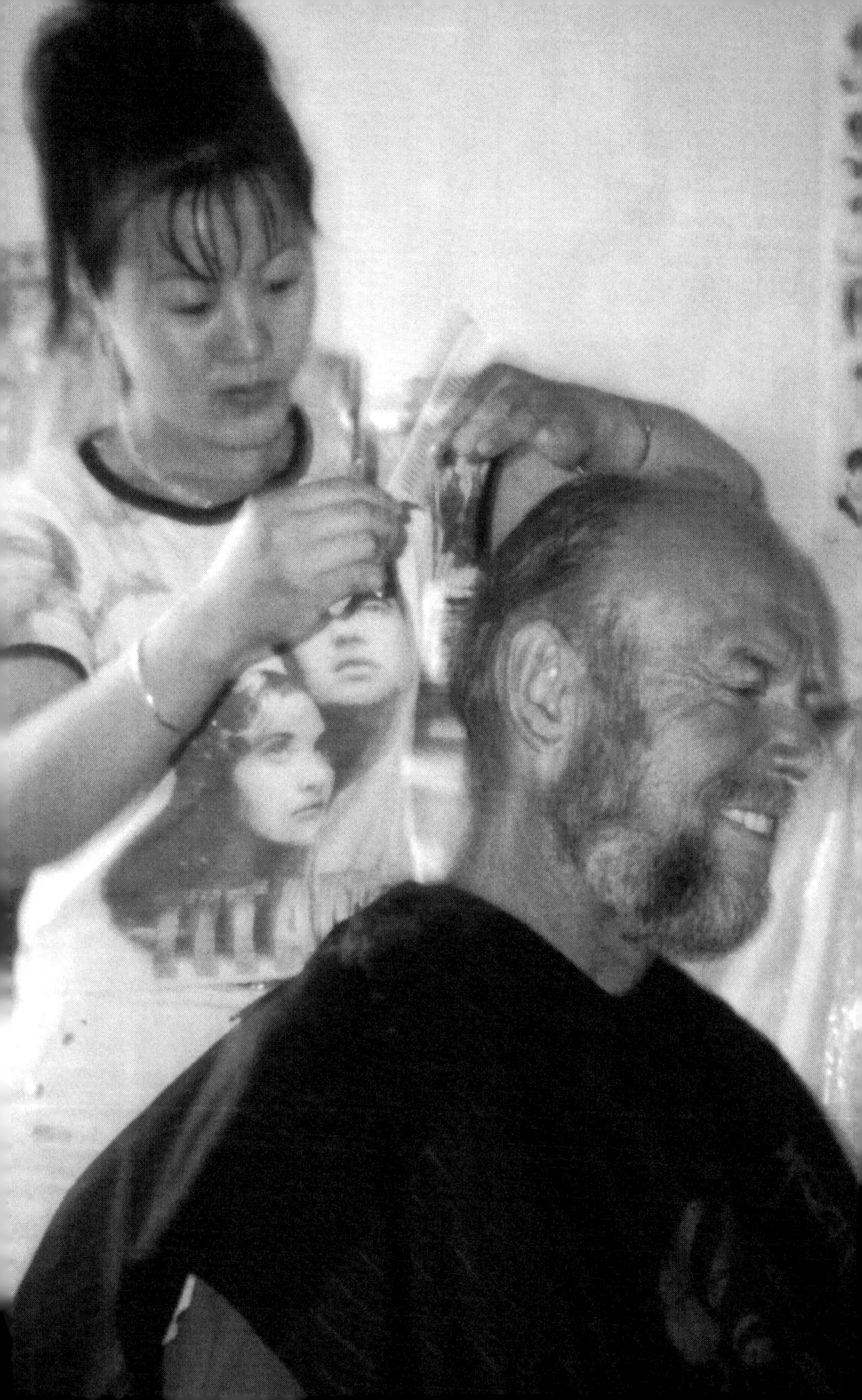

Pedaling, Paddling and Pedes 2

Instead of school bussing – a great idea

Opposite: Certainly, her first Caucasian customer

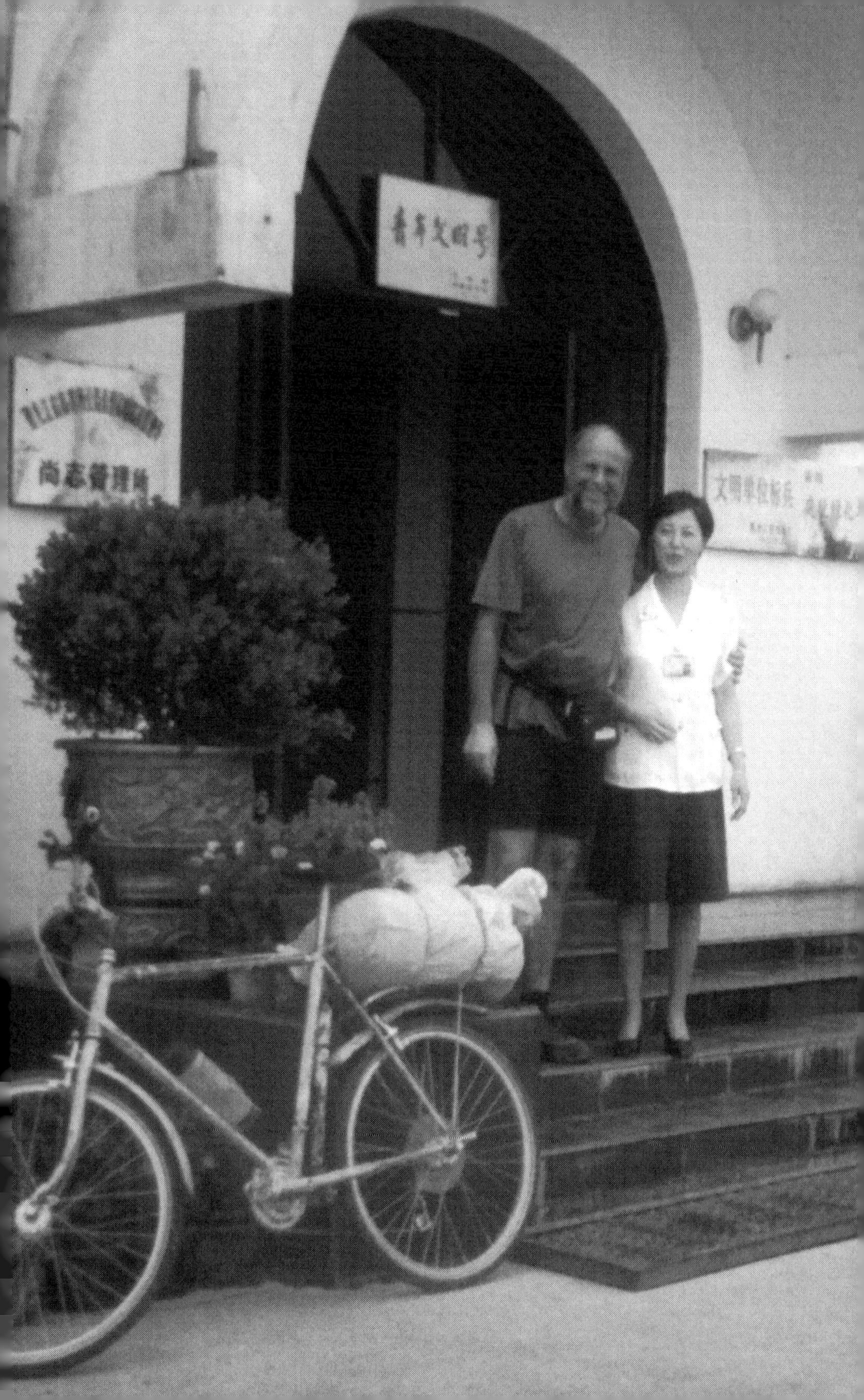

Pedaling, Paddling and Pedes 2

Reaching the Pacific Ocean in Vladivostok

Opposite: As a guest at a police headquarters

Eurasia: Land of opportunities

May Buddha's picture inspire peace

Pedaling, Paddling and Pedes 2

Traveling on a train, mother and daughter invited me for lunch

The Great Chinese wall said to be 21,967 miles (30,171 km) long

Eurasia: Land of opportunities

Tiananmen Square in Beijing

VI. North America
Across the USA, land of the free

Chapter 22

USA 1: Hawaiian Islands (09/01/2017)
The Macadamia farm on the Big Island

Should I even write about my short bike rides on the Hawaiian Islands? Several considerations propelled me to proceed: 1. These islands are located between the beginning and end points of my horizontal trek around the world namely San Francisco and Vladivostok at the Pacific coast of Siberia. Hence, these islands were a geographical fit. Thus, I concluded, an article would be a further enhancement of this undertaking and 2. I love to write. It lets me re-experience the events and adventures. Those were good enough reasons for me to share my Hawaiian experiences in this book.

    A heavy snowstorm was pummeling the Reno area when Lois and I left our home in the morning of January 12th, 2017. Our cruise ship to the Hawaiian Islands was to leave from San Diego two days later. How could we best get there with our Toyota Prius? To avoid potentially snow blocked passes, we decided on a detour via Las Vegas. Good plan! After 80 miles, the snow turned first into slush and then rain which lasted all the way into Las Vegas. We spent the night at the Flamingo Hotel/Casino. Rather heavy rain continued next day and lasted until the town of Escondido in California, just a little short of San Diego. Staying at the Holiday Inn Express in downtown had the advantages that we could leave our car there and were shuttled to the M.S, Westerdam, 'our' cruise ship. We woke up to a sunny morning. 'Little Wilhelm', my fold-able bicycle, housed in a large suitcase, was promptly delivered to our stateroom by the crew of the ship. For now, I shoved 'him' under my bed.

    I love the sea and for the next 5 days enjoyed traveling over the watery deep of the Pacific. In the morning of the 6th day we arrived in Hilo, the principal community on the east side of this Hawaiian Island, commonly referred to as the 'Big Island'. 'Little Wilhelm' and I were ready for action. Lois preferred to keep enjoying the wide range of comforts offered on the ship. Also, we had toured parts of the island on previous occasions by rental car. Since it tends to rain more frequently on this side of the island, I kept a raincoat in my knapsack, along with some basic bike parts and tools as well as sandwiches, fruit and water. So, whereto should I ride? I had about 8 hours available before the ship would continue to Kona on the opposite and normally sunny side of the island. The thought had occurred to me to ride the

119 miles across the island and get back onto the ship in Kona. I would have had until 17:00 h the following day to do so. Normally that would have been 'a piece of cake', but I had not thought of it early enough. Also, I had not talked with Lois about this possibility and further did not want to leave her alone. Also, I was not prepared to spend a night outdoors. Besides, I would have had to inform the ship's administration of my plans. Too late now!

It seems that I was the only one of the close to 2,000 passengers who had the foresight to bring a bike along. "Look, someone with a bicycle! Well, isn't that a great idea!" I welcomed those comments with a big smile and nodded. 'Indeed, this is great, wholesome fun and quite practical!' I could have answered.

Repeatedly on my global rides, I had noticed, bicycles to be perceived as dangerous. In this case, even my 'Little Wilhelm'. "Please, Sir, do not ride your bicycle within the harbor compound," I was advised by security personnel. Though there was plenty of room, I pushed my bike until I reached the exit gate.

So where to now? Lois and I love macadamia nuts. On previous tours of the island by car, we had stopped at a macadamia farm about 12 miles from Hilo. To visit it again seemed like a worthwhile destination. It felt good to have soil under my feet or more accurately under my tires again. Having escaped from a blizzard just a few days ago, I now entered the wonderfully lush world of tropical vegetation. Though light, sporadic clouds moved over the sky, it was sunny and splendidly warm. I wanted to linger and enjoy. No, let me do the bike ride first and then spend the remaining time in the Reeds Bay Beach Park, I decided.

As is typical in harbor environments, the area along Kalanianaole Ave. was industrial and unattractive. I followed it for about 3/4 mile (1.3 km) until I reached Highway 11, the main road leading west out of Hilo. Businesses and homes alternated. It started to get more attractive once I reached residential areas. Most yards were adorned with flowery garden arrangements. Vehicular traffic on this divided highway was heavy. Fortunately, I could ride on a bike lane which later turned into a highway shoulder.

It was not a major problem, but it was annoying. My seat post kept sliding downward. Though I adjusted it repeatedly, after a couple of miles it was too low again. Though I had been looking, I missed a place where I could get my problem fixed and then I was already out of town. Might I find something with which to address the situation? Did it not exist here or did I just not see it. I could not find a single piece of hard wood which I could shape to fit inside the pipe holding the seat post. Do most plants here consist of soft reed-like material? I was riding now through slightly hilly landscapes of thick brush land. Without a machete, I imagined it to be just about impossible to penetrate this thick cluster of plants on either side of the highway.

A large, colorful sign alerted me to turn left for the 'Mauna Loa Macadamia Visitor Center'. From here on, the road narrowed down to two lanes and that without bike facility or shoulder. The good news was that the traffic slowed down to a trickle, making this ride most enjoyable. From the junction, there were still nearly 3 miles (5 km) to go until it ended at the nut farm. In the beginning, the dense forest continued. When it thinned a little, I could make out papaya trees behind the foliage of a hedge. When I reached a row of what looked like some sort of tall, slender conifers with 'needles' about 7" (18 cm) long, flanking the left side of the road, I entered the nut farm property. A sign announced that there were 2,500 acres (1,012 HA) of macadamia trees. I stopped to explore and walked into the thick green foliage. No nuts? Was this out of season? No need to worry! Another sign indicated that free samples would be provided at the center. Onward then!

Typical for an orchard, the nut trees were arranged in long rows. Their average height I guessed at around 12' (3.6 m). The leaves in whorls of 3 to 6 were oblong shaped and often more than a foot long. This was the blooming season. Seeing an abundance of large blossoms, I expected a wealth of sweet smells but did not discern any fragrance. Small, whitish and tasseled flowers grew on long spikes.

I suspected that most of the folks passing me in tourist busses were from the M.S. Westerdam. Right on! I recognized some of them as they streamed into the large store facility. Most of the nuts offered were chocolate covered and packaged in boxes. About 9 different flavors were available. I tried them all and they were all good, though rather pricey. I bought a package of 10 boxes and then approached one of the fellow cruise travelers to take it back to the ship for me.

So, what else was there? In one section typical Hawaiian jewelry was displayed, primarily made from pearls and coral. Toward the back, folks were busy enjoying macadamia nut ice cream at a snack bar. From here, one could step onto manicured meadows surrounded by lush bushes, trees, and a host of flowering plants. This little paradise invited one to a stroll.

I had a new toy: A cell phone. Since this was to be my turnaround point, I called Lois to confirm that everything was fine, that I still loved her and that I would be back on time.

On returning to Hilo, when I reached the outskirts, I looked more diligently for a solution to fix my sliding seat dilemma. It should be easy if I could drill a hole through shaft and stem and placed a bolt or screw through both. The Honda car repair facility was too busy, but next to them a tire center freed a man to drill a hole on the spot I requested and inserted a bolt. Though the drill bit broke in the process, I was waived off with a Hawaiian smile when I tried to pay. I too was smiling for no longer sliding into a toddler position on my bicycle.

My next stop was Reeds Bay Beach Park, I had earlier marveled at from the distance. This tropical wonderland stretches along Kuhio Bay. I settled at a picnic table. Between catching up with my diary entries, I enjoyed a grand view. A paddle boarder was elegantly gliding across the calm water. This would have been ideal for a little kayak adventure. I switched into my swim trunks and went for a swim in this clear and warm water. Such is Hawaii!. By now it was midafternoon. Time to enjoy the sandwiches, compliment of the M.S. Westerdam. With plenty of time to spare, I arrived back on the ship.

The captain had announced that, while touring around the southern shores of the Big Island, we would pass the lava flow area around 21:30 h. It seemed that everyone wanted to watch this fantastic spectacle. Long before the time, in total darkness, folks had gathered on the decks, toting cameras and/or I-phones. Lois and I were among them. Then there it was. This was a noisy affair when the river of lava from rocky heights dropped down into the sea. Hissing steam rose high into the air, lit by the glowing fire of lava as it reached the edge and broke off from the stream, falling in sometimes vehicle sized chunks, into the water, a thrilling sight. My ordinary little Nikon camera was not well equipped to take good shots over a distance of half a mile (.8 km). The pictures showed only red globs.

The harbor of Kona does not allow for larger ships to enter. Hence, the lifeboats served as tenders. No one seemed to mind when I boarded one of them with my bicycle. Twice before on other cruises on account of strong winds and big waves, the captain had suspended trips to the shore. No problems this time. Well, not for me but certainly for those traveling on a tender which had lost power. Wind and waves were driving it through the surf towards the rocks of the shore. The vessel I was traveling on held back so as not to interfere with rescue attempts. That particular boat actually hit the seawall. Fortunately, nothing serious happened. With some effort, the tender became operational again.

 I arrived on this coastline of Hawaii for the first time. This was said to be the 'sunny' side of the island. That was easy to believe looking at the hills rising beyond the residential areas looking arid and brown. After arriving in the little harbor on a tender, I biked on narrow streets in heavy traffic through the town center. Where were the sandy beaches? None here! Big waves were rolling against a rocky coast along which resorts had been built. I asked a local for the nearest beaches. Why his hesitation in answering? I found out that the rising sea had washed out beaches. Was that the result of global warming? So, the rising of water levels was already happening.

 I biked about 3 miles south along the coast until I came to a little park. From here I enjoyed a good view of the M.S. Westerdam far out in the ocean. The traffic had gotten lighter and buildings a little rarer. Kids with dark skin were horsing around, but not in the water, not even on a beach because there wasn't any, just rocks. Rows of tables and chairs on a lawn bore witness that some festivities were in progress. Oh, yes, this was Saturday. Maybe, this was a church group. I didn't think it likely there to be attractive beaches further on and turned around. Back in town, next to the harbor in front of a hotel, I had seen a real sandy beach. Though small and a bit crowded, it had to do. Here in a bay, the water was calm. Tourists were frolicking on plastic kayaks and paddle boards. After lying in the sun and going for a swim, I caught a tender back to the ship.

Oahu (2017)
Stomping on familiar Grounds, Sharks?

The first daylight was coming up when the M.S. Westerdam entered the harbor of Honolulu next morning. With interest, I watched the process of mooring. Then I was one of the first passengers to get off the ship. After exploring the harbor area, I biked toward the fabulous Waikiki Beach. Even though it was Sunday, or was it because of it, street traffic was heavy. Riding on sidewalks and beach promenades, I came to the end of the Ala Moana Beach Park. Lost in thought, I stopped on the bridge crossing the Ala Wai Canal. Looking down on the water, in my mind, I could see my older son and me kayaking out into the ocean from here. It was in 1989. Andy was 18 years old. To avoid the surf, we had chosen this route to head for the open sea. I had visions of kayaking around the whole island of Oahu. Naturally, there would be some challenges involved. No, I would not risk my son's life. Besides, we had left my wife and our younger son behind in Waikiki. They were worried. "No, we will just go for a fun ride as long as we feel comfy with it," we had assured them.

We headed in easterly direction, leaving the long row of Waikiki Beach hotels behind. Steering toward Hanauma Bay, just a little beyond Diamond Head was when it happened. It was probably not a good thing that Andy had seen the movie "Jaws" some time ago. When a school of dolphins was heading toward us, in terror Andy yelled: "Sharks! Dad, sharks!" Sitting in front of me, I could see him freeze. Thinking the dolphins to be sharks, the horror of 'Jaws' had gotten a hold of him. "Dad, Dad, what are we going to do?!" "Son, those are dolphins!" I tried to calm him down. By this time these graceful mammals were passing on our left side. We could see them clearly now. Still, it took a little while for Andy to fully relax.

These and other exciting and wonderful moments returned to me while standing on the bridge and looking out over canal, bay and sea. Just a little further on began the Waikiki hotel and apartment building complex. In its midst, I revisited the Hilton Hawaiian Village. What an eminent layout. I walked my bike right through it. A few years ago, Lois and I had been here for a few days as the guests of Natures Sunshine Products, our most trusted supplement company.

Today, it was unusually windy. Sand whirled through the air close to the beach. Still, some brave souls hung out to lie in the sun. Of course, they may have come here mainly to get a tan and did not want to lose out on this 'important' pursuit.

Past the attractive landscaping of a park, I followed a promenade along the beach to the Fort De Russy military museum. Facing the sea, in the shade of trees with dense foliage, a row of tables and benches constructed out of concrete had been erected. This, in 1989, was our favorite hang-out, when my family of four stayed at a nearby hotel for 3 weeks. Remembering those carefree days, I wrote a letter to my sons. I missed them when I went for a swim, remembering the fun we had horsing around in the water.

Since I had all day at my disposal, I took my time to enjoy the sights and to slowly return to the ship. By the following day, still on Oahu, the wind had died. This time I rode only as far as the Ala Moana Beach Park to engage in what all tourists and seemingly many locals enjoyed; looking out at the sea, meandering around, sunbathing, reading, swimming and hoping that time would stand still.

Maui (2017)
Under the Banyan Tree, Snorkeling

On the following morning, we arrived near the shore of the town of Lahaina, on the island of Maui. Our vessel anchored close to one mile from the coast. Three of the smaller Hawaiian Islands could be seen in the distance: Molokai, Lanai and Kahoolawe. Like a white hat, heavy clouds covered the hilltops of Maui's lush green hills. This was a good moment to take pictures of this grand site. Again, we passengers were ferried by tenders into the harbor. This time, Lois came along. Even though she says she is not fond of shopping, she did a good job of it, but never found what she was looking for. Maybe it was a sort of compensation for this lack that we settled for some ice cream instead. In a square across the street, stood a mighty banyan tree. I heard it said to be the second largest of its kind in the world. Sitting on a bench in its shade, we relaxed to enjoy our ice cream cones, while watching life around us. When Lois was ready to return to the ship, I accompanied her to one of the tenders. My time for a little bike ride had now come. I headed north until I came upon a little marina. Boats were taking tourists to areas off the coast for scuba diving and snorkeling. I had brought a mask and snorkel along to do some exploring on my own. Yes, this water was substantially warmer than Lake Tahoe at its best. There was also so much more to see. I just loved to swim and dive around coral reefs. Colorful fish dashed away when I approached. Here and there we all have heard or read stories of aggressive sharks showing up. I wondered if that should happen now, would I have the fortitude not to try to dash back to the shore? Being hunters, the commotion of flight is an enticement for them to pursue and attack. Fortunately for me, it did not come to a test of my courage and resolve.

When I had returned to the ship, Lois and I fantasized about on which of the islands we would like to live. She, with her origins in farming country, would not be happy on any of them. I thought I could live on any of them but decided that Big Hawaii would be my preference.

It took us five wonderful days at sea to return to San Diego. The night before the last one, something unusual happened. We had just gone to bed when we noticed some strong vibrations and some humming sounds in otherwise calm waters. I would have slept through it. Lois called the front desk and learned that due to a medical emergency of a passenger, the captain had decided to increase the speed resulting in these vibrations.

Our next and last stop was Ensenada in Mexico. How amazing! Due to the circumstance, we arrived there 8 hours ahead of schedule. Great! With a few pesos on me, I biked into town to experience the vibrant Mexican life I love so much.

Disembarking in San Diego next day was smooth. A shuttle returned us to our hotel and our car. Would there be snow blocking us on our ride back to Reno? There was snow alright, but the highways were clear all the way home. By 22:00 h we pulled into our driveway.

In retrospect, what did I like best on this cruise? Probably, because I am hooked on biking, exploring parts of the Hawaiian Islands on my bike was what I liked most. The total number of miles I pedaled amounted to about 50 (80 km). That would have been enough to ride across any of the islands, except the big one. With all the luxuries of a cruise ship, the beauty of the land and having Lois along, this trip differed much from my usual roughing it, but still it was certainly a lot of fun.

Kauai (2019)
Chickens, Beach Dwellers

It happened already on our voyage in 2018 to Puerto Vallarta, that the security guards of the cruise line sort of 'confiscated' my bike. Now that Lois and I, a year later, were traveling with the same cruise line to the Hawaiian Islands, my suitcase containing my fold-able bicycle, was again detained. Why, when with Holland American cruise line, not only could I take my small fold-able bicycle 'Little Wilhelm', but on a different occasion even my full-sized road bike up to our stateroom? No restrictions about their use had ever been shared with us. So, what possible dangers were perceived and/or imagined this time related to a bicycle? How sad! I had come across these narrow mindsets in other places before.

So, how did I get to ride on the islands? The supervisor in the 'security' department told me that I would have to take the suitcase ashore and then assemble the bike. Their crew would watch over the empty suitcase while I went biking. By the time we reached Kauai the realization must have set in that neither I nor the bicycle were a threat. I was allowed to assemble the bike on board. Hurrah!

This would be the first time for me to ride on this so called 'garden island'. I believe it to be the most beautiful of the Hawaiian Islands. To our left, as the huge ship moored, we were welcomed by the sight of massive, steep mountains densely covered with juicy green vegetation.

Leaving the Los Angeles harbor, our first stop had been the island of Maui. While two years ago I biked for a few miles south from the port of Lahaina, this time I headed north, went for a swim with snorkel and mask and returned to sit with Lois and ice cream in the shade of the banyan tree as we had previously done. Stopping the next day on Oahu, I likewise biked a little northward and went for a swim before returning to the cruise ship. The last island to visit was the so-called Big Island. We love macadamia nuts. As I did two years ago, I biked to the giant Mauna Loa farm to sample and buy macadamia nuts. Ironically, on the way back to the ship, I stopped at a Walmart store and learned that their prices for macadamia nuts were about the same as those at the farm. Oh well, the bike ride of 24 miles (38 km) out into the country was certainly worth it.

Now where would I go on Kauai, having never ventured beyond the Nawiliwili harbor area? Studying my AAA road map, I noticed by heading north I would stay closest to the sea and come upon some public beaches. Hence, I decided to bike on Highway 51 and shortly after continued on Highway 56 to the town of Kanaa. Leaving the harbor area, I was surprised by having to labor up a steep hill. Having heard that it rains frequently on this island prepared me for the dense tropical vegetation on both sides of the street. What surprised me though, was what sounded like the crowing of roosters. Had I heard right? And then I saw them. First colorful roosters and then hens often with their little chicks, ever so cute, were freely running about. They seemed to be all over the island. It is believed that early arrivals from Polynesia brought some of these birds originally here for food. Having no natural enemies except maybe man and with plenty to feed on, they kept and still keep multiplying. As I biked on, I would repeatedly come upon them.

Once I reached the top of the initial hill, the terrain leveled out more. Soon, I got beyond commercial and residential areas and entered grasslands where healthy looking Holstein cattle were grazing. Without obstructions, I could enjoy the view into the mountains to my left and onto the ocean to my right. Paradise! I felt that this would be the highlight of the day and sang out jubilantly. I was surprised by the amount of traffic. Where were all these vehicles heading? My map showed only a few small communities ahead. Anyway, I felt safe riding on the well-marked bike routes. Though golfing is not my thing, I was pleased to pass a huge golf course, hoping folks there would have as much fun as I was experiencing.

Highway 580 branched off to my left leading to the Opaekaa Waterfalls. I turned right to the Wailua Beach instead to watch the mighty waves crashing and rolling on to a rocky beach. No surfers here I suppose on account of the massive amounts of boulders covering the shore.

Continuing on, I came upon a bike trail guiding me away from the highway and closer to the sea. Excellent, for urbanization was increasing with resorts and general businesses.

In Kapaa, this trail ended in a park overlooking a large bay. This, I decided, was to be my turnaround point. Relaxing at a picnic table, I ate the sandwich and apple I had brought along. I was not alone. Just a little above the sand beach, people were living in a well-sized tent. Best of the utensils lying around were two bicycles. There seemed to be some permanence to this setup. While a dark-skinned woman was hanging laundry on a clothesline, she was talking to a fellow inside the tent. People promenading along the beach did not seem to mind and obviously neither did the authorities. It puzzled me though wondering where and how these tent dwellers went to the bathroom. Talking of that biological need, I chose an elegant location on the way back to the ship: The Hilton Hotel. What a layout, besides having excellent toilet facilities! From the high reception area, rooms, outdoor pools and tropical landscaping were terraced down toward the sea. Very nice, but I was anxious to return to be with Lois on the cruise ship.

One more time I had a chance to ride 'Little Wilhelm' when the ship on the way back stopped for a day in Ensenada, Mexico. As we rode from San Pedro toward Reno next morning, we were wondering what the weather would be like over Donner Pass. We had heard of storms heading that way. This was February and my birthday. Would there be a surprise gift? Well, how about this; driving through Auburn, CA, it began to snow and increasingly more so as we drove on. For the last 20 miles to the summit, we had to put on snow chains and drove with them all the way literally into our garage in Reno. And so ended my 78th birthday from a little Hawaiian biking tour into a winter wonderland.

North America: Across the USA, land of the free

Chapter 23

USA 2: Golden Gate Bridge to Wyoming (2001)
Biking on I-80, separated, a deluge

In several ways, this was a memorable day. I stood next to a historic fortress just below the Golden Gate Bridge on the San Francisco side of the bay. I had been here before on several occasions. It was always a special moment for me to be at the heart of this world class point of interest, the marriage of scenic beauty and human ingenuity. Though it was heavily overcast, I was filled with exuberant joy and excitement. Were these huge waves rolling into the bay a prelude to the adventures ahead? Occasionally, they sprayed some of us onlookers. What distinguished me from them was that I had my bicycle with me. I intended to ride my bike across America all the way to the Atlantic coast as part of completing one of my horizontal biking adventures around the world. Almost for the entire trip, Lois would accompany me in our recreational van. The latter turned out to be very useful right to begin with since bicyclists were not allowed to ride on the Bay Bridge. So, after pedaling on the streets through San Francisco along the shoreline and passing Fishermen's Warf, Lois transported Wilhelm and me over the bay to Oakland.

The traffic was intense. With effort, I pedaled into the mountain range east of the city. Typically, when traveling away from the Bay Area, the sun would suddenly appear. It did not this time. Something very pleasant, however, happened: I came upon a real bike and hike trail, totally separate from the road, a much better alternative than sharing a lane with motorists.

270

Incidentally, this is the way I have seen the safety needs of bicyclists addressed all over the world. It is just beyond me why we, the richest country, keeps our cyclists in harm's way with vehicular traffic.

Houses stayed behind as I reached lofty heights. The forest of predominantly evergreens became denser. I felt so glad to have just escaped the stranglehold of urban congestion. A feeling of relief and freedom grabbed me and propelled me ahead. Now the joy of biking could begin in earnest. Typically, while riding across a country, I would avoid the large cities. In fact, the only larger communities I would later traverse on my way to the Atlantic were Sacramento, Reno and Salt Lake City. Now there was a lovely town ahead of me: Walnut Creek. I reached it just as it turned dark. We were fortunate to have been given the key to a friend's condominium. That is where we stayed in comfort for our first night.

Somewhere near Locke on the Sacramento River, surrounded by bird sanctuaries, we spent the following night in our van. It rained and the raindrops drumming on the sheet metal roof created a sensation of great coziness as we lay in our warm sleeping bags.

For some time, we stayed on the eastside of the Sacramento River. Lois wanted to grocery shop. We discussed the route to follow to ascertain where to meet again. We separated and with that trouble began. Once before, we had missed each other. That was in the heart of Australia. This here became a much longer separation which eventually involved the police.

It was about midmorning when I came upon a bridge. In lieu of crossing and riding on the west side of the river as agreed upon, I stayed on the east bank for it was less traveled, more scenic and shorter. I had assumed, Lois driving the van, would realize that if she could not find me on one side, she would check the other. Actually, the river was not wide here. I saw her approach on the opposite side. Trying to get her attention, I hurriedly got off the bike, waived frantically with both arms, jumped up and down and yelled full force. I must have been quite a sight to behold for anyone not knowing the reason for my strange behavior. Yet it was all in vain. Lois never saw me and never would until late at night. In the event of losing each other, our plan was to contact the police and to leave corresponding messages as to one's whereabouts. So, when one of us contacted the police, the other could act upon the information left there. For now, I just kept biking on for there was no police station nearby.

And while I was still hopeful to connect with Lois in daylight, the next excitement was approaching: Sinister, dark, heavy clouds. I was just reaching the outskirts of Sacramento when the downpour hit me with full force. I was somewhat prepared for rain, but this was more of a deluge. I found refuge in a supermarket. Fortunately, the tempest did not last long. When I continued biking, pools had formed which in parts where knee deep. It was one thing to pedal through these ponds, it was even worse and outright miserable when passing vehicles splashed me with a mixture of grime, dirt and water. When I got a big spray into my face, visibility for a few precarious seconds was instantly reduced to zero.

Lois, I knew, on the other hand, though riding in the comfort of a dry, warm vehicle would be worried about my whereabouts. When I contacted the police, she already had left word there for me. Late that evening in Rocklin, we were happily reunited. Oh yes, biking can have unexpected thrills.

How would I get over the Donner Pass if bicycles were not permitted on Interstate 80? The good California government has allowed the use of the freeway if there are no other alternatives, so I was told by a highway patrol officer. He had stopped me on a section I was not supposed to ride on. I had to leave for one of the side roads. Because of that I almost missed Lois again, for she expected to meet me on the freeway.

There was still snow and lots of it at the Donner Summit. Snowplows had created walls of snow, now dirty and unattractive, as high as 10' (3 m). Naturally, after the hard uphill ride, it was a pleasure, though a cold one, to coast down beyond Donner Lake. From Truckee onward to the Nebraska state line, except for Reno/Sparks and Salt Lake City, I could now bike undisturbed on I-80.

Spring was in full swing in lower regions. I found the Truckee River canyon particularly enchanting. Even the plains beyond Fernley were enriched with a wealth of wildflowers. However, no longer were there patches of juicy green grass, for the land had already turned into typical brown desert country. To begin with, the wind was with me. Riding through rolling hills on a sunny day was indeed quite pleasant. Then we came upon another river, the Humboldt. Just below, where a dam had created a lake, in the midst of trees and shrubs, surrounded by desert, we spent the night in a campsite. With delight, we watched where the water rushed out of the lake in form of a sizable cascade. We stretched the palms of our hands toward the raging water and imagined feeling its energy. If there was only a way known to fill ourselves from this power source and to store it inside of us! I could certainly have used it to draw from on my ongoing ride.

Beyond Battle Mountain, NV, it got really nasty: Strong headwinds, rain and uphill terrain. At times like this, it was a real blessing to take a break with Lois in the van, where it was dry, warm and where there was good company and food and drink. One of the advantages of our desert is that the duration of a storm is usually short. So, the following morning, the sun was out again offering a magnificent view of the snowcapped Ruby Mountain range. Beyond Wells, NV, there were actually trees next to the freeway. That changed abruptly when we entered the bright salt flats just beyond the state line of Utah. If it was not for the warmth, one could have the sensation of traveling through snow country. The wind was in my favor and with absolutely no ups and downs, I averaged better than 15 miles/hour. Biking into the darkness became a great experience for never seemed the stars so bright and close and the night canopy so gigantic.

In preparation for the Olympic Games, Salt Lake City was amid heavy construction. On top of having to deal with a confusing mass of detours, it rained. Later, when I was back out in the country, I resumed for what bike riding provides such ample opportunity, namely, to reflect, meditate and sing. I thought of the history and the noble purpose of the Olympic Games. I can appreciate the long-term training and conditioning for athletes, the challenge of competition and the sweet sensation of accomplishment and victory. Who among us would not like to be a gold medal winner, have muscles and willpower of 'steel' coupled with superior coordination? Yet, I noticed that many of these super athletes die relatively young. Why? I wondered. When you give it all you have and maybe even a bit more, do you stress your body into health threatening zones?

I thought of the role the actor Brad Pitt played in "Seven Years in Tibet". As a renegade Austrian soldier escaping from a British prisoner of war camp during World War II, he made his way into Tibet. Upon entering this theocracy, he shared with a Buddhist monk that he initially had come with a team of mountain climbers to scale "unconquered" Nanga Parpat, the world's 5th highest mountain. Coming from a deep level of wisdom, the monk then responded, and I paraphrase: "In your world someone is declared a hero who conquers a high mountain. In our world we consider someone a hero who overcomes his ego." What a beautiful thought and wonderful concept to live by.

East of Salt Lake City the freeway snaked through a canyon to higher regions. Was this the route the early Mormon scouts and pioneers had taken coming down into the large Salt Lake Valley? As far as Nebraska and Iowa, we came upon historical markers reminding us of this great trek for religious freedom. Amazing, that religious persecution had to happen in our own country! Ironically, it was not all that long ago that folks had fled religious persecution in Europe coming to America. I thought of a statement from Mahatma Gandhi, a practicing Hindu, to the effect of: If we come together on the basis of the Sermon on the Mount, all the problems of the world could be solved. How true, I felt. If we could connect via the spiritual and moral values of religions and not be divided by them, we could all become brothers and sisters and grow into the family of mankind, we, I believe, are meant to be. That is my dream.

Two days later we reached Wyoming.

Chapter 24

USA 3: Wyoming, Nebraska and Iowa (2003)
Antelopes, Buffalo Bill, visiting family

"Home on the range, where the deer and the antelope play, where seldom is heard, a discouraging word and the sky is not cloudy all day." I was riding lonely stretches of hilly prairie when the song came to my mind. I sang it repeatedly as I rode through Wyoming. This was September 22nd, 2003, indeed a sunny day. At about 13:00 h, free of any luggage, I swung on the used road bike I had just bought for this trip. In anticipation of good road conditions, I dared to ride on tires barely 1 1/8" (2.9 cm) wide. These allowed me greater speed but were very sensitive as I was soon to find out. I averaged 2 punctures a day. Free of any luggage? Yes, because Lois was accompanying me again in our recreational van.

However, there were also some challenges. One of them manifested itself on this very first day. Had we 'progressed' to cell phones or walkie-talkies, this concern could have been easily avoided. Having traveled in this fashion across the USA thus far, we were not as careful in reviewing the location of our next rendezvous. Lois wanted to buy some victuals. According to our map, Green River was the next larger community, albeit 30 miles further on. So, I suggested to Lois to drive there and wait for me at the eastern on-ramp from that town. I had no food and only little water with me, plus I was somewhat out of shape. So, when I finally reached Green River, I was hungry, worn out and anxious to meet with Lois. But where was she? Not at either of the two on/off ramps. There had been ongoing construction on both locations. Had that confused her? Had we miscommunicated and had she understood to go to Rock Springs, the next even larger community? Remember, in situations like this, our backup plan was to contact the police. Doubting, that little Green River would have a station, I decided to ride on to Rock Springs, 11 miles (18 km) further on. It was almost totally dark when I arrived there. Just as I exited on the first off-ramp, Lois caught up with me. The day was saved!

What had happened? Lois had felt that I was overdue and had driven back on the freeway, probably just when I rode through the community of Green River. Not seeing me broken down anywhere, she correctly concluded that I had gone on. We made sure that such situations would not reoccur and they did not.

My most recent previous bike ride had taken me through South Africa. There was a great similarity in the landscape: Rolling, grassy hills, occasional bushes, trees only along stream beds and far apart lonely ranches. Here and there, small herds of cattle or sheep were separated from the road by barbed wire fences. Even the antelopes resembled those in Africa. What did not were the prairie dogs. Well nourished, they appeared ready for winter. Oh, how cute when they stood on their hind-legs like little people and observed my approach, but only for so long. Realizing that I could mean danger, they would abruptly dash for their dens. It amazed me how, at great speed, they would drop into vertical openings which seemed narrower than their bodies. Incidentally, all animals I encountered seemed to be less bothered by even the noisiest truck then by my quiet, humble appearance on a bicycle.

It was early on my 3rd day that a herd of about 50 antelopes took off in wild flight at my approach, ironically not really away from me, but running almost parallel with me. Eventually, I left them behind for this became my fastest day ever: 135 miles (216 km) in 11 hours – not subtracting the times taken out to rest and eat.

The night before, we had spent at the foothills of the Snowy Range Mountains, a nature reserve. A sign there explained this to be the windiest area of Wyoming. As if to prove that to be correct, strong, icy winds howled around us and rattled our vehicle as we cuddled in our cozy 'home', a luxury I did not have in South Africa. In the light of the sinking sun, we had seen patches of fresh snow not far above us.

My hands froze when I took off biking in the morning until eventually the sun came to my aid. Fortunately, the wind actually blew in my favor, though considerably gentler.

Beyond the town of Laramie, the freeway began a long ascent ultimately reaching a height of 8,350 feet (2,530 m). Long before arriving at the peak, I had entered dense forest. Why would I come upon these woods only here in the protection of a state park? Had the prairie been covered with trees at one time? Are we experiencing progressive erosion? Right here the forest was just as thick and lovely as we find it in Oregon and Washington. There was another attraction; this one was man made: The Lincoln Memorial. Near the top of this elevation a huge figure portraying the great president had been placed. At a nearby rest stop between forest and this inspiring monument, Lois and I met for lunch.

Enjoying the benefits of a long downhill grade and the wind in my back, I passed through Cheyenne by midafternoon. The landscape had changed from rugged hilly prairie to level fields of corn, soybeans and occasional pastures. That night, we spent in Pine Bluffs, just a stone throw from the Nebraska state line. It was brisk in the morning, being only a little above freezing. Here I had to leave Interstate 80 for Nebraska does not allow cyclists to ride on it. Actually, that was good news. Highway 30 runs parallel to I-80 and was almost free of traffic, a biker's dream. I felt like I owned the road. I could hear the birds or listen undisturbed to the silence within. The sun was up, the wind was with me. I moved along swiftly and exuberantly. Here and there I came through villages ever so sleepy and laid back. I hardly saw a soul. A sign said: "Population 174". But where was everybody? Even the county park near Bushnell which Lois had picked for our breakfast site was deserted. Surrounding a lake, cottonwoods had turned colorful. A pier, partly resting on pontoons, seemed to be the ideal spot to set up our camping table and chairs. It had been so cold earlier that I had to put on gloves. Now I even took my T-shirt off to bask in the warm sunshine. Breakfast is actually our favorite meal. For optimal health it is suggested for it to be the largest and dinner the smallest.

The landscape was totally flat by now, as is almost all of Nebraska. Most of the rich fields, we passed, had not been harvested yet except for some corn being cut. Here and there fields had been plowed. The smell of fresh, moist earth filled the air. Of the livestock out on pastures, I liked the Black Angus the most. They are so cute and appear so gentle. Lois confirmed that they are. She would know, having raised them on the farm she and her late husband once owned and managed in Iowa. Toward noon, I came upon a bunch of strange looking, out-of-place appearing animals though not too long ago they roamed these regions by the millions: Buffaloes. I thought of the stories, I am sure we all have heard, of how they were wantonly and senselessly killed just for 'sport' and 'kicks' until they were almost extinct.

North America: Across the USA, land of the free

Here is one of the beauties of bike riding: It re-establishes an earth connectedness, an openness and desire to protect and save our environment. Overjoyed was I to watch a sizable herd of them to peacefully graze.

From bison we came to Buffalo Bill, the famous Wild West showman, whose real name was William Cody. I had sort of associated him with Wyoming and was surprised as I entered the town of North Platte to see signs pointing to his home. Currently, Lois was ahead of me. I had to ride through this so typical prairie town to catch up with her. Then my so wonderfully agreeable soulmate and I drove back to see the elaborate spread of this so internationally known man. Ironically, worlds away, only four weeks later while biking in Africa, I came upon a fellow whose T-shirt read "The Buffalo Bills".

What a treat this visit was! Buffalo Bill's entrepreneurship had resulted in considerable wealth. We felt taken back to observe opulence of 150 years ago. There was a spacious mansion, food storage cabins built into the ground, quarters for service personnel and then, most impressive to us were the huge stables. Oh, he was quite a performer and loved to be photographed with Indian chiefs of fame such as Sitting Bull, Yellow Horse etc.

As we left this fascinating site, now a state monument, I kept wondering what life and country were like over a century ago. As then, I mused, these are still regions with plenty of peace and quiet, fertile soil and good crops – a land of abundance.

Somewhere we had switched to highway 34 and headed right to Lincoln and on to the Missouri River. Crossing over an old-fashioned one-way toll bridge, we arrived in Iowa. Beyond the wide river valley, we entered hilly country. This, like a homecoming on a sunny Sunday morning, had the air of a celebration.

The further east we traveled, the richer the farms appeared, prettier and more orderly as well. Flowerbeds often decorated the front yards of beautiful farmhouses. Barns were commonly painted in a reddish-brown color with white trims, all surrounded by a bright white painted wooden fence.

Two days later we arrived in Ottumwa, Iowa where Lois grew up and spent most of her early life. The whole next week there became a celebration of sorts with Lois' children, their families and her friends as well as a statement to the cause of natural healing and wellness. A year prior, we had hoped to get the 'stone rolling' in this community fairly dormant toward alternative health approaches. Now we were delighted to be asked for information and advice and felt honored to respond. One of the many highlights of our visit here was a trip to nearby Fairfield, known also as the world's headquarters for the Maharishi Yogi movement associated with Transcendental Meditation. Besides visiting their facility, we stopped in a well sized health food store/restaurant to eat and buy provisions. We asked for xylitol. This wonderful natural sweetener not only prevents but actually reverses cavities, osteoporosis and any other bone decay. We were surprised that no one had heard of it here. The manager became involved. He got a little annoyed with me when I suggested he bring xylitol into his center. Anyhow, I shared with him that we owned a health food store ourselves in Reno. I had not left my business card with him, nor my name, neither my address. To our great surprise, he called me later at Everlasting Health Center in Nevada, sort of apologizing. Now that he had done some research and discovered the great values of xylitol, he wanted to know where he could best get it, which I gladly shared with him.

Thus ended this segment of my bike ride across our country on a course of supporting natural healing methods and the use of certain supplements to achieve and maintain wellness.

Chapter 25

USA 4: From Iowa to the Atlantic (2003)
Civil War battlefield and people of peace

Was this the heart of our country? We were traveling through amazingly rich farmland on little known back country roads of southeastern Iowa. In particular corn and soy were growing so abundantly that one could believe here were enough protein and carbohydrate sources to feed the whole world. Lois suggested that it could also be used to produce ethanol and thus lessen our dependency on fossil fuels. When I just referred to the heart of America, I was thinking of something else, something much bigger namely the people living here. What is a true American to you and me, if not a freedom loving, God fearing person with strong moral backing, earth connected and generous? Those you will typically find in the Midwest also referred to as the Heartland.

It was a very hot day in September when we left Ottumwa. Coming from dry desert country, the humidity was rather impressive if not even oppressive. A crescendo of crickets and grasshoppers which would never stop, day and night, convinced us that summer was still in full swing but soon to be over. At Ft. Madison, we had intended to cross the Mississippi into Illinois. Alas, we did not make it that far on our first evening. Just 10 miles (17 km) short of our destination, I had a flat. While I patched the puncture, I noticed a sign pointing to a county park. That prompted us to explore. What a wonderful surprise to discover a well-sized lake. It was getting dark, and we were all alone. Great! We made this beautiful place our home for the night.

Can you imagine the sensation of going for a swim in total darkness? This was not for Lois and with some apprehension she watched as I let myself glide from the pier into refreshing coolness. Aaaahhh!

For breakfast next morning, we stopped at a riverboat casino and heard the familiar clatter of slot machines. Lazily, the murky waters of North America's largest river flowed past us. Certainly, the Mississippi must have been cleaner in 1964 when a little further north in Davenport, I enrolled in the original Palmer College of Chiropractic. As I thought back about those days, it reminded me that people in many countries around the globe are healthier than most Americans. Could one of the reasons be that typically in Europe, for instance, families take four weeks or more vacation at a time? What health benefits could be gained by doing that? Since most of us here lead a stressful life, getting thoroughly away from it for a while would help to balance and revitalize body-functions and the nervous system. When we in addition engage in wholesome activities coupled with healthy foods, all body systems are wonderfully reactivated, toned and balanced.

While vacationing in Hawaii for three weeks some time ago, I observed that folks had hardly gotten used to the swing of a relaxed life, when they started to pack for their departure again. When I talked with people about why they chose such short getaways, most answered, that was all the vacation time they could get, or they could afford. Though this may be valid, I wish to submit not to overlook the principle: "A stitch in time saves nine!" Resting and restoring body, mind and soul may be a cost-effective way to avoid potential larger medical and work loss expenses. Also, vacationing does not have to be costly as my biking adventures demonstrate.

Once across the Mississippi, I continued biking through the fertile lands of Illinois and Indiana. We were about halfway across Ohio, when we decided to take a side trip with 'Hermann'. That is the name we used for our camper van. We marked the spot on our map for we had to come back to this very location. However, instead of continuing from here, we would reverse direction. I would begin my bike ride at the Atlantic coast and return to this point. Lois had never seen the Niagara Falls. Well, why not now! So, we headed there next. What a spectacular sight! We switched to the Canadian side, took a boat ride and got sprayed by the mist which could hardly dampen our excitement and enjoyment.

Lois also wished to experience the well-known autumn colors in the maritime states and Canadian provinces. We drove next through the states of New York, Vermont and New Hampshire. When we crossed the border into Quebec near Sherbrooke at 5:00 in the morning, we had an interesting experience. We were the only tourists at this early hour. A Canadian customs official decided to search our van. He never asked us whether we had illegal drugs, weapons or any other harmful substances. "Did you bring any melatonin or DHEA?" he inquired. Well now, had the medical establishment convinced the Canadian government that these wonderful hormones which our body produces should be the objects of a search? We did not have any of these 'dangerous drugs' with us and were allowed to proceed on.

In 1962 and 1963 I had lived in Quebec City. We headed toward this provincial capital, known as 'little Paris'. It rained on route which made the *"couleur"* (French for color) of the foliage even more brilliant. By the time we reached the city, the sun had come out. *'Le Chevalier'* (meaning horseman or knight), a health center in the gorgeous Chateau Frontenac hotel, no longer existed. That is where I had worked. Only a few old-timers vaguely remembered the place. Therefore, I could treasure the great time I had here only in my memories.

We visited the sites of interest in the old city and then headed on to the Gaspé Peninsula. In route Lois' wish for autumn colors was generously fulfilled. The highlight was a walk through the Forillon National Park at the most eastern tip of the peninsula.

From there we drove south and eventually entered the city of New York. The World Trade Center was still standing in Manhattan. We traveled by ferry past the Statue of Liberty to Staten Island and drove on to Atlantic City. The familiar sights, sounds and smells of casinos aside, we loved to walk out on the boardwalks and piers and to watch the Atlantic Ocean. Early on the next morning, we arrived in Havre de Grace on the Chesapeake Bay, just a little north of Baltimore. A plaque marked the spot where on May 3rd in 1813, American Lieutenant John O'Neil single-handedly manned a canon against a British battleship. How was that for patriotism? He was wounded, captured by the British and later released. At this historic point, I remounted my bicycle and headed west biking on backcountry roads through Maryland. Then we swung north into Pennsylvania. The latter became my favorite state. Wooded mountains enhanced the serene farmlands and townships, their foliage now at the peak of autumn colors. The tourists had deserted the lakes, picnic grounds and parks. Peace and quiet lay over this beautiful land in full season attire.

Suddenly the sound of bugles, trumpets and drums, the battle cries from thousands of soldiers and the deafening roar of cannons and rifles. The land was covered with blood and the agony of the maimed, wounded and dying, over six thousand in number, many still in their teens. The year was 1863 (July 3rd). We had slept the night prior in an apple orchard nearby. At dawn we arrived on the Civil War Gettysburg battlefield. We walked through heavy fog as if through rifle and cannon smoke. Low hanging clouds of a gloomy day swept across the fields where men fought and died for the whims of politicians. "What if they called for war and no one came," I thought again as so often, "there must be a better way but violence to solve differences. The famous historian Howard Zinn so wisely declared: "Dissent is the highest form of patriotism." In my heart I felt "only love prevails". Later president John F. Kennedy would say that wars result from stupidity. They certainly are the outcome of incompetency on the part of the rulers.

In the museum we lingered in the medical section. Crude surgical instruments looked more like torture tools. To our delight there was a display of homeopathic remedies, so popular in the 19th century as an effective alternative to barbaric medical procedures. We became aware on this Civil War battlefield of another war fought today with even considerably higher casualties. "Big Pharma" and the medical establishment with the support of the government and media have just about routed homeopathy. Today there is a cry for natural healing. Hopefully, homeopathy and other harmless, yet effective modalities, will soon overcome the three major killers in our country: #1 medical intervention, # 2 heart failure, #3 cancer. When I was biking again, my mind kept dwelling on the essence of these two wars.

Two days later, as it was getting dark, we arrived in the little town of Berlin, certainly an intriguing name for a German traveler like me. A gentleman, I asked for directions, turned out to be the president of the local historical society. He confirmed and explained German settlements in Pennsylvania. He introduced us to Bill Glessner, a former seed salesman, who was well acquainted and befriended with areal Amish families. With him we spent all of the following morning visiting their homes, farms and workshops. We even chatted with their bishop partly in German. The Amish maintain an old version of our language, no longer spoken in Europe and therefore a little challenging for me to understand. He then produced a hymn book. I had no difficulty reading the German text.

What a wonderful experience! We were deeply touched. While we, in the 'civilized' world don't even know yet how to slow down the destruction of our planet, these people do not do a single thing that harms the earth. Also, they do not allow themselves to be abused by any authority to kill other human beings as we had just experienced on the nearby battlefield. That is how I had imagined true Christianity. Maybe, I thought when I was back on my bike, as the consciousness of spirituality grows globally, we will learn to live in harmony and peace as brothers and sisters. Then we can turn this planet we have been given as our home into a paradise with abundance for all and treat our bodies as divine entities to be kept at optimum levels of health and wellness... At this moment, I felt particularly elated that I had chosen a modest bicycle as my mode of transportation.

There were two more events of interest before we reached the place where we had interrupted the bike ride. The first one happened south of Pittsburgh. Motorists and bike riders are not always on good footing. The following illustrates how helpful, I as a cyclist, had the chance to be toward two motorists. We had just finished breakfast in a restaurant and were walking back to our van, when we noticed some commotion around the vehicle next to ours. A young man and women seemed enormously frustrated. They had locked themselves out of their car. As annoying as that can be at any moment, the timing in this instance was as inappropriate as it was hilarious. These two souls were scheduled to get married within the hour, but needed to drive into Pittsburgh, still an hour's ride away. I got to the next phone with my AAA membership card and made sort of an SOS call on their behalf. Rescue arrived quickly. When the couple took off, they literally hurried into their marriage. We later received a nice "thank you" card from them.

When we entered a small section of West Virginia, it occurred to us to call our friend Patch Adams M.D. We had hosted his appearance at UNR's medical school and the Pioneer Theater in our hometown Reno. Maybe we could make a detour and see ourselves how far his project had progressed. In the movie "Patch Adams" his life and work are portrayed by the actor Robin Williams. It shows a plot of land donated to him in this state where he wants to build a health resort with openness to all healing modalities and where payment for treatments is voluntary. The resort will be operated from contributions and by volunteer staff members. What a noble concept! Alas, when I reached his office, I learned he was out of town. So, on we traveled.

Late afternoon, we crossed the Ohio River into Ohio. The following day, I had a chance to test the rain gear we had brought along, for it rained heavily all day long. I could not really determine whether the water eventually seeped through the material. Did the rain just keep running from my face down my neck and all over my body or was it collectively my own body moisture? Regardless, I was miserably wet most of the day. It was such a blessing to have Lois with our van nearby.

Two days later, we arrived at our destination in central Ohio, where we had decided to interrupt my bike ride in favor of the aforementioned excursion with our van. The sun was appropriately smiling as I finished my bike ride across our great nation. What part of our beautiful planet would come next? Would I be trekking vertically or maybe diagonally or possibly kayaking or hiking? With adventure in my heart and mind, I mused about what would come next.

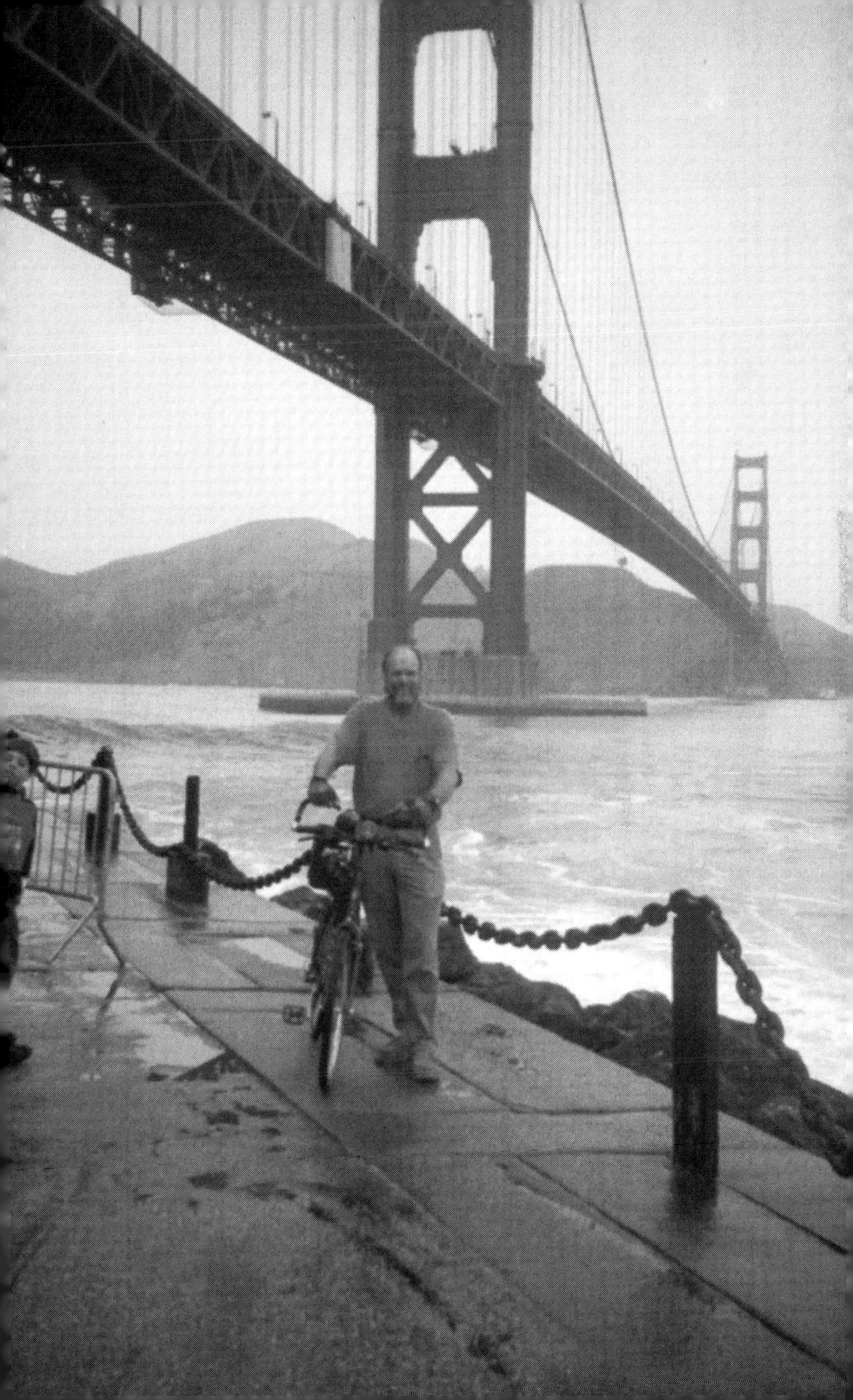

North America: Across the USA, land of the free

Trolly in San Francisco

Previous page: Golden Gate Bridge, San Francisco – starting from the Pacific on a rainy day

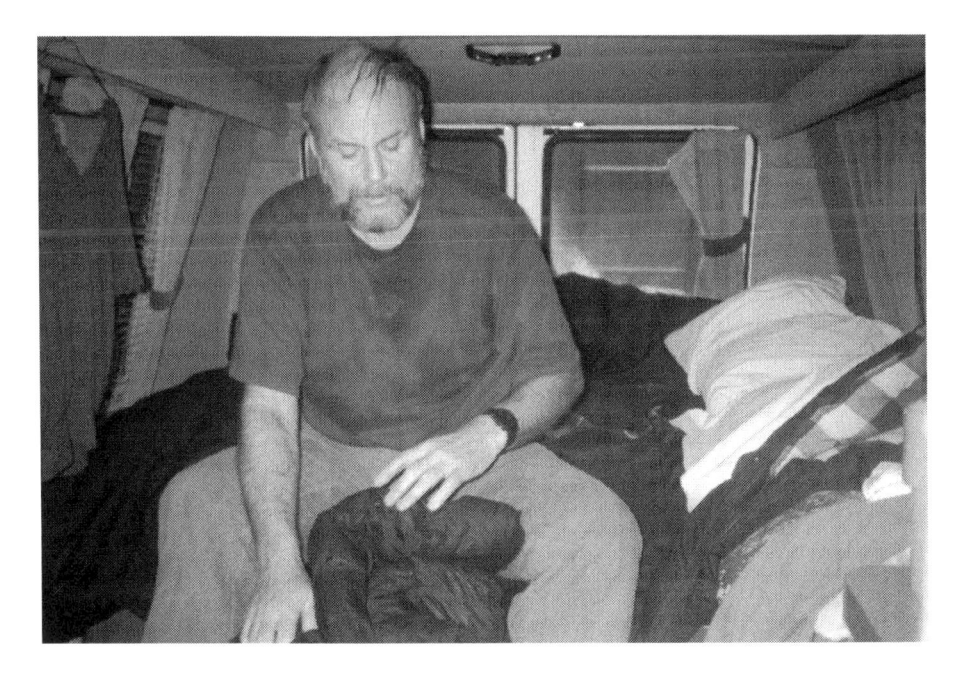

Drying clothes and warming up in our camper

North America: Across the USA, land of the free

Man crosses U.S. on bicycle

The Macomb Journal 10/2/98, IOWA

Bicyclist dreams of travelling all continents

By Lisa Anderson
Journal Staff

COLCHESTER — Hans Frischeisen, 59, is headed to Atlantic City, N.J., ... on a bike ... from San Francisco. He figures it'll take four weeks.

On his way east, Frischeisen rode on U.S. 136 Thursday morning. He spent Wednesday at Lake Argyle in Colchester.

Frischeisen says he rides about 100 miles per day. Lois Eckroat, his wife of three years, drives a van alongside, finding places for them to park for the evenings and making sure her husband eats right. They own the Everlasting Health Inc. based out of Reno, Nev., a health food store and clinic staffed with five doctors ranging from chiropractors to homeopathy.

Originally from Munich, Hans Frischeisen came to the United States in 1961 for the first time. His interest in the U.S. came from the German writer, Karl May. May wrote books about the cowboys and Indians of the American west. After reading so much about the west he decided to come and see for himself.

After coming to the U.S. for the first time he decided to stay. He married a woman from the U.S. and settled down.

He worked for IBM in Iowa and Reno, Nev., as a sales representative until 1990, when he was offered early retirement as part of company cutbacks.

Frischeisen has been riding bikes since he was 5 years old, however the serious interests began when he had a dream of himself riding across many continents of land. After the dream it seemed to him that IBM became more of a secondary element in his life and the biking become a primary interest, an interest he believes will never stop.

Since retiring, he has crossed Australia, all of Europe, parts of Asia, the Americas and the north shore of Canada going as far as Guatemala. He says he likes riding because it's healthy and doesn't hurt the environment. He says motorized transportation is a curse, and he's concerned the world will be out of fossil fuel in 25-30 years.

Starting in San Francisco and on his way to Atlantic City, New Jersey, Hans Frischeisen is traveling across the U.S. on his bike. Frischeisen, who is 59 has been biking seriously since 1980, he travels approximately 100 miles per day and plans to be across the U.S. in four weeks. Wednesday he traveled through Colchester and stopped at Lake Argyle for a rest.

Newspaper article from The Macomb Journal, located in Illinois

Opposite: Donner Pass – Hans is front of a wall of snow

288

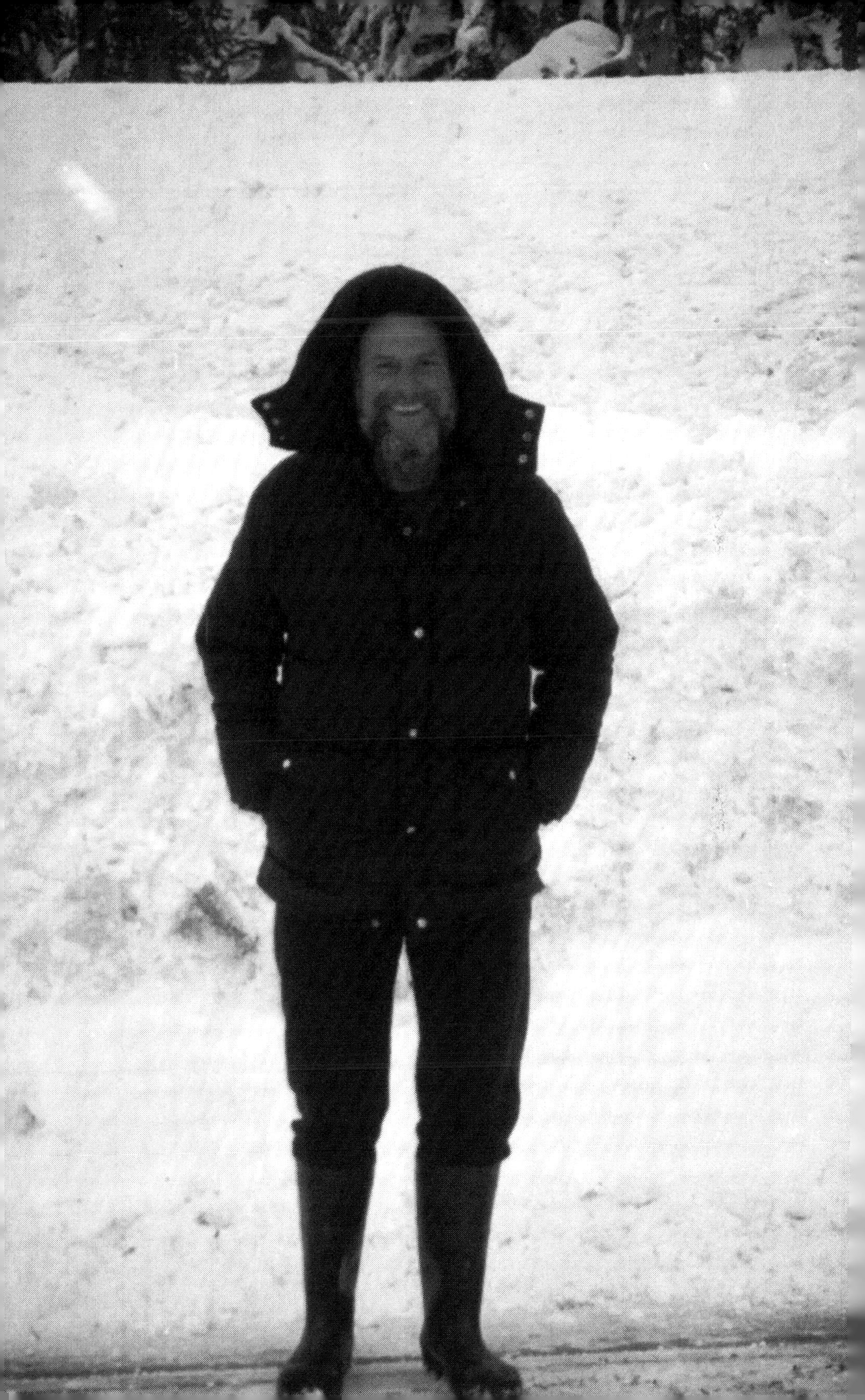

North America: Across the USA, land of the free

Donner Lake, CA

Pedaling, Paddling and Pedes 2

A Reno greeting

The Nugget Hotel and Casino in Sparks, NV

North America: Across the USA, land of the free

Like snow, salt flats west of Salt Lake City, UT

Downtown Salt Lake City, UT

Mormon Temple in Salt Lake City, UT

Antelopes in Wyoming

Buffalo Bill museum in North Platte, NE

A typical Iowa farm

With Lois' son and daughter and their families in Ottumwa, IA

Autumn colors in Ohio

North America: Across the USA, land of the free

Gettysburg battlefield

Meeting the Amish in Pennsylvania

Havre de Grace where in 1813, John O'Neil single handedly took on a British battleship

Conclusion

Global warming is already having effects on our planet and great calamities are said to come upon us if we do not act immediately and thoroughly. I am jubilant, knowing that my mode of traveling supports that vital thrust. It is my hope and the purpose of this book to inspire you to play the utmost role in the wholesome stewardship of our beautiful home; 'Spaceship Earth'. We, in America, believe we are the 'good guys' on earth. Right on, so do I, yet there are many other good people wherever you go. Would we not be even 'better guys' if we assumed a leadership position to protect our planet? I hope my book has shown you there is a wonderful world out there to be explored, ideally, in the spirit of pronoia. It is my great hope and wish that you now will consider non-fossil fuel-based transportation whenever possible and reasonable, that even more so you will pursue a healthy, wholesome life and above all practice love, joy and peace. To advance that, is the mission of my life and the purpose of this, and my preceding book and the books to follow of this series.

Let us all ask ourselves: Is the world really as evil and dangerous as the media continuously and, yes, fairly forcefully tries to pound into us? In contrast, would you believe that we are actually living in the most peaceful and humane times in history? Yes, hard to believe, isn't it? But that is what historians have firmly concluded by establishing a ratio between the amount of violence and the number of people living on earth at that time, starting from our earliest recorded beginnings. And that is also what I have observed and shared in this, and my other books. I have experienced amazing friendliness, caring, compassion and loving kindness on my nearly 6 treks by 'muscle fuel' around the world. Surprisingly, the most human warmth I experienced was in areas of our world which our governments, and the media, have labeled "hostile" proving that people around the whole world want to live in peace, brotherly and sisterly love, everywhere. In my lifetime of traveling the globe, I have found that I have, without exception, always found an echo if I travel and live with a positive, loving and caring disposition.

Are you ready to experience the wonders of this planet we live on? Are you a modern-day adventurer, like myself, or would you rather learn about the beauty of human nature unfettered by fear and fear mongering, from your own arm chair as you read about my experiences just as they happened. Either way, I believe my books will be an inspiration for you to travel with a pronoia described here, in detail, and see for yourself how wonderful our planet and its inhabitants really are. Or if you wish to know more about this wonderous world and it's enormously interesting peoples and places and, as well, how privileged we are to live here at this time, in this place….happy and mindful traveling!

About the Author

Hans Frischeisen was born in 1941 in the town of Insterburg in the province of East Prussia in Germany. Thus, he was exposed to some of the horrors of World War II at a very young age. As refugees from the invading and brutal Soviet Forces, his mother escaped with him, as a 4-year-old, sitting on the rack of her bicycle. His early experience of unimaginable violence is one of the factors why, throughout his life, he has pursued a course of pacifism. Hans grew up and began his education in West-Germany and continued on to further education in the field of natural healing. In 1961 he immigrated to Canada and two years later, into the USA. In 1964 he moved to Alaska where he became a sales rep. for IBM. Pursuing his interest in health, after his retirement from the company in Reno, Nevada in 1990, he founded Everlasting Health, a large center for natural healing, which he sold 21 years later. By means of 'muscle fuel' i.e., biking, kayaking and hiking, and with a 'pronoia' disposition, he carried a message of peace, love and health nearly 6 times around the globe across all major land masses. Hans passionately shares how much loving kindness and longing for peace there is in the world, which he experienced as he trekked over 81,000 adventuresome miles, more than twice horizontally, twice vertically and once diagonally around the world as an ambassador of peace and true health.

For more information, contact the author (healthmomentum@gmail.com).